Teaching
Emotional Intelligence

SECOND EDITION

*To my parents, Zeev and Corinne Bloom,
who respected my ability to choose and
taught me to do so wisely.*

Teaching
Emotional Intelligence

**STRATEGIES AND ACTIVITIES
FOR HELPING STUDENTS
MAKE EFFECTIVE CHOICES**

SECOND EDITION

ADINA BLOOM LEWKOWICZ

CORWIN PRESS
A SAGE Publications Company
Thousand Oaks, CA 91320

For information:

Corwin Press
A Sage Publications Company
2455 Teller Road
Thousand Oaks, California 91320
www.corwinpress.com

Sage Publications Ltd.
1 Oliver's Yard
55 City Road
London EC1Y 1SP
United Kingdom

Sage Publications India Pvt. Ltd.
B-42, Panchsheel Enclave
Post Box 4109
New Delhi 110 017   India

Printed in the United States of America

Library of Congress Cataloging-in-Publication Data

Lewkowicz, Adina Bloom.
Teaching emotional intelligence : strategies and activities for helping students make effective choices / Adina Bloom Lewkowicz. — 2nd ed.
    p. cm.
Includes bibliographical references and index.
ISBN 1-4129-4057-5 or 978-1-4129-4057-3 (cloth)
ISBN 1-4129-4058-3 or 978-1-4129-4058-0 (pbk.)
    1. Emotional intelligence. 2. Emotional intelligence—Study and teaching. 3. Emotional intelligence—Activity programs. I. Title.

BF576.L49 2007
152.4071′2—dc22   2006027350

This book is printed on acid-free paper.

06   07   08   09   10   10   9   8   7   6   5   4   3   2   1

Acquisitions Editor:	Cathy Hernandez
Editorial Assistants:	Charline Wu and Megan Bedell
Production Editor:	Astrid Virding
Copy Editor:	Jackie Tasch
Typesetter:	C&M Digitals (P) Ltd.
Proofreader:	Ellen Brink
Indexer:	Juniee Oneida
Cover Designer:	Michael Dubowe
Graphic Designer:	Lisa Riley
Illustrator:	Robert Griesen

Contents

Preface   vii

Acknowledgments   viii

About the Author   x

Introduction: A Teacher Laments   1

SECTION 1: Developing Emotional Skills   9

  1. Understanding Choice-Making   10

  2. Developing Group Choice-Making   16

  3. Identifying Feelings   21

  4. Understanding Assumptions   25

  5. Examining and Lowering Anxiety   32

  6. Becoming Aware of Feelings   39

  7. Dealing With Anger   46

  8. Examining and Accepting Responsibility   53

  9. Choosing Happiness   60

SECTION 2: Developing Social Skills   67

  10. Developing Self-Acceptance   69

  11. Examining Self-Measurement   73

  12. Evaluating Unrealistic Expectations   78

  13. Promoting Friendship   84

  14. Strengthening Family   91

  15. Learning About Put-Downs   98

  16. Dealing With Peer Pressure   104

  17. Examining Prejudice   116

SECTION 3: Developing Life Skills   **123**

   18. Looking at Manipulation   125

   19. Strengthening Active Listening and Feedback Skills   128

   20. Developing Assertiveness   132

   21. Learning Communication and Negotiation   135

   22. Building Study Skills   139

   23. Clarifying Values and Consequences   142

   24. Investigating Cheating   147

   25. Investigating Stealing   151

   26. Investigating Bullying   155

   27. Investigating Abuse of Alcohol and Other Drugs   158

   28. Getting Help   163

   29. Taking Risks and Setting Goals   166

Epilogue: A Teacher Rejoices   **170**

Resource A: Reproducible Masters   **173**

Resource B: Summary Activities   **203**

References   **207**

Index   **209**

Preface

The poignant words of an 18-year-old boy inspired the writing of this book. In my second year of graduate school in social work, my field placement was with an agency that served chemically dependent adolescents. On the final day of my internship, that boy came up to me and said, "Adina, I'm so happy that I became addicted and that I'm now in recovery because I came out so much better a person!"

I was rendered speechless, dumbstruck by the riveting thought that what he received through the recovery process could have been his birthright. The knowledge and skills with which to develop positive, healthy, successful children and prevent future problems are available and teachable.

Armed with the words of that 18-year-old boy, a fervent belief in the potential of each individual to be fully actualized, a background in education, psychology, theater, and social work, and an unbridled desire to save the world, I chose to write this book. Teaching youngsters to make informed, effective choices regarding their emotional, physical, mental, and social well-being can lead to the development of happy, healthy, high-functioning adults.

Teaching Emotional Intelligence will do just that. This is not a pipe dream, nor is this a book of gimmicks and catchphrases. It is a curriculum based on the understanding that students think and behave ineffectively because they lack the skills and information with which to make more effective cognitive and behavioral choices. This curriculum provides teachers with the tools to transmit those important skills and that vital body of information.

As more and more children grow into adults who feel good about themselves, manage their emotions effectively, communicate clearly, learn how to resolve conflicts, and how to meet their needs in positive ways, we can move as a society toward the development of a healthy, high-functioning civilization. At the very least, we will end up with healthier, higher functioning classrooms and happier students and teachers.

I am very grateful to Corwin Press for the opportunity to publish a second, even more comprehensive, user-friendly edition of this book. This edition reflects an understanding that the curriculum is most effective for use in second through sixth grades and secondarily in seventh and eight grades. Modifications are provided for these last two grades. The chapter and section headings have been reorganized for greater clarity. The introduction has been greatly expanded to reflect current research as well as to clarify the theoretical framework of the lessons. A session on bullying has been added as well as an epilogue to offer the reader some examples of success stories from using the lessons.

The scenes in each section have been rewritten to enhance understanding of the process of assumptions influencing thoughts, affecting emotions, and leading to actions and to simplify the enactment of the scenes. In addition, following each scene, a series of questions with accompanying answers have been provided for a more in-depth analysis of the scene. Also, certain sections have additional suggested activities.

■ ACKNOWLEDGMENTS

I would like to thank those educators who share my vision and will attempt to bring it to fruition, one child at a time. I would also like to thank SkyLight for the initial opportunity to try to leave the world a better place than I found it. In particular, I would like to thank Jean Ward, who was the first to share my vision, Sue Schumer, and Dara Lee Howard, who edited the manuscript.

I would like to thank Cathy Hernandez at Corwin Press for allowing the vision to continue and for her patience with my revision process. I would also like to thank Astrid Virding, production editor, and Jacqueline Tasch, copy editor, for their help in getting my book ready for publication.

I thank my children, Ellis and Zanna, for putting up with all the hours devoid of "Eensy, Weensy Spider" and with all the mom-free games of "Trouble." I thank my husband, Zvi, for all the hours he had to sing "The Wheels on the Bus" and mediate sibling spats, for all the years of supporting me while I wrote both editions of this book, and for all the hugs and reassurances throughout the process. I give thanks to my mother for being my secretary/wife, nanny/friend. I thank my mentors, Zeev Bloom, Ken Simpson, Howard Goldstein, and Mitchell Fields, for their inspiration. And I thank an 18-year-old boy for giving me the final impetus to write *Teaching Emotional Intelligence*.

■ PUBLISHER'S ACKNOWLEDGMENTS

Corwin Press gratefully acknowledges the contributions of the following reviewers:

Sherri Becker
Eighth grade English teacher
Mitchell Middle School
Mitchell, South Dakota

Jennifer Betters
School counselor
Sugar Creek Elementary School
Verona, Wisconsin

Cheri DiMartino
Gifted and talented specialist
Eva Wolfe Elementary School
North Las Vegas, Nevada

Jane Hampton
Principal
Oak Mountain Elementary School
Birmingham, Alabama

Deborah Hardy
Guidance and counseling chair
Irvington High School
Irvington, New York

Elizabeth B. Lengle
School counselor
Warrior Run School District
Turbotville, Pennsylvania

Greg O'Connell
Assistant principal
Grant Wood Elementary School
Cedar Rapids, Iowa

Diane Smith
School counselor
Smethport Area School District
Smethport, Pennsylvania

About the Author

Adina Bloom Lewkowicz, L.I.S.W., is a prevention specialist, curriculum consultant, therapist, actress, and mother of twins. Most recently, she was the coordinator of the SAY (Social Advocates for Youth) Coalition of Bellefaire JCB in Cleveland, Ohio, providing prevention programs and materials for adolescents. Adina has had extensive experience as an expressive arts therapist, working with individuals ranging in age from toddlers through senior adults. Adina speaks and consults nationally on teaching emotional intelligence, as well as on using expressive arts in education, prevention, and therapy. Adina developed a curriculum for an afterschool day care program using the expressive arts to complement the standard school curriculum. As artist-in-residence with the Ohio Arts Council/National Endowment for the Arts Artist-in-Education program, Adina traveled throughout the state of Ohio, providing in-school drama residencies for youngsters of all ages. In addition, Adina has performed as an actress and singer throughout the East Coast in summer stock and dinner and regional theaters.

Introduction

A Teacher Laments

I have just about had it up to here! One more argument or fit of tears and I think I will scream. I know that I am supposed to be a super teacher with an endless supply of patience and energy, a technique for every situation, and a solution for every problem, but sometimes. . . . I cannot believe that he just crumpled up his assignment again because it was not exactly the way he wanted it to be. How can I get through all my lesson plans? Oh terrific. There she goes, grabbing his pencil yet one more time. I can see the headlines now: "Youth who stole pencils in her formative years arrested for grand theft!"

I want these children to grow to be happy, successful adults. I do everything I can. I talk with them and reason with them, but sometimes it is as if I were talking to the air. The same things keep happening over and over again. With youngsters being the way they are, it's difficult enough to get all the subjects covered that must be taught. Now you want me to teach something else? How can I find the time? Why should I bother?

WHY TEACH EMOTIONAL, SOCIAL, AND LIFE SKILLS?

Teachers in the twenty-first century have the formidable job of educating a nation of youth at risk. A significant number of young people have a strong potential for dropping out of school or becoming involved with youth violence, teen pregnancy, and substance abuse (Weissberg, Wahlberg, O'Brian, & Kuster, 2003). Studies indicate that a relatively few youths possess the kinds of skills, values, and supports that would protect them against these kinds of risks and promote their engagement in positive behaviors (Benson, Scales, Leffert, & Rehlkepartain, 1997).

Classrooms are filled with youngsters displaying a wide range of concerns and behavioral problems that teachers have little time and few techniques to address. Students may suffer from poor self-awareness, low concentration, lack of motivation, little self-discipline, low self-esteem, poor communication, an inability to express feelings effectively, difficulty in resolving conflicts, and a significant amount of emotional pain.

1

Anxious, unhappy, angry youngsters do not make ideal students. As they try to focus their attention on getting their needs met and feeling better, little concentration is left for learning. Searching for—and finding—inappropriate outlets for their emotions, they misbehave, often creating conflicts between students. Teachers spend too much valuable class time dealing with issues between students (Frey, Nolen, Estrom, & Hirschstein, 2005). Encouraging a classroom full of such students to learn effectively can be very time consuming and frustrating.

The question we need to ask is this: If children are struggling academically because other issues are occupying their minds, will giving them more academics help? Or do we want to educate them to deal effectively with their feelings, needs, and relationships so that they can then absorb the academics? (Elias, 1997).

It might be helpful to enlarge our definition of the *intelligence* we want our students to acquire so that it includes *emotional intelligence* (Mayer, Caruso, & Salovey, 2000). Howard Gardner (1983), in his definitive work, *Frames of Mind,* suggests that educators consider promoting other intelligences, including different kinds of emotional intelligence. He describes *intrapersonal intelligence* and *interpersonal intelligence* as two of the multiple intelligences people possess and describes the need to develop these intelligences, thus developing each individual to the fullest.

Research indicates that supporting emotional and social development is the missing piece in the education of our youth. Researchers from various fields of inquiry have come to similar conclusions—the importance of educating not just the mind, but the whole person. There is mounting evidence to support a strong link between social-emotional learning and academic performance; research also suggests an increased likelihood that youths who build social-emotional competencies will develop the values and attitudes that lead to safer, less risky life choices (Elias et al., 1997).

In his groundbreaking research on emotional intelligence, Daniel Goleman (1995) asserted the great need for developing mastery over the emotional realm so that people can get their needs met in healthy ways. He spoke of the need to develop social and emotional competencies, indicating that these can be learned and that the school environment is an ideal context in which to do so. This seems logical, as schools have access to youths, a history of effective presentation of knowledge and skills, and highly competent professionals to transmit the information.

More and more educators seem to be agreeing with Goleman, supporting an educational agenda that includes the promotion of students' social-emotional competence, character, and health. This is evidenced by a growing number of school-based prevention and youth development programs, focusing on producing students who are skilled socially, who know how to manage emotions, to get their needs met effectively, and to make choices based on their deepest held values (Elias et al., 1997).

The values clarification movement of the 1970s focused on helping individuals determine whether or not their choices were in line with their values, allowing the individual to determine what the values were (Raths, Harmin, & Simon, 1978). The current character education movement predetermines values to teach (Lickona, 2004). I propose that when people have the knowledge and skills to make informed, positive, independent choices regarding their social, emotional, and mental well-being, they will be more likely to make choices in line with their values, which are universal.

If people can deal effectively with their emotions and know how to meet their needs effectively, they are more likely to embody values such as responsibility; if they know how to feel good about themselves, they are more likely to embody values such as perseverance; if they know how to get along effectively with others, they are more likely to embody values such as kindness and empathy.

As teachers help to promote social and emotional learning, they will be able to lessen their students' frustrations, helping them to get their needs met in positive, healthy ways; they will also make classroom time more productive, prevent behavioral problems, build students of character, and increase academic prowess. They will be able to do so by providing their students with a body of information and a set of skills with which to make informed, positive, independent choices regarding their social, emotional, and mental well-being (Dewhurst, 1991; Zins, Elias, Greenberg, & Weissberg, 2000). This book provides teachers with the tools to do just that.

It is important to clarify the nature of the information and the kinds of skills teachers need to provide in order to promote effective emotional, social, and ethical decision making. The underlying theme to all of the areas covered in this book is making effective choices. William Glasser (1998), in his discussion of *control theory*, explains that every behavior people exhibit is based on their best attempt to meet a need. He further explains that each action, thought, and, indirectly, feeling is based on unconscious choices. To make the most effective choices possible, people need to examine and reformulate their thoughts.

Daniel Goleman's (1995) research on emotional intelligence indicates that to develop social and emotional competencies, youngsters must develop the skills to challenge their often inflexible thoughts. He spoke to the importance of checking thoughts against available evidence, thus offering cognitive guidance before the emotional switch goes into effect, triggering ineffective choices.

Albert Ellis (2001), one of the pioneers of the cognitive-behavioral approach, further describes the crucial process of checking thoughts against evidence. He explains the importance of examining erroneous beliefs—assumptions—which lead to thoughts, triggering emotions, prompting people to behave in particular ways. To affect the ultimate behavioral choice, it is necessary to evaluate the assumption for errors in logic. This book is centered on that exact process.

The book begins by showing that every thought, feeling, and behavior is based on a choice that has been made. Often, however, these choices are made by default, out of habit, or based on faulty information or none at all. The curriculum helps the teacher to help students make choices con-sciously and effectively by developing students' abilities to think before they feel and act.

The lessons in this book help students to examine the assumptions that inform their thoughts, trigger their emotions, and ultimately lead to their behavioral choices. Students are taught about what assumptions are; some basic errors in logic that lead to assumptions; how to examine their assumptions and thoughts for errors in logic; how to change the assumptions to provable beliefs and then change their thoughts, feelings, and finally their behavioral choices. They then are taught to apply this fundamental process across many situations. Assumptions are explored as they relate to dealing with a variety of emotions; issues of self-acceptance; issues related to a variety of relationships and ethical choices. The examination and reframing of underlying assumptions helps students learn how to stop, think, and choose well and in alignment with their values, rather than merely comprehending their options at a conceptual level.

This curriculum is designed to provide a wide range of active experiences in this choice-making process. The information and skills addressed are presented in a way that affords youngsters the opportunity to learn the material through application. In this way, material can be learned and used rather than merely understood (Sloboda & David, 1997).

■ TEACHING STRATEGIES

Drama

Many lessons in this curriculum utilize drama as a primary method with which to observe and evaluate choices and rehearse alternate options. The thought of using drama may seem daunting, as it conjures up images of talented actors and actresses performing great works of theater on a stage. In this book, the use of drama is nothing like that. Neither talent nor previous experience is necessary. Drama is used not to produce a high-quality play but rather to fully experience and examine the concepts in the curriculum.

Drama calls for participation at the physical, verbal, emotional, and intellectual levels. Using drama as a tool to explore choices allows for a more complete involvement in that exploration than merely discussing the concept. Drama becomes a mirror students use to observe the nuances of their own as well as others' choices in ways that other methods do not afford. In addition, as students involve themselves in the dramatization process, they are less likely to distance themselves from the concepts being explored than they might if they were exploring that concept through discussion alone (Mayer, 1990; McCullough, 2000).

Drama provides students a context within which to discuss and evaluate choices by reflecting on past situations and examining possible future consequences. By playing another person, effectively putting themselves in someone else's shoes, they can experience actions taken, the meanings of those actions, and the feeling of being answerable for those actions. They can determine whether these actions would express their values and whether or not the consequences would be acceptable to them. The information gained from such an exploration is more likely to be understood and applied than simply providing students with information about choices and consequences and expecting them to accept it at face value (McCaslin, 2005; Wilhelm & Edmiston, 1998).

Most of the lessons in this book include a series of scenes focused on the choices being explored. You are welcome to use the scenes in their entirety, as a jumping off point, or to create your own with input from your students, based on their experiences.

Each scene is designed to help students examine the assumptions that inform their thoughts, trigger their emotions, and ultimately lead to their behaviors. This approach was inspired by a method called *psychodrama*, which uses drama techniques to gain psychological insight. Practitioners of this method have discussed its application to affective education as a very effective tool to promote self-awareness (Blatner, 1988).

In psychodrama, an individual is encouraged to explore life situations by acting them out in a group setting, using others present as other actors in his or her "life drama." The others present can also take on other specific roles: as a mirror reflecting the feelings of the main character in the drama or as a double, reflecting the inner thoughts of the main character.

The scenes provided in this book reflect universal life situations as opposed to situations based on individual students' stories. However, the scenes are designed to promote self-awareness and psychological insight as students examine their life situations in light of the scenes presented. Also, the roles of double and mirror are used, and an additional role of assumption or belief has been added to facilitate far greater awareness, insight, and opportunities for change.

The first scene enacted and examined in every lesson reflects the thoughts, feelings, and behaviors based on a particular assumption. The assumption, thoughts, and feelings are highlighted in the actual dialogue of each scene. Then, the scene is investigated in light of some of the basic errors in logic that lead to assumptions–*crystal-balling*, when one claims to know what will happen in the future; *generalizing*, when one exaggerates by stretching the truth, using words such as *always, never, everyone,* and *no one*; and *awfulizing*, a form of generalizing in which one claims that something is awful, horrible, or terrible.

The investigation is followed by a discussion of the scene, including how the assumption affected the character's thoughts, feelings, and behaviors; how to change the assumption to a more provable belief; and how that new belief would alter the character's thoughts, feelings, behaviors, and final outcome. A second scene is then enacted reflecting the thoughts, feelings, and behaviors based on the provable belief.

This dramatic enactment, evaluation, and reenactment of the process of making choices (from assumption to thoughts to feelings to actions) offer a powerful opportunity to experience the process and rehearse ways to change behaviors by first changing beliefs and then rehearsing new thoughts and actions stemming from them. Dramatizing this process is as close as possible to experiencing it in real life, thus making it more likely that this learning will be applied in the students' own lives.

It will be necessary to make copies of both scenes for your students so that they may participate in them. The scenes are enacted simply. Use chairs and desks to represent furniture, and use simple hand-held objects as necessary. Or choose to have students imagine everything. Students can move around as much or as little as the scene indicates. Putting the scene in the center of the room allows other students to surround the enactment. This can foster greater group involvement. The front of the room is another option.

To involve as many students as possible, allow different students to act in each scene. As students play the characters, encourage them to express the thoughts and feelings of the character through their bodies and voices. Those not involved in the scene may be active observers, looking for nuances of body language and vocal inflection that might further illuminate the concept and listening for evidence of illogic in the character's assumption, thoughts, and behaviors. In addition, some scenes ask the observers to take on roles such as members of a jury, which can further engage them.

You can discard or modify the provided scenes or use them as jumping off points, allowing your students to create scenes that more closely reflect their own life experiences. The process of creating a scene helps students to thoroughly explore the assumption being discussed and apply it to their own lives. This also builds other skills such as sequencing and creative writing.

To develop their own scene, students must focus on the assumption being investigated. They determine which event might best depict the outcome of a belief in that assumption, giving preference to situations that the students have experienced. For example, when creating a scene dealing with an assumption that leads to anxiety, ask the students, "In which situations might you feel anxious? In what setting would that take place? What characters would be needed to enact the scene? What kind of thoughts and feelings might the assumption lead to in the main character? What would happen at the beginning, middle, and end of the scene as a result?" Make sure students adapt the same investigation/discussion process to their own scene so they can explore and correct the errors in logic that led to the assumption. Then, have the students create a second scene reflecting the thoughts, feelings, and actions based on the provable belief. The scene can be either written out and read or outlined and ad-libbed within the framework created.

Skill Development

To execute increasingly effective life choices rather than merely understanding how to make them, youngsters must develop a range of skills or human competencies. In his book, *Emotional Intelligence,* Goleman (1995) cited a number of highly effective emotional education programs. A common thread in each of these programs is a focus on developing these skills. Other researchers have also pointed out the importance of providing opportunities for intrapersonal and interpersonal skill development (Cowan & Clover, 1991; Deline, 1991; Erin, Dignan, & Brown, 1991; Jones, Kline, Habkirk, & Saler, 1990; Rolan, 1991; Rotheram, 1982; Sloboda, 1997; Tobler & Stratton, 1997). One of the strengths of this curriculum is that it addresses a comprehensive range of skills fundamental to making increasingly effective life choices. Students are initially exposed to building skills in cooperation. There are activities infused throughout that continue to support the acquisition of this skill. Not only is this an important life skill but it supports the teaching of the curriculum, as many of the activities are of a cooperative nature.

The first section of the book offers a range of dramatization activities as well as exercises that build emotional skills. Fundamental stress-management skills are addressed at the beginning of the curriculum and throughout. The second section promotes the development of social skills, and the third section provides activities that further develop life skills, such as values clarification, communication, negotiation, assertiveness, conflict management, and goal setting.

Detective Metaphor

Envisioning the choice maker as detective is a metaphor that is sparingly included throughout the book. I recommend this metaphor for your use and can say that I have found it very helpful in teaching this material. If asked to play the role of a "choice detective," students frequently respond with enthusiasm and a freedom of expression that is not always comfortable for them "playing themselves." The metaphor is not applied heavily in the text, however, so that there is latitude to include personalized versions of detective activities or ignore the suggestion if desired. My use of the term *choice detective* for choice maker, the Inquiry and Investigating Procedures sections of some of the student handouts, and the dramatic activity titled *scene investigation* are intended simply as suggestions for including the metaphor in your presentation of the material.

HOW TO USE THIS BOOK ■

This book is designed for anyone who works with young people and has the context within which to develop the knowledge and skills described. It can be used, for example, by teachers, school counselors, day care providers, club leaders, program directors, camp directors, and parents. The curriculum is most appropriate for children in Grades 2 through 6. It can be used for middle school students, as well, and modifications have been provided for these grades.

The activities fall most directly within the curricular areas of health, social studies, and language arts. However, additional activities are provided to extend the lessons into the areas of math, science, and history. These activities can be expanded to more fully address these curricular areas, and additional activities can be developed to extend the lessons into other areas of the school curriculum. Also, if a lesson does not fully address your needs on a particular topic, expand the lesson as necessary to address specific issues in greater depth.

Multiple intelligences are addressed throughout the curriculum, including intrapersonal, interpersonal, bodily/kinesthetic, verbal/linguistic, visual/spatial, and logical/mathematical.

Lessons

Each lesson begins with an introduction that outlines the salient points of the topic being addressed. This introduction is used to inform the teacher of the focus of the lesson. The material from the introduction will then be shared with students after some initial activities to engage their interest in the topic. The heart of a lesson is the activities, which include exercises and scenes designed to move step by step toward acquisition of the knowledge and skills related to that topic. Some suggested activities require students to behave in ways that are unusual in some classroom settings. For example, some activities require that students move around rather than sit in chairs. Other activities, such as brainstorming, may lead to overlapping conversations rather than each student speaking in turn.

Although these activities may demand a certain flexibility in the classroom, they do not lack structure. Each activity is designed with a specific outlined framework to maximize its effectiveness. As a result, these techniques provide students with a high level of involvement in the topics explored. In addition, the activities can be adapted to your level of comfort. For example, you may prefer to try some of the more physical activities with a smaller portion of the class. Or, if you are concerned about the noise level in the classroom, you may want to structure an activity such as brainstorming so that students raise their hands before they speak.

In most activities, one or more handouts for students are provided. These handouts are collected in Resource A near the end of the book. You are encouraged to photocopy and use them for instructional purposes in your classroom.

One section that recurs in many of these handouts is the Inquiry section. This section is an opportunity for each student to express feelings, opinions, and experiences; to explore a certain topic and develop material for further exploration; and, if shared with another, to find out that other classmates may have similar experiences and feelings. An inquiry is presented in the form of an unfinished sentence that students complete, based on the first thing that comes to mind. There are no right or wrong answers. If the student shares a personal response during a class discussion, no one should comment on it, and the handouts are not to be evaluated.

A number of the handouts are variations of four worksheets. These four worksheets, which are also provided in Resource A, are used in more than one activity. As a result, before use, teachers will need to add titles, label columns, and provide directions. The activity description will identify which worksheet to use and provide the information needed to tailor the handout for that activity. You will need to briefly share the results of the worksheet on a separate day from the actual lesson. This lets the students know that to create positive change, it is important to work on their choice-making awareness and skills daily and not just during the actual lesson time. Consider suggesting that students collect the handouts as part of a personal journal. The collection provides a good review source outside the classroom.

Following Resource A, Resource B provides summary activities that supplement the chapters. It includes additional suggestions for ways to reinforce the knowledge and skills by using them throughout the school day. I strongly recommend using these suggestions to make this approach to choice-making a part of the classroom culture. This will contribute greatly to the likelihood that the knowledge and skills taught will be applied.

Section 1

Developing Emotional Skills

This first section focuses on the development of effective skills in dealing with emotions. Daniel Goleman's (1995) research on emotional intelligence indicated a great need for mastery over the emotional realm and spoke of the importance of providing the opportunity for each person to develop positive emotional habits. Other researchers have pointed out the benefits of enhancing emotional abilities, tying these skills to greater academic achievement (Zins, Weissberg, Wang, & Wohlberg, 2004), social adaptation (Greenberg et al., 2003), and as a predictor of positive life outcomes (Mayer et al., 2000).

The first four lessons in this section introduce the basics of informed choice-making. In succeeding lessons, students develop an understanding of what it means to make a choice, examine how choices may be made as a group, become aware of and investigate how emotions affect choice-making, and discover how to become aware of and examine assumptions that underlie choices.

The next five lessons offer opportunities for students to apply their understanding of the choice-making process to their own decisions about their emotions. They develop an awareness of how they are feeling and explore choices about when, how, and how intensely they would like to experience a variety of emotions and the ways in which they would like to deal with them. Using their knowledge of the assumption-thought-feeling-action chain, students examine effective choices across a wide range of situations. The lessons explore assumptions believed and choices made regarding three emotions (anxiety, anger, and happiness) and two issues influencing emotions (hiding feelings and responsibility).

1

Understanding Choice-Making

Youngsters have the ability to make healthy, positive choices about how to think, feel, and behave when they are given the tools and the context to do so. Teachers have the opportunity and ability to offer both. When teachers encourage the development of their students' emotional intelligence, students will be able to apply that intelligence to the choices they make.

The development of emotional intelligence and conscious and effective choice-making begins with self-awareness. Dealing with self-awareness as a global concept is a rather daunting proposition. Instead, let us start at the beginning and start small.

To make effective choices, people must first understand the definition of choice, the kinds of choices that are made, the process by which choices are made, and the ways that choices affect people. To make a choice, people decide which of two or more possibilities or alternatives is best. People make choices every moment about their every thought, feeling, and action. Often, these choices are made very quickly and below a person's level of conscious awareness. People do not know that a choice has been made or that there was the option to make other choices. Even when aware that a choice existed, a person's range of choices may be limited. Choices frequently are made by default or out of habit; are based on choices of others, such as friends, family, and the media; or are based on faulty information or none at all.

Choices lead to consequences. The accumulation of choices, whether made consciously or unconsciously, and the consequences that follow add up to the person one is. People have the ability to design themselves as they would like to be by consciously choosing among alternatives. They can slow down their decisions and make effective, thoughtful, fact-based choices.

This lesson describes this deliberate choice process and gives students experience with it. Students act as increasingly adept choice makers, or choice detectives, looking for facts to determine the best possible feeling, thought, and behavioral choices. Activity 1 provides a definition of choice and an opportunity for participation in the choice-making process. Activity 2 helps students understand the wide range of daily choices that they make. Activity 3 offers active analysis of the choice-making process. Activity 4 helps students gain awareness of the importance of conscious and effective choice-making and invites their commitment to becoming informed choice makers.

In addition to the actual lessons, there are many ongoing classroom opportunities for developing an awareness of and active participation in the choice-making process. Students learn that each of their thoughts, feelings, and behaviors is based on a choice that they have made and for which they are responsible. Therefore, when they are demonstrating a particular thought, feeling, or behavior, students can be reminded that they are making a choice to think, feel, or act in that particular fashion. For example, if a student is feeling angry and breaking pencil points, rather than merely telling him or her to stop that behavior, remind the student that he or she is choosing to behave in that way. Then, help the student apply the choice-making process to examine whether this was an effective choice and explore and rehearse a more effective way to deal with his or her angry feelings. In this way, the student has a structure within which to deal more appropriately with the feeling the next time it occurs (see Figure 1.1).

This is not to say, however, that this structure is easy to apply. Choice-making is based largely on habit, so youngsters need guidance at first and then a great deal of practice. This may seem frustrating and time consuming at the onset of the curriculum. With practice, however, youngsters are able to make increasingly effective choices on their own, soon demanding less and less of the teacher's time. They will not need to be told to stop their ineffective behavior. Rather, they will make effective behavioral choices on their own because they know how to do so.

Figure 1.1   Making Choices

1. Look at alternatives

2. Choose an alternative

3. Act on the choice

4. Evaluate the choice

5. Keep the choice or make a new choice

Students will be participating in a program that can be enjoyable and can help them to become the very best people that they can be. However, let them know that they will be experiencing new activities, some of which they may feel uncomfortable doing. If they find an activity uncomfortable, let them know that they can tell you how they feel and that they will be allowed to pass on the activity the first time it is introduced and rejoin the activity when they feel more comfortable.

Also, it may be harder for students to stay in control because of the difference in structure between some of these activities and the regular classroom activities to which they have become accustomed. For example, in this curriculum, they will be moving around as opposed to sitting in their seats. Let them know that it will be helpful if they can work hard to keep themselves in control and to ask for help when they are finding that difficult to do.

▶ Activity 1: STANDING UP FOR CHOICES

1. Explain that when making a choice, a person decides what is best out of two or more possibilities, also known as alternatives. Remind students that people are always making choices between alternatives. They make choices about what to believe, how to think, and how to act. Many of these choices are made without planning. It is important to plan their choices so they make the best choices possible.

2. Present two alternatives and ask students to choose one, standing up when the alternative is read to indicate their preference. Examples of choices to present to students:

    Do you prefer Burger King's or McDonald's hamburgers?

    Do you prefer sports or art?

    In your free time, do you study or do you watch television?

    If there was someone in class whom no one liked, would you stay away from or go up and talk to that person?

    If you had no money and you saw some on your parent's dresser, would you take just a little bit for something you really wanted, or would you leave the money there?

3. Add other choices based on your knowledge of the choices your students make. Provide a range from simple to increasingly difficult choices.

4. Explain that many choices are made without thinking, and discuss this with students. Choices are made this way sometimes because a person follows what a friend does. It is important to think before choosing so that the choice made is the best for both the chooser and other people. It is helpful for students to think of the choice process as pushing the "pause button" on the "VCR of life," to stop and think about whether or not they want to make a choice before it is made. In this way, it is more likely that the choices made will bring the best results both immediately and in the future, as people are a result of the accumulation of all the choices that they make. Choice detectives make the best possible choices by slowing down and looking at available

alternatives, the consequences of choosing those alternatives, and which choice is in line with their values. Doing so offers a much greater chance of being happy, healthy, and successful in the future. Which choices are easy to make, and which are more difficult? Who and what influences the choices that are made?

▶ Activity 2: BRAINSTORMING DAILY CHOICES

1. Explain that students are going to brainstorm together. Explain that brainstorming means they will search their minds for and share as many possible ideas as they can come up with about a particular topic. There are no right or wrong ideas, and they are not looking for one particular answer. Encourage students to feel free to share any idea that comes into their minds and to withhold comments about or evaluation of the ideas until a later time.

2. Students brainstorm about the daily choices that they make, those their parents make, and those their teacher makes, to get an idea of the great number and variety of choices made by people every day. Examples of choices that might be identified include

    Student: what to wear, whether or not to get angry in response to a sibling's action

    Parent: what to make for dinner, whether to keep working or take a coffee break

    Teacher: whether to reprimand a student's action or let it go, how much time should be spent on a particular subject

▶ Activity 3: THE CHOICE WALK

1. Ask a volunteer to walk from one side of the room to the other. Ask the rest of the class to watch very closely as the volunteer crosses the room.

2. Following the walk, ask the observers to describe the choices the person made as he or she was crossing the room. How fast did the person walk, where did the person look? Then ask the walker whether he or she thought about other choices that may have been available before taking action, or did the person make the choices quickly without thinking about them? (Most students will reveal that the choices were made without thinking.)

3. Explain that to slow down choice-making and help a person look at other possible choices, a series of choice-making steps can be used. In a way, it will be like using the pause button on the VCR before the choice is made and then making the choice in slow motion. Ask the same student to walk across the room again. This time, have the student focus on one choice—for example, speed when walking—to demonstrate the choice-making process:

    First, look at the available possibilities, that is, the alternatives. What alternatives are there in terms of speed of walking? (A person could walk slowly, at a moderate pace, quickly.)

    A person then chooses one of the alternatives. (Student chooses.)

Explain that after a choice is made, a person takes action based on that choice. (Student walks across the room at the chosen speed.)

Explain that a person can then evaluate the choice made to see whether he or she is happy with the results. (Student evaluates the choice. For example, he may not have liked that he walked fast because he got tired, or he may have liked that he looked straight ahead because he seemed confident.)

If a person is not happy with the chosen alternative, a person can make a new choice and take a different action. (Student chooses whether to make a new choice.)

4. Summarize the steps of the choice-making process, using Figure 1.1.

Extension

Students analyze the process of making choices for the task of walking across the room. For example, how did the student find the alternatives? How did the student evaluate the alternatives? How did the student decide whether to change the choice?

▶ Activity 4: BECOMING INFORMED CHOICE MAKERS

1. Explain that the students may use the choice-making process—demonstrated in Activity 3 for the simple choice of how fast to walk—to make the best choices for themselves in every area of their lives. Students can slow down their choice-making and look for clues to determine the best possible choices to make.

2. Ask students to commit themselves to more deliberate choice-making and the use of the choice-making process by taking the Choice-Detective Pledge. Ask each to raise his or her right hand and repeat: "I will make choices deliberately, making sure that I look for clues when choosing how I will think, feel, and act."

3. Have students design a pledge form and sign it in a collective ceremony.

Extension

Write a diary entry reflecting the daily choices made by a person in a certain period in history or the choices made by a particular historical figure or literary character being studied.

Middle School Modifications

STANDING UP FOR CHOICES—Add examples, such as

If someone offered you a drink at a party, would you take it?

If you had not studied for a test and could see someone's paper out of the corner of your eye, would you look?

If you were pressured to do something you were uncomfortable doing and if you did not, you would lose a friend, would you do it?

Pass a paper around and ask students to write about times when they stood up for a choice they or someone else made that may have differed from others' choices. Have a student read the list aloud.

BRAINSTORMING DAILY CHOICES—Have the students draw a timeline to include choices they were able to make in the past, the choices they can make now, and the choices they will be able to make in the future. Give examples of past choices (what to eat, what to wear), of present choices (what activities to do, what to do on a date, where to apply to college), and of future choices (whom to marry, where to live, where to work). Have students discuss how the kinds of families people are born into affects their range of choices. Students might write and deliver a speech titled "The Effects of Geographic Location and Economic Status on the Range of Choices Available to Us."

An additional activity might be to have students draw a picture and discuss all the choices made during the activity, for example, choice of medium, color, whether to talk during the activity, and whether to copy someone else's idea.

2

Developing Group Choice-Making

The first lesson provided students with a basic awareness of the choice-making process and how it affects them. This lesson helps students generalize that awareness to how their choices affect others and how group choices occur. Students begin developing an understanding of and experience in cooperation and develop a set of rules to govern their behavior.

Examining and experiencing the process by which collective choices are made lays the foundation for the development of several emotional domains. Students expand their knowledge of the choice-making process and begin to practice self-control and management of their emotions. Understanding the importance of the search for ways to make choices that benefit the greatest number of people—and experiencing joy in doing so—develops the foundation for empathy and for handling relationships.

Exploring group choice-making in a school context requires acknowledging the inherent hierarchical setup of a classroom. A class is not a democracy by nature. The teacher is responsible for a relatively large group of youngsters in a setting that demands certain kinds of behaviors but rejects others. It is a setting that requires that the teacher transmit a great deal of information in a few short hours. Therefore, the teacher makes choices for the group, setting schedules and rules so teaching can be effective. Students are expected to adhere to the rules and cooperate with the teacher and each other. They receive a strong message that they are expected to obey authority.

Although this is an important message, it is not necessarily the only one that it is desirable to teach students. Nor is it necessarily the best message with which to encourage cooperation and positive behavior. By teaching the meaning and benefits of cooperation and eliciting participation in the development of classroom rules, teachers send the message that students know what is necessary for a smooth-running classroom and are capable of achieving it. The act of developing those rules is an opportunity to explore necessary behaviors as well as actively experience group choice-making.

There are several ways in which the group choice-making process can occur (see Figure 2.1).

A choice can be made for a group through the use of authority. In this situation, one person in charge chooses and imposes the choice on the group. There may be several rules in your classroom that are nonnegotiable and that must be decided in this way. It would be helpful to explain to your students why this is so and the reasons behind the rules, such as safety, state laws, and so forth.

A choice can be reached by group consensus. This means that every person in the group agrees on the choice before it is implemented. An example of group consensus is a jury verdict, in which all jurors had to agree.

Also, a choice can be reached by a majority of the group members agreeing on it. An example of this would be an election for class officers. There may be several rules that students can choose by majority or consensus, offering active participation in the group choice-making process.

It will be helpful for students to understand that working together well, or cooperating, can make a group more enjoyable and each person in it happier. However, to cooperate is a choice that each individual group member must make. It is not always easy to cooperate because it sometimes means that people have to wait their turn, share something that they are enjoying, or agree to something that is not their preference. However, the benefits of cooperation are that each person is guaranteed a turn at some point, all group members are expected to share, and there are many times when an individual's idea becomes the group's choice. When members exercise some self-control and tolerate some frustration, the

Figure 2.1   How Group Choices Are Made

Authority	One person in charge makes choices for the whole group.
Consensus	Each person in the group agrees on the choice.
Majority	More than half of the people in the group agree on the choice.

group works well, accomplishes great things, and is an enjoyable experience for each of its members.

The activities in this lesson explore these areas of cooperation and group choice-making. Activity 1 offers an experience in and an understanding of the benefits of cooperation. Activity 2 elicits participation in the development of group rules. Activity 3 presents an opportunity to make a group decision about the rules that will govern classroom behavior as well as how they are implemented.

In addition to the actual lesson, other opportunities can be found for encouraging cooperation, reinforcing skills, and helping to improve the classroom atmosphere. The entire class can encourage everyone's responsibility for effective choice-making. Students can be taught to help each other use the choice-making process to examine choices and to offer alternatives, and they can support each other for positive choices made.

▶ Activity 1: ALPHABET

1. Before starting, create a space in which the students can move about freely.

2. Explain that you will call out a letter and that everyone in the class will join to make a physical picture of the letter. To do this, students stand up and move together to form the letter as quickly as possible. However, tell students that they may not speak while forming the letter. They are to form the letters as a group, in silence.

3. Begin with simply shaped letters such as T and O and gradually move on to more complex shapes such as N and R.

4. Discuss with students how the letters were formed. What did they have to do to make it work? What would have made it more difficult? Students may use the word *cooperation* and leave it at that. However, encourage them to be specific in terms of the ways in which they cooperated. For example, perhaps a student looked for a part of a letter not yet formed and went to that place, or one student took another student and placed him or her in an available spot. If students fought for the same spot, it would have made the activity more difficult to accomplish.

▶ Activity 2: BRAINSTORMING GROUP RULES

1. Students are going to make a group choice about the kinds of rules they think are needed to work together smoothly as a group. Tell them that their choices affect other people. It is important to make choices that have the best effect on the most people.

2. Ask students to brainstorm as many rules as they think they will need. You may give general areas where rules may be needed, such as disruptive behaviors, noise level, or ways to participate. Ask for a student volunteer to record the rules that are suggested. An example of some rules that might be suggested:

No one may put down anyone in the class.

Everyone will listen to instructions.

No one will speak when another person is speaking.

If the noise level becomes too high, a signal will be given and will be followed by silence.

Everyone will be in charge of keeping themselves in control.

Extension

Ask students to turn the brainstorm list into a song by coming up with a melody of their own or by putting the words to a song that they already know.

▶ Activity 3: RULES VOTE

1. Use the information in the introduction of this lesson to discuss the different ways that group decisions can be made.

2. Explain that although rules may often be decided by someone in authority, to make their group choice about the kinds of rules they want, the students will vote, inviting everyone to participate in the choice-making process and allowing the majority to make the final choice.

3. Explain that you will read their list of rules, and they are to raise their hand to vote to include that rule. They may vote for as many rules as they think they need. After the vote, ask the recorder to list the accepted rules and post it as a reminder. Give a copy of The Cooperation Rules We Choose by Majority (see Resource A) to students and suggest they record the rules for their own journals.

4. Explain that the students have just participated in the choice-making process. They looked at the alternatives available and chose the alternatives they wanted. However, the process is not yet complete. The next step is acting on the choices they made. They are in charge of acting according to the rules they chose. This may mean that they will need to remind themselves and their classmates of the rules that were chosen if someone has forgotten to follow them for the moment. Also, after acting according to the rules for a period of time, students may want to evaluate the rules they chose and change them if they think changes are necessary.

Extension

Ask students to write and deliver a speech as an expert about one of the group choice-making methods. For example, they might consider the way a jury reaches a verdict (consensus), the way in which a president is voted into office (majority), or the way in which the U.S. Constitution was developed (majority).

Middle School Modifications

Ask students to give examples of choices made by consensus, authority, and majority, and discuss the benefits and drawbacks of each method. Have them discuss various contexts and the different ways in which rules become established and decisions get made within these contexts.

ALPHABET—If students catch on quickly, have them make letters within a certain time limit or create words and sentences.

BRAINSTORMING GROUP RULES—Ask students to brainstorm implicit rules, such as social rules among peers, as well as rules that are currently in place that they believe should be modified or eliminated. Students might then work in small groups to develop songs, jingles, or raps. A good follow-up for this activity is to ask students to create a timeline, detailing the rules people have to follow as children, teenagers, and then as adults.

3

Identifying Feelings

To be able to manage emotions, which leads to greater emotional intelligence and more effective choice making, a person must first be aware that emotions exist. At every moment, people are experiencing particular feelings or a combination of feelings. Often, these feelings inhabit a person's being with little awareness or conscious choice by the person. Emotions affect people in many ways, including their physiology, movement, and speech. The ways people are affected by their feelings and how those feelings are expressed vary widely from person to person.

Without realizing it, people are propelled by their feelings to act to change them, remove them, or keep them. This can lead to choices that bring no result, the opposite result, or results not in a person's best interests. With increased awareness of feelings and how to respond to them, people begin to move toward conscious and effective choice-making. People can work toward choosing and rehearsing how they would like to feel and how to express their feelings.

First, however, they need to become aware that they are experiencing an emotion and look to their bodies for clues as to the nature of that emotion. Bodies and voices provide those clues (see Figure 3.1).

This lesson focuses on identifying feelings. Its activities help students to identify emotions they are experiencing. Activity 1 reinforces cooperation. Activity 2 presents an opportunity for students to connect an imagined situation to its corresponding feeling. Activity 3 gives students a chance to experience and identify a variety of feelings in their bodies. In Activity 4, students communicate a variety of emotional messages with their bodies alone.

In addition to the lesson, there are other opportunities for identifying feelings in the classroom. You may act as a model for your students,

Figure 3.1   How to Know What You Are Feeling

How parts of the body are held

Posture

Tension

Gestures

Facial expressions

Eye contact

Voice rate

Voice pitch

Voice volume

sharing your feelings in whatever way you are comfortable. Also, identify body language that is observed in students, offering them the opportunity to discuss their feelings, should they choose to do so.

▶ Activity 1: ALPHABET

Do the same activity as in Lesson 2, Activity 1. Following the activity, ask students what specific things they did or did not do to form the letters. Was it different than the first time they did this? How?

▶ Activity 2: "HOW WOULD YOU FEEL IF . . ."

1. Explain that people are always feeling a certain way, such as happy, sad, or angry. Sometimes people know what they are feeling and why, and sometimes they do not. It is important for people to be aware of how they feel so they can choose how they want to feel and how best to deal with those feelings. People show their feelings in different ways, for example, by the looks on their faces, how they speak, and how they act. They can choose how they would like to feel and how they show their feelings. The first step is paying attention to how they are feeling right now. They can do this by looking at their bodies and listening to their voices.

2. Explain that you are going to make a number of different statements. Ask students to listen to the statement and imagine how they would feel if the statement was meant for them personally. Examples of statements that might be used:

   I am so proud of you.

   Your work is improving nicely.

   You have five more minutes to complete the test.

The doctor will see you now.

I'll be your best friend if you give me some of your candy.

I don't think I'll ever be able to trust you again.

Nobody likes you.

You can never do anything right.

I've got your book bag, and I'm not going to give it back.

3. Ask students to share some of the feelings they experienced as they listened to the statements. How did they know they were experiencing those feelings?

▶ Activity 3: FEELINGS GAUGE

1. Ask students to stand up and allow for a little elbow room between themselves.

2. Explain that you will call out a series of different feelings. After you call out a feeling, the students are going to imagine what their bodies might be going through if they were experiencing that feeling. Then, starting at the top of their heads and moving down to their toes, they are to act out that feeling with each part of their bodies. Examples of feelings that you might use are sadness, joy, anger, surprise, or fear.

3. Ask students to focus on the way in which parts of the body are held, tension, facial expressions, eye contact, gestures, and posture.

▶ Activity 4: MESSAGES

1. Explain that people can tell a great deal about how they and others are feeling by paying attention to their bodies. Often, they give messages to each other using only their bodies.

2. Tell students that you will call out a series of messages. After you call out a message, the students will express that message using only their bodies. (Have half of the class stand and half sit, so that students see that body language exists regardless of position.) They can use the way in which they hold different parts of their bodies, tension, facial expressions, eye contact, gestures, and posture, but they may not speak. Examples of messages that might be used include:

I'm so tired.

I'm bored.

I didn't do anything wrong!

Please let me answer the question.

I'm very proud of you.

I can't believe you just said that!

One more word out of you, and you've had it!

I'm so nervous.

Please don't look at me.

See how wonderful I look.

3. Ask students what other messages they give and receive. Did everyone give the same message in the same way? What were some of the similarities and differences between the ways in which the messages were given?

Middle School Modifications

Ask students for specific examples of the ways in which their feelings are expressed in their bodies, voices, and actions.

HOW WOULD YOU FEEL IF . . . ?—Add examples such as "He thinks you're cute," "I'm ashamed to call you my son," "I don't care what your curfew is, I want you home by 11:00!"

FEELINGS GAUGE—As a feeling is expressed, have students freeze, look around, and describe the specific similarities and differences in the way the feelings are expressed.

MESSAGES—Have students add their own examples of messages they give each other and those that are given to them.

FEELINGS IN BODY—Have students help each other outline their bodies on a large piece of paper. Then, each student chooses a feeling and colors the parts of their body outline that are affected by that feeling. Remind them to include facial expressions, muscles, heart rate, pulse, and so forth.

4

Understanding Assumptions

To make and execute effective choices, it is not enough to simply understand the definition of choice-making. People must understand the basis for their choices. This lesson illuminates choice-making at that fundamental level where choices are truly made—underlying beliefs.

The choices people make are often based on unquestioned assumptions. Although these assumptions are beliefs but not provable facts, they inform thoughts, lead to feelings, and motivate actions. However, the assumption-thought-feeling chain happens so quickly that a person is rarely aware that it occurs. As long as the process is beneath conscious awareness, it becomes difficult or almost impossible to influence any part of the chain to make a different choice.

To make more effective choices, people must become aware of the assumptions and evaluate them for exaggerations and other errors in logic. Then, they can change the assumptions to provable beliefs, alter the corresponding thoughts and feelings, and explore and rehearse new choices based on this process. The first step is understanding the basic nature of assumptions, which this lesson clarifies. Ellis (1990) identified three concerns when examining assumptions (see Figure 4.1). These concerns, couched as three questions for student deliberation, open a previously closed assumption to fresh consideration.

Three basic errors in logic lead to assumptions. One error in logic is crystal-balling: when someone wrongly claims to know what will happen in the future. Clearly, it is stretching the truth to believe that anyone can predict the future exactly. However, people might steer clear of new activities because they are sure they would do badly. If this assumption is rewritten to a provable belief, they could then see a realm of future possibilities. They might do badly, but there is also the possibility that they would be average or even good at the new activity.

Figure 4.1 Concerns When Examining Assumptions

Am I crystal-balling?	When one claims to know what will happen in the future
Am I generalizing?	When one exaggerates and stretches the truth
Am I awfulizing?	When one claims that something is awful, terrible, or horrible

SOURCE: Based on A. Ellis, *How to Stubbornly Refuse to Make Yourself Miserable About Anything, Yes, Anything* (New York: First Carol, 1990).

One way to help students to correct the error of crystal-balling is by helping them to change their language from absolutes to shades of gray. For example, instead of saying and believing that they know what *will* happen in the future, they can talk about a range of possibilities that *might* happen.

Another error is generalizing, or exaggerating the truth, for example, when people believe that every single person has to like them. Clearly, this is unlikely. To hold this belief is not logical, however, many assumptions and choices are based on hanging on to this kind of thinking, despite its inherent lack of logic.

For example, if people believe that everybody must like them, they might constantly agree to do things for other people despite personal situations, such as lack of time. They would fear that if they said no, someone might not like them, and that would be intolerable. But would it? Students can be helped to look at the facts and not the beliefs, rewriting the assumption to make more sense, using language that represents shades of gray. They can say that a person might *prefer* to be liked by everyone, but it is stretching the truth to believe that everyone will do so. The worst thing that could happen is that some people might not like a person. That might not be thrilling but it would be tolerable.

The third basic error in logic is awfulizing, or claiming that something is awful, horrible, or terrible. Looking at possible outcomes on an awfulness scale, more negative weight must logically be put on situations dealing with factually bad circumstances, such as bad health or death. However, sometimes, something is labeled as awful when the situation is less than awful. It is really just a situation a person doesn't like. This may lead to a variety of negative feelings, clearly out of proportion to the situation. How many people have hyperventilated and wasted valuable down time while stuck in traffic? The students can be helped to discuss certain outcomes as *undesirable* or *disliked* as opposed to *awful*.

Activities in this lesson provide students with the opportunity to become acquainted with these errors in logic. Activity 1 provides additional opportunity for experiencing and examining cooperation.

Activity 2 further builds awareness of the effects of emotions in one's body, and Activity 3 develops an awareness of the effects of emotions on one's voice. Activity 4 highlights the difference between facts and beliefs. Activity 5 offers experiential opportunity to explore assumptions and their effects on bodies, voices, and choices. Activity 6 provides information about the basic errors in logic and provable beliefs, and Activity 7 provides an experiential opportunity to apply that information.

In addition to the lesson, it would be helpful to explore assumptions behind students' actions when an occasion arises in class. Rather than merely correcting a behavior, explore the assumption that led to that behavior. For example, if a student were throwing homework away before it was completed, explore the possibility that the student was awfulizing and held the assumption that the homework had to be perfect. Work toward an understanding that imperfection is not awful and that attempts, even failed attempts, are worthwhile and important steps in learning.

▶ Activity 1: ALPHABET

Do the same activity as in Lesson 2, Activity 1. Try a few letters, with the students acting as if they are experiencing a number of different emotions. Then ask students how they feel when they are cooperating. How do they feel when they are not cooperating? How might this activity be affected if they were feeling angry? How might this activity be affected if they were feeling shy?

▶ Activity 2: SIT/STAND

1. Explain that, as learned in the previous lesson, the way people feel affects their bodies. People even express how they feel by the way they stand up and sit down.

2. Tell students that you are going to ask them to stand and sit as if they are thinking a number of different thoughts and feeling a number of different feelings. They are to stand and sit, showing what they are thinking and feeling using only their bodies. Examples that might be used include:

   Sit as if you really wanted to be out of your seat and running around

   Sit as if you were in a class that you really liked

   Sit as if you did not want anyone to see you

   Stand as if your name was just called in class and you did not know the answer

   Stand as if you were about to answer a question in a class with a teacher who was very tough on students

   Stand as if you were threatening someone

3. Have the students focus on the way the body is held, and on tension, energy, and so forth.

▶ Activity 3: SUBTEXT

1. Explain to students that feelings affect not only a person's body but also his or her voice. People use their voices in different ways to deliver different meanings.

2. Tell students that you are going to call out several phrases and several meanings for those phrases. After you count to three, they are to say the phrase together, using their voices to get across the different meanings. Have the students focus on rate of speech, pitch, and volume. Examples of things to say:

   Say "I'm sorry" as if you are being coerced to say it by a parent

   Say "I'm sorry" as if you have just stepped on your best friend's foot

   Say "Who, me?" as if you've just won a million dollars in the lottery

   Say "Who, me?" as if you've been asked to answer a question on an oral exam for which you have not studied

3. Ask students how the rate of speech, pitch, and volume changed meanings. What sentences could they add to the phrases that would tell what else they are saying in addition to the phrase itself? For example, in the first meaning of "I'm sorry," you might be saying, "I'm not really sorry. I'm being made to say this to you."

▶ Activity 4: BELIEF VOTE

1. Explain to students that choices that are made about feelings, thoughts, and actions are based on beliefs. Beliefs are things that people think are true but which may or may not be true in fact. Things that may not be true are also called assumptions. To make the best possible choice, people must know that their beliefs are true; they search for facts to determine if something is true or false.

2. Tell students that you will first tell them two possible beliefs and then call out the beliefs one at a time. They are to choose one belief, making their choice by standing up after you call out the one they choose. Examples of choices might be

   McDonald's hamburgers are the best or Burger King's hamburgers are the best.

   The moon is made of green cheese or the moon is not made of green cheese.

   The Earth is flat or the Earth is round.

   The United States is the best place to live or Canada is the best place to live.

3. Ask students how they chose which hamburger was better. Are their choices influenced by anyone other than themselves? Who and what might influence their choices? How do they know what the moon is made of? Did people always know that? How do they know the shape of the Earth? What choice might have been made several centuries ago? What influence do available facts have on choices? Which country would someone living in Toronto,

Canada, choose as the best place to live? How about someone who lives in Cleveland, Ohio? What influence does personal experience have on choices made?

▶ Activity 5: ASSUMPTION WALK

1. Divide the class into two groups, and have the groups stand on opposite sides of the room. Clear a path so that students can cross from one side of the room to the other. (Have only one group walk for this activity, and use the second group for Activity 7.)

2. Explain that you are going to tell one group an assumption that will be a secret from the other group. Use the assumption, "When I cross the room, everyone will look at me and think I look stupid, and that will be awful." After you tell the group the assumption, ask them to walk halfway across the room, expressing that assumption with their faces and bodies as they walk.

3. Ask students to stop in the center of the room and say hello in a way that expresses that assumption through their voices. Then, have them cross the rest of the way, still expressing that assumption through their bodies.

4. As the group crosses, the other group that is observing tries to determine what the assumption is, looking for the specific ways in which that assumption is expressed through body and voice. The observers will find it easier to describe what they think the walkers are feeling than the assumption that led to the feeling. They may need some help in doing so. Discuss how assumptions influence actions, as, for example, the way it affected the bodies and voices of the students as they crossed the room.

▶ Activity 6: EXAMINING ASSUMPTIONS

1. Help the students begin to understand the basic errors in logic by applying them to the previous activity. Use the information from the introduction to educate them about the errors in logic that inform assumptions. Then help them to change the assumptions to provable beliefs by using language that represents shades of gray as opposed to absolutes.

2. Explain that crystal-balling is when a person claims to know exactly what will happen in the future. Ask the observing students if the students who crossed the room were crystal-balling. You can explain that an example of this was the first group's assumption that others would think they were stupid. Explain that it is impossible to predict exactly what will happen in the future and that doing this is not based on facts. There is a possibility that others *might* think a person is stupid, but there is no proof that this is the case. There are many other possibilities as well. You can ask the students for other options or provide the options. Others might not think anything at all about the person as a result of his or her walk, or they may think that he or she looked great. People cannot predict what may happen in the future.

3. Explain that generalizing is to exaggerate or stretch the truth. Ask the students if the students who crossed were generalizing. You can explain that an example of this was the first group's assumption that *everyone* would think they were stupid. Explain that it is stretching the truth to believe that every single person in the class is thinking the same thing; such a conclusion is not based on facts. There is a possibility that *some* might think they were stupid, but students should remember that provable beliefs are not based on possibilities.

4. Explain that awfulizing is stretching the truth by claiming that something is awful, terrible, or horrible. Ask the students if the students who crossed were awfulizing. You can explain that an example of this was the first group's assumption that being thought of as stupid by others would be *awful*.

5. Explain that it is usually exaggerating to believe that something is awful, terrible, or horrible, and that such a belief is not based on facts. A person might *prefer* not being called stupid, but that doesn't mean it would be awful. Beliefs are based on facts, not exaggerations. The worst thing that may happen if someone is called stupid is that the person may not like it. However, no one can prove that this would be the most awful thing that could happen to a person.

▶ Activity 7: PROVABLE BELIEF WALK

1. Remind students that the first group's assumption was unprovable.

2. Do Activity 5 again, using the group that observed before to do the walk this time. Help them to come up with or give them a provable belief that is not based on crystal-balling, generalizing, or awfulizing. (You can use "When I cross the room, some people might look at me.")

3. Ask students to reflect on the differences they saw in the two groups' behaviors during their walks. Ask them if they think making an assumption affects their behavior, and if so, in what ways?

Extension

Follow up by suggesting that the students write about scientific assumptions that, based on new evidence, have changed over time. They can present these as scientists giving a lecture. Or they can create before and after pictures of an initial scientific assumption and then the belief based on proof (such as thinking the Earth is flat and then finding evidence that it is round).

Middle School Modifications

ALPHABET—Have students discuss the specific ways the activity changed as the emotions changed. Discuss the ways in which other kinds of activities might be similarly affected.

SIT/STAND—Have students discuss the specific ways the movements were affected by the circumstances. Have the students demonstrate ways in which body language can lead to unwanted consequences.

SUBTEXT—Have students provide specific examples of the effect of subtext in their daily lives. Have the students demonstrate ways in which vocal inflections can lead to unwanted consequences.

ASSUMPTION WALK—Have students demonstrate other assumptions that affect the way they enter a room and carry themselves.

EXAMINING ASSUMPTIONS—Have students create posters, describing in words and graphics personal examples of crystal-balling, generalizing, and awfulizing.

PROVABLE BELIEF WALK—Have students discuss the contexts in which changing assumptions and the ways in which they carry themselves would be beneficial.

5

Examining and Lowering Anxiety

Anxiety is an emotion based partly on the assumption, "If something seems fearsome, I must get terribly upset." When a person believes this particular assumption and applies it across a wide range of situations, that person can spend quite a bit of time feeling anxious.

It can be helpful to look at the physiological origins of anxiety. Human beings and other animals have a natural ability to produce a great amount of energy and strength to use in running away from or fighting a perceived danger. People experience this energy in the form of adrenaline; their hearts go faster, and they perspire. In prehistoric times, this energy gave the cave dwellers a chance to survive by fighting off or escaping from such dangers as saber-toothed tigers.

Often, however, people respond to fairly safe situations as if they were as dangerous as an attack by saber-toothed tigers; as a result, they fill their bodies with the kind of energy it would take to fight off that kind of danger. Not all situations are that dangerous, nor do they all call for that amount of energy. By examining their assumptions and thoughts related to anxiety, people can teach themselves not to respond automatically. Students begin to understand that they have the choice to feel many ways about situations, not just terribly upset, and that not all situations are awful or horrible. They can determine the level of danger and find the right amount of energy with which to respond.

The activities in this lesson examine assumptions believed and choices made with regard to anxiety. Activity 1 helps students examine the physiological responses to anxiety, building their awareness of when they are feeling this emotion. Activity 2 increases awareness of situations that trigger anxiety. Activity 3 provides experience in examining one's thoughts. Activity 4 teaches students a useful relaxation technique. Activity 5 provides an opportunity to explore the assumption that leads to anxiety by developing and enacting a series of dramatic scenes based on exploring the assumption.

In addition to these activities, there are other ways of becoming aware of and lowering anxiety. Students can be encouraged to explore their feelings at stressful times such as exams. Also, by offering them opportunities to practice in class, you can encourage them to use relaxation techniques on a regular basis.

▶ Activity 1: BRAINSTORMING STRESS INDICATORS

1. Explain that there are times when people may feel nervous or anxious, such as when they have a big test coming up or when they have to see a doctor. It is important for them to look at their bodies and listen to their voices so they can identify that they are feeling anxious.

2. Ask students to brainstorm the physical things that their bodies and their voices do when they are anxious and to demonstrate those things through movement. Examples of things that they might suggest include stuttering, shaky voice, shaking body, sweating, stomachache, headache, or forgetting.

3. Share the information about the physiological origins of anxiety from the introduction.

▶ Activity 2: INQUIRY

1. Prepare an Anxiety Assessment Scale using the two-column scale form in Resource A. Write the title at the top of the page. Label the columns *Day* and *Amount of Anxiety*. Add the directions: "Fill in the day and show the amount of anxiety you feel on the scale." Add the word *anxiety* to each scale value. Make copies of this assessment, and of the Anxiety form, which is also in Resource A.

2. Ask students to complete the inquiry sentence—"I am anxious when . . ."—on the Anxiety form.

3. Introduce the Anxiety Assessment Scale at the end of the lesson, and ask students to fill it out during the week.

▶ Activity 3: SELF-TALK

1. Explain that people are always thinking about something, even when they are not aware of it. Ask students to sit silently and close their eyes for one minute. During that time, ask them to pay close attention to all the thoughts going through their minds.

2. After a minute, ask who would like to share one of the thoughts they were able to catch. (Have the students share several examples.)

3. Explain to students that the thoughts they think lead to the feelings they experience. For example, certain thoughts can lead to feelings of anxiety. Ask students to imagine that a very important test is about to be given and that they do not feel prepared. Have students sit silently and close their eyes for a minute. During that time, they are to pay close attention to all the thoughts that might be going through their minds, knowing that an important test is about to begin.

4. Ask who would like to share one of the thoughts they were able to catch. (Have the students share several examples.) Examples they might share include

I'm going to flunk this one.

I wish I could get out of here.

I knew I should have studied.

I had better hide my report card when it comes out.

▶ Activity 4: RAGS

Note: This activity is an excellent relaxer. You can use it when students seem stressed or need to loosen up and unwind.

1. Have the students stand with enough room in front of them so they can bend over without hitting each other or the furniture. Explain that this exercise will help them relax their bodies.

2. Ask them to imagine that the muscles in their bodies are slowly changing to rags. Beginning with the top of their heads and slowly moving down their backs, they are to imagine that one muscle group at a time is going to disappear and be replaced with a collection of limp but clean rags.

3. Rags cannot hold up any part of a body: tell students that when a body part has changed to rags, they should allow it to hang loosely. When their bodies are made entirely of rags, ask them to hang limply for a few seconds, paying close attention to the sensation of being made of rags rather than muscles.

4. After hanging, ask them to return to a standing position very slowly, by adding just enough muscle to the rags to get themselves to stand, but no more than is absolutely needed. Have them try to fill their body with a mixture of rags and muscles.

5. Ask students what it felt like to be made of rags. Was it more difficult for a certain part of their bodies to turn into rags? When do they think they might be able to use this exercise?

6. Tell students that the rags exercise also can be done sitting in a chair and that there is no need to hang all the way over to feel the sensation of rags. The exercise also can be used to focus on a particularly tense part of the body, such as a hand that is holding a pencil too tightly.

▶ Activity 5: SCENE INVESTIGATION: STRESSING OUT

1. Scene 1: Based on Unprovable Assumption

Explain to students that they will be acting out a scene that examines this assumption:

If something seems fearsome, I must get terribly upset.

The scene will reflect the assumption and the thoughts, feelings, actions, and consequences that arise from belief in that assumption. Have the students choose roles, and stand in front of the class. Feel free to change genders of the characters and pronouns accordingly. Also, feel free to adapt the scene or create another one that more closely reflects your students' concerns. Instruct all students to express the dialogue with their bodies and voices. Have Carlos sit, with the assumption, thoughts, and feelings standing behind him, as if they are a part of him. As they and the narrator speak, have the student playing Carlos reflect what they are saying with his body and voice. Have the observers watch for evidence of illogic in thoughts, feelings, actions, and consequences.

Scene 1: Stressing Out?

Narrator:	The teacher announces that a test is about to begin. She says:
Teacher:	Class, please put your books in your desks and take out pencils for your math test.
Narrator:	Carlos worries a lot about tests. He assumes:
Assumption:	When something seems scary, I must get terribly upset.
Narrator:	He thinks:
Thoughts:	I won't remember anything. I'll never do well. I'm going to fail. My parents will kill me. I won't go to high school or college and I'll be a failure!
Narrator:	He feels:
Feelings:	I'm so nervous and stressed!
Narrator:	Carlos fidgets with a pencil and asks the teacher:
Carlos:	May I go to the washroom?
Narrator:	She answers:
Teacher:	No Carlos, you'll have to wait until after the test.
Narrator:	The teacher hands out the tests. Carlos stares at the questions and writes very little on his paper. The teacher collects the papers, calls Carlos over and says:
Teacher:	I'm disappointed, Carlos, I know you know the answers and could have done a lot better.

2. Assumption Examination

Remind students that the assumption of this scene was, "If something seems fearsome, I must get terribly upset." Have the student choice-detectives examine the assumption by exploring the ways in which it reflects the three errors in logic. Ask the students the questions below and help them by providing as much of the answer as is necessary. As the lessons progress, they will need decreasing amounts of help.

Was the assumption based on crystal-balling?

The assumption says that a person knows with certainty that something will happen in the future that is to be feared. Choice-detectives know that it is impossible to make this prediction.

Was the assumption based on generalizing?

The assumption says that getting terribly upset is the only possible choice. Choice-detectives know that using the word *must* is an example of exaggerating. *Must* means that there is no choice, that a person could not live without getting terribly upset. But the fact is that the only things people must have to live are related to physical safety: air, water, and food. When people feel, at the moment, that they have no other choice besides becoming terribly upset, they allow themselves to feel this way. However, after examining the assumption, a person realizes that he or she does not have to feel terribly upset, that there are many other ways to feel.

Was the assumption based on awfulizing?

The assumption says that something that seems fearful is awful and horrible and cause for becoming terribly upset. A choice-detective knows that it is stretching the truth to believe that everything that seems fearsome is worth becoming terribly upset. In certain situations, a person might have reason to take action with regard to what seems fearsome. However, all situations do not demand this.

3. Scene Examination

Tell students that you will ask them some questions to help them apply their understanding of the errors in logic to the assumption; rewrite the assumption so that it becomes a provable belief; rewrite the thoughts based on that belief; redefine their feelings based on these thoughts; and finally, predict the actions and consequences arising from the new belief, thoughts, and feelings. Their responses will be reflected in the dialogue in the next scene, and the goal is that they will be ultimately applied in their personal choices. Have students answer the following questions. Answers are provided if necessary.

Applying assumption examination:

Do you think that everything that seems scary gives you a reason to be terribly upset? (No, we can exaggerate the scariness of many situations.)

Can you name some things that you thought were scary that are now less scary than you once thought? (Getting shots, math, meeting new people.)

Do you think that Carlos exaggerated what would have happened if he didn't do well on the test? What do you think would have been the worst thing that could have happened? (Yes, he exaggerated. He might have missed a few problems or even failed the test. However, he would not have flunked the grade or been killed by his parents.)

Rewriting assumption to a provable belief:

What might have been a better belief for Carlos to have when something seems scary? (If something seems scary, I can look closely to figure out what the risks really are.)

Rewriting thoughts to reflect new belief:

What thoughts would that lead to? (I may not do as well as I would like on the test, but I might do fine. If I don't do well, the worst that can happen is I'd have to take the test again. I'll try to remember what I was taught.)

Redefining feeling based on thoughts:

What feelings would that lead to? (Calmness, hope.)

Predicting actions and consequences based on new belief:

How do you think the scene might have ended differently, in a way that would get Carlos's needs met and help him to persevere? (Carlos might have taken deep breaths, done the rags exercise, worked his hardest, and done well on the test.)

4. Scene 2: Based on a Provable Belief

Tell the students that they will be acting out a scene that reflects the provable belief:

If something seems scary, I can look closely to figure out what the risks really are.

The scene will reflect the belief and the thoughts, feelings, actions, and consequences that arise from that belief. Have different students play the roles in this scene to offer a larger number of students the opportunity to act. The same instructions that were given before the first scene apply, in terms of adapting scene, placing actors, using body and voice, and instructing observers. Please take note that in the previous scene, there was the character of "Assumption" and in the revised scene, the character is called "Belief."

Scene 2: Stressing Out?–Revised

Narrator:	The teacher announces that a test is about to begin. She says:
Teacher:	Class, please put your books in your desks and take out pencils for your math test.
Narrator:	Carlos now believes:
Belief:	If something seems scary, I can look closely to figure out what the risks really are.
Narrator:	He now thinks:
Thoughts:	I may not do as well as I would like on the test, but I might do fine. If I don't do well, the worst that could happen is that I'd have to take the test again. I'll try to remember what I was taught.
Narrator:	He now feels:
Feelings:	I feel a little nervous but hopeful.
Narrator:	The teacher hands out the tests. Carlos takes a slow, deep breath, thinks through the answers, and slowly completes the test. The teacher collects the papers, calls Carlos over, and says:
Teacher:	Carlos. I'm so proud of you. You took your time, tried hard, and it really shows!

About a week after this lesson, give students the opportunity to share highlights from their Anxiety Assessment Scales and to discuss their experiences and behavior choices regarding anxiety during the week. Additional activities could include drawing a double-sided picture, one side representing the effects of the assumption and the other reflecting the provable belief.

Middle School Modifications

BRAINSTORMING STRESS INDICATORS—Use age-appropriate examples, such as a first date, college decision making, an opening night performance, or a big game.

INQUIRY—If students are uncomfortable sharing feelings, these can be written anonymously and read aloud.

SCENE INVESTIGATION—Encourage students to develop their own scenes with the one given as a reference.

6

Becoming Aware of Feelings

Sometimes people find it difficult to identify or express their feelings. It may seem at times that people are not supposed to let out their emotions, to cry, or to talk about how they feel. People might try to hide their feelings hoping that they will go away, but they do not disappear, they just hide out. Stifled feelings may be responsible for what are known as psychosomatic diseases. Also, they may affect choices made without a person being aware that this is happening. For example, when a person is angry with someone but does not deal with the anger immediately, he or she may display anger against someone else in an unrelated situation. Students who are upset about something and try to ignore it may find themselves acting out in class.

Awareness of feelings enables people to consciously choose and manage their emotions, understanding when these feelings occur, how often, and how they are expressed.

This lesson examines beliefs and choices made with regard to covering or uncovering feelings. Activity 1 reinforces and gives practice in cooperation as a life skill. Activity 2 provides additional rehearsal in relaxation skills. Activity 3 provides an opportunity to experience masking feelings, whereas Activity 4 offers a chance to examine feelings hidden and feelings shown. Activity 5 builds an awareness of situations in which feelings are covered up. Activity 6 explores the assumption, "I must never let out my feelings, or it will be awful" through a series of scenes.

Additional ways to encourage expression of feelings are through modeling; sharing your feelings when appropriate and in ways you are comfortable with; encouraging students to share their feelings about events in school as well as in their lives, as appropriate; and developing anonymous ways students can do so, such as feelings boxes in which students can write down issues and feelings they want to talk about, act out, or explore.

▶ Activity 1: MIRRORS

1. Have the students stand in a circle. Ask one student to pretend he or she is looking into a very large mirror. The volunteer slowly moves different parts of his or her body. The remaining students form the mirror and follow the volunteer's movements exactly.

2. Explain that everyone must focus on the volunteer and work together to be a believable mirror. If any one of the mirror students does not follow the movements exactly, it will seem as if there is a crack in the mirror, and the mirror is supposed to be in excellent condition.

3. Discuss with students how the mirror students did. What did they have to do to make the mirror work? What might they have done to make the mirror even more believable? What would have kept the mirror from working well? Was it easy to be the mirror students?

▶ Activity 2: RAGS

Repeat Activity 4 in Lesson 5. Following the activity, ask students if they experienced sensations that were different than the first time they did this relaxation exercise. What was different this time? What might they do so the exercise can help them relax even more? When might they use this exercise to help them relax?

▶ Activity 3: MASKS

1. Explain that some people want to cover up what they are feeling, so they make sure that their feelings do not show on the outside. This may be because they are afraid that others won't understand and will laugh at them or because they are following some unspoken rule in their minds, such as big children or boys don't cry, neither of which is true.

2. Ask students to imagine that they are experiencing one particular feeling. Before the feeling shows, however, they will put an imaginary mask over their faces and show a different feeling on the outside. Examples that might be used here include

   Imagine that you are feeling sad. Now, put a happy mask over your face so that everyone can see you smiling, and no one will know that you are sad.

   Imagine that you are feeling afraid on the inside and would like to scream. Put a show-off mask over your face so that everyone can see that you feel confident, and no one will know that you are afraid.

3. Students can perform this activity by drawing and then putting on a mask with each side showing a different emotion, or they can pantomime the two feelings.

4. Ask them what it feels like to be experiencing an emotion but to be unable to express it.

▶ Activity 4: IDEA TREE

Ask students to draw an idea tree with the word *feelings* in the trunk. They are to write the feelings they tend to cover up in the roots and those they show to people in the branches.

▶ Activity 5: INQUIRY

1. Using the four-column form in Resource A, prepare a Feelings Checklist. Write the title at the top of the page. Label the columns *Day, Feeling, Covered,* and *Uncovered*. Add the directions: "Fill in the day and the feeling you felt. Put a check mark under the column labeled *covered* if you covered up the feeling or under *uncovered* if you let your feeling out." Make copies of this form and of the Uncovering Feelings handout, which is also in Resource A.

2. Ask students to complete the sentence, "A time when I kept my feelings inside was . . ." on the Uncovering Feelings handout.

3. Introduce the Feelings Checklist at the end of the lesson, and ask students to fill it out during the week.

▶ Activity 6: SCENE INVESTIGATION: SHARING FEELINGS

1. Scene 1: Based on Unprovable Assumption

Explain to students that they will be acting out a scene that examines the assumption:

I must never let out my feelings, or it would be awful.

Have the students choose roles, and have all but Muneo stand in front of the class. Muneo will be seated with the assumption, thoughts, and feelings standing behind him, as if they are a part of him. Remind everyone to express the words with their bodies and voices, and have the student playing Muneo reflect what the others are saying with his body. Have the observers watch for evidence of illogic in thoughts, feelings, actions, and consequences.

Scene 1: Sharing Feelings

Narrator:	A teacher is returning a test to the students. He says:
Teacher:	Here are your tests back. I know that most of you did the best you could. Some did very well, and some were not as successful.
Narrator:	A student, Muneo, is upset about his grade on the test. However, he doesn't like to let his feelings show. He assumes:
Assumption:	I must never let my feelings out, or it will be awful.
Narrator:	He thinks:
Thoughts:	I'm so upset about this grade. I can't believe I did so badly. I'd better not let anyone know how I feel, or they'll think I'm weird.
Narrator:	He feels:
Feelings:	I'm sad and disappointed and scared of what my parents are going to say. I'm also really nervous that my friends will see how I feel.
Narrator:	Muneo tries to smile to cover up how he really feels. A friend wonders how he did on the test. He asks:
Friend:	How did you do?
Narrator:	Muneo snaps:
Muneo:	Why do you want to know?
Narrator:	The friend turns away, angry with Muneo. Muneo tries to ignore how upset he is, but his head begins to hurt and his stomach starts to feel funny. He says to the teacher:
Muneo:	I don't feel well. May I go to the nurse?
Narrator:	The teacher answers:
Teacher:	Certainly, Muneo, I hope you feel better.

2. Assumption Examination

Remind students that the assumption was, "I must never let my feelings out, or it will be awful." Have the students examine the assumption by exploring the ways in which it reflects the three errors in logic. Ask the students the questions below and provide as much of the answers as they need.

Was the assumption based on crystal-balling?

The assumption states that it would be awful if feelings were expressed. Choice-detectives know that it is impossible to predict what would happen if someone lets out his or her feelings. There are all kinds of possibilities as to how it would be, but no one can prove that it would be awful.

Was the assumption based on generalizing?

The assumption states that people must never let out their feelings. Choice-detectives know that using the word *must* is an example of exaggerating and that they do have a choice about whether they let out their feelings. The word *never* is also an exaggeration and leaves no room for other possibilities. People who believe the assumption may feel that covering up their feelings is their only choice. However, if they examine the assumption, they see that there is another choice—to let out feelings when and how they like.

Was the assumption based on awfulizing?

The assumption states that letting out feelings would be awful. Choice-detectives know that it is stretching the truth to believe that something terrible or awful would happen if feelings are let out. People who believe the assumption and cover up their feelings may be uncomfortable. They might prefer to show their feelings, and they can see by examining the assumption that nothing terrible would happen if they did.

3. Scene Examination

Have students answer the following questions. Answers are provided if necessary.

Applying assumption examination:

Do you think it would be awful to share your feelings? (It might feel uncomfortable at first for some people, but it would definitely not be awful.)

Do you think that Muneo's friends would have thought he was weird if they knew how he felt? (No, they probably would have understood and even helped him because they might have felt the same way.)

What might happen if you didn't share your feelings and kept them inside? (You might get a stomachache and a headache, or you might be mean to someone you didn't want to be mean to.)

What might happen if you did share your feelings? (You might feel better and get help to deal with your feelings.)

Rewriting assumption to a provable belief:

What would be a better belief for Muneo to have about sharing his feelings? (It will not hurt and it might even help to let out my feelings.)

Rewriting thoughts to reflect new belief:

What thoughts might that lead to? (I'm upset about this grade. Maybe I'd feel better if I let someone know how I feel.)

Redefining feelings based on thoughts:

What feelings might that lead to? (Hope that he might feel better.)

Predicting actions and consequences based on new belief:

How might the scene have ended differently, getting Muneo's needs met and helping him to be kinder? (He might have talked about his feelings, gotten support from his friend rather than angering him, felt better about his test, and avoiding feeling sick.)

4. Scene 2: Based on Provable Belief

Tell the students that they will be acting out a scene that reflects the provable belief:

It will not hurt and it might even help to let out my feelings.

Have different students play the roles in this scene. Give the same directions as the first scene in terms of placing actors, using body and voice, and instructing observers.

Scene 2: Sharing Feelings–Revised

Narrator: A teacher is returning a test to the students. He says:

Teacher: Here are your tests back. I know that most of you did the best that you could. Some did very well, and some were not as successful.

Narrator: A student, Muneo, is upset about his grade on the test. He now believes:

Belief: It will not hurt, and it might even help to let out my feelings.

Narrator: He now thinks:

Thoughts: I'm upset about this grade. Maybe I'd feel better if I let someone know how I feel.

Narrator: He now feels:

Feelings: I know that I'm sad and scared. I am hopeful that if I talk about how I feel, I might start feeling better.

Narrator: A friend wonders how Muneo did on the test. He asks:

Friend: How did you do?

Narrator: Muneo tells his friend how he feels. He says:

Muneo: I'm upset that I got a bad grade on the test and scared about what my parents will say. I don't know what to do.

Narrator: His friend says:

Friend: I know how you feel. I feel the same way when I get a bad grade. Maybe you can get some help so that you can do better next time.

Narrator: Muneo asks the teacher for some extra help. He says:

Muneo:	I don't think I understood the questions on the test. Could you help me with it?
Narrator:	The teacher answers:
Teacher:	I would be happy to help you and I'm proud of you for asking for help. I know that you'll do better next time!

About a week after the lesson, give students the opportunity to share highlights from their Feelings Checklist and to discuss their experiences with sharing feelings during the week.

Middle School Modifications

MIRRORS—Have students do the activity in pairs, trying not to let anyone see who is leading and who is following.

MASKS—Have students choose emotions from their personal experiences. Have them discuss their observations of the effects of masking on body and voice. They can present these observations as a lecturing psychologist or show it in a mime.

SCENE INVESTIGATION—Change the situation to one in which a girl is told that her date for a dance has asked someone else to go with him. Revise the scene as appropriate, using the lesson scene as reference.

7

Dealing With Anger

All of us become frustrated or angry at times, and for some, this occurs frequently. The only way infants can express their feelings and needs is by crying. Toddlers are told to "use their words." This is difficult, at first, and when toddlers are discouraged from crying, they sometimes express their feelings in temper tantrums. As children grow older, that frustrated toddler inside may bubble over and lead them to make ineffective choices regarding anger. Various situations trigger anger, and people react in various ways. Some might try to make themselves feel better by hurting themselves or others. Others might keep anger inside and create an illness. Or sometimes, they might keep their feelings inside for a while until they boil over in ways and places they did not intend.

Choosing to become frustrated and angry is based partly on the assumption that "It is awful, and I must get angry when things don't go the way I want them to go." This lesson helps students realize that they have a choice of how to react to anger, from letting go of the situation to dealing with it effectively. This can lead to getting their needs met in more effective ways and allowing them to embody virtues such as patience and respect.

This lesson examines beliefs and choices made regarding anger. Activity 1 reinforces cooperation skills. Activity 2 provides a new relaxation method. Activity 3 builds awareness of feelings of anger and shares strategies that students may use. Activity 4 explores the choice of letting go of unpleasant situations or dealing with them. Activity 5 explores the assumption, "It is awful, and I must get angry when things don't go the way I want them to go" through a series of scenes.

Additional ways to explore choices around anger include modeling assertiveness and dealing with class situations that elicit anger by discussing choices made and the assumptions on which they were based, and by choosing and rehearsing new options.

▶ Activity 1: MIRRORS

1. Explain that the students will be creating a mirror as they did in Lesson 6, Activity 1. The person looking into the mirror will move as if he or she is feeling angry. As the mover shows anger through face and body, the rest of the students will mirror him or her exactly.

2. How did the mirror work this time? How was the anger expressed? Are there other ways in which one can express anger? Did they feel any anger as they copied the movements?

▶ Activity 2: SLOW BREATHING

1. Explain that this is another exercise that can be used to help a person relax.

2. Ask students to close their eyes for a moment and to pay attention to the natural rhythm of their breathing. Their breathing is the slowest when they are the most calm and when they are sleeping. As they become more and more anxious or emotional, their breathing becomes more rapid.

3. To calm themselves, they can purposely slow their breathing. Ask them to inhale to a slow count of four, using all four counts to take in a full breath. Without holding their breath, they immediately exhale to a slow count of four. (Do this several times.)

4. Ask the students how they feel. Was this exercise different than the rags activity? How do they think they might use this exercise?

▶ Activity 3: INQUIRY

1. Using the two-column scale format in Resource A, prepare an Anger Assessment Scale. Write the title at the top of the page. Label the columns *Day* and *Amount of Anger*. Add the directions: "Fill in the day and indicate the amount of anger you felt on the scale." Add the word *Anger* to the scale values. Make copies of the Anger Assessment Scale and of the Anger handout, which is also in Resource A.

2. Ask students to finish the sentence "A time I got angry was . . ." on the Anger handout.

3. Introduce the Anger Assessment Scale at the end of the lesson, and ask students to fill it out during the week.

▶ Activity 4: LETTING GO

1. Use the information from the introduction to explain the variety of responses to anger. Tell the students that when something happens that is not to their liking, they have the option of letting it go or dealing with it. Read the situations below, and take a vote to determine whether students would let go of what happened or deal with it.

Someone brushes up against you in the hall.

Someone calls you a name.

Your brother or sister gets a bigger piece of cake for dessert.

A classmate throws something at you.

Your teacher assigns extra homework.

2. Have the students brainstorm additional situations and discuss the criteria for letting go of something or dealing with it (e.g., letting go of situations that cannot be changed, that happen by accident, that have less impact on one's life).

▶ Activity 5: SCENE INVESTIGATION: CONTROLLING ANGER

1. Scene 1: Based on Unprovable Assumption

Explain to students that they will be acting out a scene that examines the assumption

It is awful, and I must get angry when things don't go the way I want them to go.

Have the students choose roles and stand in front of the class, except for Alisha and her friend, who will be seated. Have the assumption, thoughts, and feelings stand behind Alisha as if they are a part of her. Remind the actors to use their bodies and voices, and remind the observers to pay attention to thoughts, feelings, actions, and consequences.

Scene 1: Controlling Anger

Narrator:	Alisha and her friend are playing checkers in Alisha's room. Alisha's sister Samaya stands at the door and watches. She asks:
Samaya:	Can I play, too?
Narrator:	Alisha assumes:
Assumption:	It is awful, and I must get angry when things don't go the way I want them to go.
Narrator:	She thinks:
Thoughts:	I can't believe she won't leave me alone. This is awful. She's out to make me crazy. I hate her.
Narrator:	She feels:
Feelings:	I'm frustrated and furious.

Narrator:	She says:
Alisha:	No way, leave us alone.
Samaya:	Why not, I know how to play, too!
Narrator:	Alisha gets angrier and angrier and says:
Alisha:	Go away, you're a little baby. Play by yourself.
Samaya:	Please, I promise to be quiet.
Alisha:	I said, get out right now, or you're going to regret you're my sister.
Narrator:	Samaya doesn't move. Alisha gets up. Goes over to her sister and starts to raise a hand to push and hit her. At that moment, their mother passes by the bedroom, sees Alisha's raised hand, and says:
Mother:	I see that you're still having problems getting along with your sister. You need to ask your friend to leave so that we can talk about what we can do to help you to get along better.

2. Assumption Examination

Remind students that the assumption was, "It is awful and I must get angry when things don't go the way I want them to go." Ask the students the questions below, and provide as much of the answers as necessary.

Was the assumption based on crystal-balling?

Choice-detectives know that it is impossible to predict what will happen if things don't go the way people want them to go. There are many possibilities, and no one can prove that it will be awful.

Was the assumption based on generalizing?

Choice-detectives know that it is an exaggeration to use the word *must*. People do not have to get angry if things don't go their way. There is a choice about how to feel, even though it may be difficult to make that choice, at first.

Was the assumption based on awfulizing?

Choice-detectives know that it is stretching the truth to believe that it is awful if things do not go the way someone would like. A person may prefer things to be different, but no one can prove that it is awful if they are not different.

3. Scene Examination

Have students answer the following questions, and provide help with the answers as necessary.

Applying assumption examination:

Is it really awful when things don't go your way? (No, I would like certain things to be different, but it is not awful if they are not.)

When things don't go the way you want them to, is your only choice to get very angry? (I have a number of choices, including ignoring certain situations and trying calmly to change certain situations.)

Did Alisha get what she wanted in the first scene? (No, her friend had to leave.)

Rewriting assumption to a provable belief:

What might have been a better belief for Alisha to have about times when things don't go her way? (Sometimes I would like things to be different, but I can deal with them calmly or let them go.)

Rewriting thoughts to reflect new belief:

What thoughts would that lead to? (I'd rather play with my friend than my sister. I'll explain myself calmly to her.)

Redefining feelings based on thoughts:

What feelings would that lead to? (Hope.)

Predicting actions and consequences based on new belief:

What would she do differently? (Talk to her sister, get help from her mom.)

How would the end turn out differently so that Alisha could have her needs met while being kinder and more patient? (She would be able to come up with a compromise that would satisfy her sister and still allow her to play with her friend.)

4. Scene 2: Based on Provable Belief

Tell the students that they will be acting out a scene that reflects the provable belief:

Sometimes I would like situations to be different, but I can deal with them calmly or let them go.

Have different students play the roles in this scene, and give them the same directions as to placement, use of body and voice, and observers.

Scene 2: Controlling Anger–Revised

Narrator:	Alisha and her friend are playing checkers in Alisha's room. Alisha's sister Samaya stands at the door and watches. She asks:
Samaya:	Can I play, too?
Narrator:	Alisha now believes:
Belief:	Sometimes I would like things to be different, but I can let them go or deal with them.
Narrator:	Alisha now thinks:
Thoughts:	I'd rather play alone with my friend. Maybe I'll explain that calmly to her.
Narrator:	She now feels:
Feelings:	I'm hopeful that I can take care of this.
Narrator:	Alisha takes a slow deep breath so that she will be able to answer calmly. She says:
Alisha:	We'd like to play by ourselves.
Samaya:	Why? I know how to play, too!
Narrator:	Alisha thinks:
Thoughts:	I'm not going to get angry. I'll try to explain myself to her.
Narrator:	Alisha says:
Alisha:	Sometimes I like to play with you, but sometimes, like today, I like to play alone with my friends.
Samaya:	Please, I promise to be very quiet.
Narrator:	Alisha thinks:
Thoughts:	I don't know what to do. Maybe mom can help.
Narrator:	At that moment, their mother passes by the bedroom. Alisha says:
Alisha:	Mom, we want to play by ourselves right now, but Samaya wants to play with us. I tried to get her to understand, but she won't take no for an answer.
Mother:	Thank you for trying to explain yourself to your sister and not yelling. I'm proud of you for asking for help rather than fighting. Your sister and I will do something together. Maybe after you and your friend have had some time alone, Samaya can join you for one game. Is that all right with you?
Alisha:	Yes. Thanks, mom.

Extension

Discuss and demonstrate the boiling point of water, allowing the water to boil over. Or do a pantomime of being "boiling mad," first boiling over and then showing a different way to handle anger.

Also, a week or so following this lesson, at any day or time convenient to you, give students the opportunity to share highlights from their Anger Assessment Scale and to discuss a time since the lesson when they felt frustrated or angry and how they dealt with those feelings.

Middle School Modifications

Have students give examples of the different ways they have handled anger, discussing, drawing, or acting out the changes in body, voice, and consequences based on each choice.

MIRRORS—Do a series of mirrors revealing a continuum of anger from slightly perturbed through enraged. Discuss the similarities and differences between each.

8

Examining and Accepting Responsibility

Many times, people do not know what they are responsible for, what they have directly caused, and what are the responsibilities of others. Sometimes they understand that they are responsible for their choices; sometimes they believe that they are not responsible for their own choices; and sometimes they believe that they are responsible for others' choices as well as their own.

It is important for people to determine responsibility based on facts and not assumptions, so that they acknowledge appropriate responsibility but not inappropriate guilt. Two related assumptions serve as the foundation for this assumption: "I am responsible for everything. I am responsible for nothing."

This lesson examines assumptions related to one's degree of responsibility for various choices. Activity 1 encourages active examination of students' assumptions relating to responsibility. Activity 2 builds the students' ability to determine when they are responsible for something. Activity 3 explores the twin assumptions "I am responsible for everything, I am responsible for nothing" through a series of scenes.

Additional ways to encourage the assumption of appropriate responsibility are modeling and discussing choices for which students are responsible, rather than accepting phrases such as "I had no choice."

▶ Activity 1: RESPONSIBILITY VOTE

1. Tell students that they are going to vote to determine situations in which they would take responsibility and those in which they would not take responsibility. Explain that some people assume that they are not responsible for their own choices. Some people assume that they are responsible for others' choices as well as their own. It is important to examine these assumptions so that a person can determine what is and is not his or her personal responsibility.

2. Explain that you will describe a number of different situations and give the students two choices to vote for: responsible and not responsible. Students who would accept responsibility should raise a hand after you say "responsible." Tell them that their answers are to be based on their personal opinions. Examples of situations that might be used include these:

   Your homework is not where you thought you left it. Are you responsible for your homework?

   Your den is messy after a friend has been over to play with you. Are you responsible for the mess?

   You said, "I wish you were dead" to someone, out of anger, and that person became ill. Are you responsible for their illness?

   Your parents have been fighting, and you overhear your name being mentioned during the fight. Are you responsible for their fighting?

3. Discuss the process of determining responsibility by examining the facts and asking questions such as: Did the situation happen as a direct result of what I did? Was the situation a result of my choice, even though I may have made the same choice many others made? Was the situation a result of someone else's choice or of something else? Could I have made a different choice?

▶ Activity 2: INQUIRY

1. Using the two-column format (without scale) in Resource A, prepare a Responsibility Checklist. Write the title at the top of the page. Label the columns *Day* and *Situation*. Add the directions: "Fill in the day and the situation. Then, write the word or words that best describe how much of the situation you felt you were responsible for: *everything, certain things, nothing*." Make copies of the checklist and of the Responsibility handout, which is also in Resource A.

2. Ask students to complete the inquiry sentence, "A time I felt totally responsible or not responsible was . . ." on the Responsibility handout.

3. Introduce the Responsibility Checklist at the end of the lesson, and ask students to fill it out during the week.

▶ Activity 3: SCENE INVESTIGATION: DETERMINING RESPONSIBILITY

1. Scene 1: Based on Unprovable Assumption

Explain to students that they will be acting out scenes which examine the assumptions:

I am responsible for everything. I am responsible for nothing.

Have the students choose roles; all but the two defendants will stand in front of the class. The defendants will sit, and their assumptions, thoughts, and feelings will stand behind their defendant as if they are a part of them. Remind students to use their bodies and voices to reflect the dialogue. Tell the observers that they are to imagine that they are the jury for the cases being tried: They need to listen carefully to the assumptions, thoughts, and feelings to determine the level of responsibility of each defendant.

Scene 1: Examining and Accepting Responsibility

Narrator:	The judge calls the court to order. She says:
Judge:	The court is now in session. In the first hearing, the defendants will describe their situations. They will describe what happened and the part they played in what happened. They will then state whether they feel they are responsible or not responsible for what happened. I would like the jury to listen carefully. Following the hearing, you will determine the responsibility of each defendant. Defendant No. 1, please describe your situation.
Narrator:	Defendant No. 1 assumes:
Assumption:	I am responsible for everything.
Narrator:	He thinks:
Thoughts:	I hope I get punished for this because it was my fault.
Narrator:	He feels:
Feelings:	I feel so guilty and ashamed.
Narrator:	He says:
Defendant No. 1:	Well, your honor, I was angry with my mother because she wouldn't let me sleep over at a friend's house. I'm working on doing better with my anger, but it's still a new thing for me. Well,

(Continued)

(Continued)

	when I was angry with my mother, I thought to myself. "I wish you were dead." My mother has been sick for the past few days, and I know that it must be because of me, because of what I thought. It's my fault that she's sick. I take all the blame. I'm sorry for making her sick. I'm completely responsible and must be punished.
Narrator:	The judge calls on the second defendant. She says:
Judge:	Defendant No. 2, please describe your situation.
Narrator:	Defendant No. 2 assumes:
Assumption:	I am responsible for nothing.
Narrator:	She thinks:
Thoughts:	I don't really know why I'm here. It's not my fault.
Narrator:	She feels:
Feelings:	I'm confused and frustrated.
Narrator:	She says:
Defendant No. 2:	I guess I'll tell you what happened, even though it had absolutely nothing to do with me. We were working on a project in class, and the teacher had asked us to work in silence. Well, everyone was talking anyway, and we got in trouble. I don't know why I'm here though. Everyone was talking so I had to talk, too. If someone says something to you, you have to answer them. I had no choice. It's not my fault. Don't blame me because I'm not responsible.
Narrator:	The judge says:
Judge:	Members of the jury, please answer the questions you will be asked to determine the responsibility of the defendants. Court will be in recess while the jury reaches a decision.

2. Assumption Examination

Remind students that the assumptions were "I am responsible for everything. I am responsible for nothing." Have the jury examine the assumptions by exploring ways in which they reflect errors in logic. Ask the students the following question, and help them by providing as much of the answer as is necessary.

Were the assumptions based on generalizing?

Choice-detectives know that using the words *everything* and *nothing* are examples of exaggeration. It is not possible for a person to be responsible for every single thing that happens. It is not possible for a person to be responsible for absolutely nothing that happens. A person might be responsible for some things. A person can look at the facts to determine his or her responsibility.

3. Scene Examination

Have students answer the following questions. Answers are provided if necessary.

Applying assumption examination:

> Do you think that it's possible to be responsible for every single thing that happens? (No, some things but not everything.)

> Do you think that it's possible to be responsible for not one single thing? (No, some things are likely to be my responsibility.)

> What can a person do to determine responsibility? (Examine the facts by asking questions such as: Did the situation happen as a direct result of what I did? Was the situation a result of my choice, even though I may have made the same choice many others made? Was the situation a result of someone else's choice? Could I have made a different choice?)

Changing assumption to provable belief:

> What would be a better belief to have about responsibility? (There are certain things for which I am responsible and certain things for which I am not responsible.)

Applying new belief:

> Do you think that Defendant No. 1 was responsible for his mother's sickness? (No, he is not responsible for his mom's sickness, as it was not a direct result of what he did. People can't make someone sick by what they think or say.)

> Do you think that Defendant No. 2 was responsible for talking in class? (Yes, even though others in class made the choice to talk, she made that choice as well. She could have made a different choice, but she chose to talk, so she is responsible for her action.)

4. Scene 2: Based on Provable Belief

> Tell students that they will be acting out a scene that reflects the provable belief:

> There are certain things that I am responsible for and certain things that I am not responsible for.

Have different students play the roles in this scene. The same instructions that were given for the first scene apply in terms of placement of actors, use of voice and body, and observers playing jury members.

Scene 2: Examining and Accepting Responsibility–Revised

Narrator:	The judge calls the court back to order. She says:
Judge:	The court is back in session. Jury, I thank you for reaching the correct verdict. I have read your answers to the defendants, and I believe that you will see that they have reached different conclusions, thanks to you. I will now give the defendants a chance to restate their cases based on the new facts they received.
Narrator:	Defendant No. 1 now believes:
Belief:	There are certain things that I am responsible for and certain things that I am not responsible for.
Narrator:	He now thinks:
Thoughts:	I don't believe that my mother's illness was my fault. Her sickness was not in my control.
Narrator:	He now feels:
Feelings:	I feel sad that my mom is sick, but I don't feel guilty any more.
Narrator:	He says:
Defendant No. 1:	Your honor, I was very angry at my mother because she wouldn't let me sleep at a friend's house. When I was angry, I thought to myself, "I wish you were dead." My mother has been sick for the past few days, but I know that I am not at fault for that. I do not have the power to make her sick. Her illness is not a direct result of what I thought. I would like her to feel better, but I can't help her to feel better by taking responsibility for something for which I am not responsible. All I can do is help her any way I can and stop blaming myself. Your honor, I know now that I am not responsible for my mother's illness.
Narrator:	Defendant No. 2 now believes:
Belief:	There are certain things that I am responsible for and certain things that I am not responsible for.
Narrator:	She now thinks:
Thoughts:	I believe that I was responsible for talking in class. Even though others were talking, I made my own choice to talk when I could have kept quiet.
Narrator:	She now feels:
Feelings:	I feel proud of myself for taking responsibility.

Narrator:	She says:
Defendant No. 2:	Your honor, we were working on a project in class, and the teacher had asked us to work in silence. Well, everyone was talking anyway, and we all got in trouble. Even though everyone else was talking, I made my own choice to talk. It might have been difficult to stay quiet while others were talking, but I could have done so anyway. Next time the situation comes up, I will remember that I have a choice to make. Your honor, I am responsible for talking in class.
Judge:	Thank you, defendants and jury. I am proud of all of you for being excellent citizens! Court is dismissed.

Middle School Modifications

RESPONSIBILITY VOTE—Use additional examples, such as: Are you responsible for your basic body type? Are you responsible for keeping a secret if revealing that secret could protect someone? Also, brainstorm the excuses used for shirking responsibility.

SCENE INVESTIGATION—Change Defendant No. 1's situation to reflect that he was angry with his mother because his mother insisted that he return home after a party by 11 p.m. Change the situation for Defendant No. 2 to that of drinking at a party.

9

Choosing Happiness

It is natural to feel and express sadness. However, some people get sad about certain things when they could choose not to be upset; as a result, they are sadder more often or more deeply than they have to be. Some people believe that something outside of themselves brings them happiness. Some may hold off being happy until everything in their lives is exactly as they want, believing that will bring them happiness. Some may choose to wait until people act toward them the way they would want before they allow themselves to be happy. Or, others may choose to wait until they possess all they would want, such as toys, popularity, or clothes, before they choose to feel happy. Others may focus on the things that they are lacking rather than appreciate the things that they have.

This lesson looks at choices made with regard to happiness. Activity 1 builds students' awareness of the ability to choose happiness in their daily activities. Activity 2 explores the effects of happiness on body and voice, giving students the opportunity to identify the characteristic body language of happiness. Activity 3 provides experience in the use of guided fantasy to enhance emotions. Activity 4 provides an opportunity to brainstorm and diagram positive and negative methods of enhancing happiness. Activity 5 helps the students learn to focus on appreciating what is positive in their lives rather than focusing on the negatives. Activity 6 explores the assumption "I can never be happy, and life will be awful unless certain things are a certain way" through several scenes.

Additional ways to encourage the choice of happiness are modeling, sharing realistic ways of dealing with sadness while not staying in that emotional place, and encouraging students to focus on positive thoughts and behaviors.

▶ Activity 1: INQUIRY

1. Using the three-column format in Resource A, prepare the Happiness Checklist. Write the title at the top of the page. Label the columns *Day, Unhappy,* and *Happy.* Add the directions: "Fill in the day and mark *Unhappy* if you were unhappy that day or *Happy* if you were happy that day." Make copies of the Happiness Checklist and of the Happiness handout, which is also in Resource A.

2. Ask students to complete the inquiry sentence—"A time when I felt unhappy was . . ." on the Happiness handout.

3. Introduce the Happiness Checklist at the end of the lesson, and ask students to fill it out during the week.

▶ Activity 2: MOVING SCULPTURE

1. Explain that everyone in the class is to combine wordlessly to create a sculpture that would express happiness through their collective bodies.

2. After the sculpture is formed and on the count of three, the sculpture moves in a way that would express happiness (open, connected, fluid, with energy).

3. On the next count of three, students add to the sculpture sounds, words, or melodies that would express happiness through their voices (with energy, volume).

4. Ask students how the sculpture formed. What made it more or less difficult to do this? How were decisions made about movement? What were the pictures, movement, and sound qualities that expressed happiness? How can the students move and speak in ways that express happiness to increase the happiness that they are feeling?

▶ Activity 3: GUIDED FANTASY

1. Explain to students that when people daydream, they are able to see all kinds of pictures in their minds.

2. Tell students that you are going to help them to see a particular kind of picture in their minds right now. Ask them to close their eyes and listen to the sound of your voice. Reassure them that because everyone's eyes are closed and there will be nothing to see, they can feel comfortable about keeping their eyes shut. As they listen to the sound of your voice, ask them to picture in their minds what you are describing.

3. Tell students that right now, they are sitting in chairs in a classroom. Ask them to imagine that their chair and the classroom have disappeared and that they are now sitting on the grass in the middle of a huge field. Tell them to feel the softness of the grass beneath them. This grass is allergy free, so there is no need to be concerned about health problems.

4. Ask them, in their minds, to look around them. It is a beautiful place, filled with all the things that they find beautiful. Tell them to look in front of them and see what is there; to listen carefully to the sounds around them; to hear all their favorite sounds; to breathe deeply; and to smell all the wonderful fragrances that surround them.

5. Explain that this is a safe place, a place where they are always happy. They can be alone here, or they can bring people they like with them. In their minds, they are to see themselves doing all the things that they enjoy in this special place and to pay attention to all the positive happy thoughts they have here.

6. Tell them that they are going to leave this place in a few moments. However, this is a place that they can come back to on their own whenever they want to feel happier. In their minds, they say good-bye to this special place for now, knowing that they can return.

7. Ask them to pay attention to the feeling of their chair underneath them and the sounds and smells of the classroom and to slowly open their eyes.

▶ Activity 4:
BRAINSTORMING A VENN DIAGRAM

1. This activity requires that students know about Venn diagrams.

2. Explain that the students are to brainstorm as many positive ways of becoming happier as they can. Then, they brainstorm as many negative ways of becoming happier as they can. Explain that positive ways would not harm themselves or others and do not go against the law or their beliefs. Negative ways would be harmful to themselves or others and are against the law or their beliefs.

3. Have them create a Venn diagram to illustrate their findings. Examples of ways of becoming happier might include the following:

Positive
    Thinking positive happy thoughts by counting their blessings
    Doing something they like to do
    Taking themselves to their special place
    Helping another person to feel happier

Negative
    Acting out
    Trying to make someone else feel bad
    Doing something to excess, such as staying in a fantasy world, spending a
        lot of money, or overeating
    Stealing
    Taking a drink

▶ Activity 5: ATTITUDE OF GRATITUDE

1. Draw a glass half-filled with water on the board. Ask your students to raise their hand if they think the glass is half full or half empty. Explain to the students that they can look at a glass (their lives) as half full and focus on what is positive in their lives, or they can look at their lives as half empty,

dwelling on the negatives. Add the information from the introduction to elaborate on this.

2. Tell the students that to help them focus on the positives, they will be developing their own gratitude posters. On a large piece of paper, have the students write and draw all the things in their lives for which they are thankful. Have the students share them with each other. Discuss the importance of looking at the positives in their lives rather than the negatives.

▶ Activity 6: SCENE INVESTIGATION: CHOOSING HAPPINESS

1. Scene 1: Based on Unprovable Assumption

Explain to students that they will be acting out a scene which examines the assumption:

I can only be happy when things are a certain way, and life will be awful until then.

Have the students choose roles and stand in front of the class. Instruct all students to express the dialogue with their bodies and voices. Have the assumption, thought, and feelings stand behind Tina as if they are a part of her. As they and the narrator speak, have the student playing Tina reflect what they are saying with her body and voice. Tell the observers that they are the studio audience watching a talk show and that they are to watch for evidence of illogic in thoughts, feelings, actions, and consequences.

	Scene 1: Choosing Happiness
Host:	Welcome to the Happiness Makeover Show where our experts will tell you exactly what you need to do to be happy! Our guest today is Tina, and boy, is she in need of a makeover! Tina has the assumption that:
Assumption:	I can only be happy when things are a certain way, and life will be awful until then.
Host:	She thinks:
Thoughts:	Things have to be a certain way, and they're not always the way that I want them to be. Life is always going to be awful. I can never be happy.
Host:	She feels:
Feelings:	I'm so sad and hopeless.
Tina:	Yeah, that's why I'm here. But I don't think it will do any good.
Host:	Well, do we have the answers for you! And here he is, the well-known happiness expert, Mr. Stuff. Please

(Continued)

(Continued)

	give Tina your expert advice on how she can be happier.
Mr. Stuff:	My dear, you absolutely must have every hair on your head exactly perfect, every outfit in your wardrobe in style, and every popular toy out there. Only then will you be happy.
Host:	It is now one week later, and Tina has taken his advice. Let's see how she feels now. Tina, how does it feel to look amazing and to own everything you could possibly want? You must be happy now, right?
Tina:	Well, no, actually. I thought for sure it would work, because Mr. Stuff was telling me exactly how to get things to be a certain way that I knew would make me happy. But it didn't work. For a while, I liked how I looked in the mirror, and I did play with the toys for a few days but then I wasn't interested any more. Those things just didn't really make me happy.
Host:	Well Tina, I'm sorry, but it looks like our expert was not the right one for you. I think that we will have to look to our studio audience and see how they can help. What do you think would help Tina to feel happier?

2. Assumption Examination

Remind students that the assumption was "I can only be happy when things are a certain way, and life will be awful until then. Have the "studio audience" examine the assumption by exploring the ways in which it reflects the three errors in logic. Ask the students the questions below and help them by providing as much of the answer as is necessary.

Was the assumption based on crystal-balling?

The assumption says that when things are a certain way, the person will be happy. Choice-detectives know that it is not possible to predict happiness in the future—even if things were a certain way.

Was the assumption based on generalizing?

The assumption says that the only way a person can be happy is when things are a certain way. Choice-detectives know that the word *only* is an exaggeration. It is stretching the truth to say that this is the only way to be happy. There are other choices for paths to happiness.

Was the assumption based on awfulizing?

Choice-detectives know that it is stretching the truth to believe that life would be awful if things were not the way a person would like them to be. A person might prefer that things were a certain way, but there's no way to prove that life would be awful if they were not.

3. Scene Examination

Have students answer the following questions. Answers are provided if necessary.

Applying assumption examination:

> Do you think that you can only be happy when things are a certain way and that life will be awful until then? (No, I have other choices of paths to happiness.)
>
> Do you think that the happiness expert gave Tina good advice when he told her to focus on how she looked and what she had? (No, looking good and having things she wanted ultimately did not make Tina happy.)

Changing assumption to provable belief:

> What might be a better belief for Tina to have about becoming happier? (I can choose to be happy even if things aren't exactly the way I want them to be.)

Rewriting thoughts to reflect new belief:

> What thoughts might that lead to? (I know that there are some things in my life that I would prefer to be different. But whether or not they are, I can choose to feel good.)

Redefining feelings based on thoughts:

> What feelings would that lead to? (Acceptance, happiness.)

Predicting actions and consequences based on new belief:

> How do you think the scene might have ended differently, getting Tina's need met and building optimism? (Tina might have realized that the expert was not the expert for her but that she was the expert on her own happiness and was able to control it. She might have thought about the things in her life that are going well, acknowledged but not become upset about the things that are not, and used her imagination to help her.)

4. Scene 2: Based on Provable Belief

Tell students that they will be acting out a scene that reflects the provable belief:

> I can choose to be happy even if things aren't exactly the way I want them to be.

Have different students play the roles in this scene. The same instructions that were given for the first scene apply in terms of scene adaptation, placement of actors, use of body and voice, and observers' role.

Scene 2: Choosing Happiness–Revised

Host: I'd like to thank our studio audience for their brilliant ideas on how to feel happier. We have shared them with Tina, and it made a huge impression. Tina now believes:

Belief: I can choose to be happy even if things aren't exactly the way I want them to be.

Host: She now thinks:

Thoughts: I don't have to focus on and become overly upset over everything. I can let the things go that aren't exactly the way I want them to be.

Host: She now feels:

Feelings: I am much happier, more of the time.

Tina: Smiling feels really good. It's nice to know that I can choose how I feel, that the situations around me don't determine my happiness—I do.

Host: Thank you once again, studio audience, for helping Tina realize that she is able to give herself her own happiness makeover! See you next time.

Create a scientific formula for happiness. Also, a week or so after this lesson, give students the opportunity to share highlights from their Happiness Checklist and to discuss when they felt happiest and how they arrived at that feeling. They may read from their Happiness Checklist or talk about their week. No one comments unless students who share would like comments or ask for suggestions.

Middle School Modifications

MOVING SCULPTURE—Discuss the specific ways happiness is expressed in bodies and voices on a day-to-day basis. Also, talk about how people allow themselves to express happiness in different ways as they get older.

GUIDED FANTASY—Have students draw a picture of their special place. You can create a collage or mural with all the pictures.

BRAINSTORMING A VENN DIAGRAM—Discuss personal, peer, and societal pressures to engage in negative methods of enhancing happiness.

ATTITUDE OF GRATITUDE–The students can share what they are grateful for in each other, their friends, and their families.

SCENE INVESTIGATION—Change the situation so that Tina believes that if she had all the friends she wanted, she would be popular and happy.

Section 2

Developing Social Skills

This section will focus on the development of social competence and the building of social skills. Various researchers have pointed out the importance of teaching social skills as a necessary part of the educational process, as well as the positive outcomes associated with doing so (Goleman, 1995; Greenberg et al., 2003; Zins et al., 2004).

One positive outcome of note is that training students in how to handle relationships contributes to greater ease in classroom management (Evertson, Emmer, & Worsham, 2005).

The first relationship that needs to be addressed is the one that people have with themselves. If people are able to treat themselves with respect, they have a much better chance of doing so with others as well. If they know how to feel good about themselves in positive ways, they are less likely to make themselves feel good at the expense of others, which contributes to unhealthy relationships. Nathaniel Branden (1994), a pioneer in the field of self-esteem, detailed the importance of integrating the development of self-esteem into the school curriculum and linked a high level of self-esteem to the prevention of a host of negative outcomes, including early pregnancy and drug abuse.

The first three lessons in this section introduce students to the ideas of self-worth and self-measurement. Students examine their concepts of themselves and consider different methods of evaluating their self-worth. In the next two lessons, students begin to apply their informed choice-making understanding to relationships. Students examine how they behave toward friends and family and consider how they may choose behaviors to improve their friendships and relations with family members.

The final three lessons expand on the previous concepts by exploring choices made regarding dealing with others. The lessons examine skills and behaviors needed to develop interpersonal intelligence and build empathic understanding. Students have the opportunity to develop an awareness of how they and others react to behaviors that demonstrate both negative (put-downs) and positive (complimentary) appraisals of others. Students examine the reality of peer pressure from both the giver's and the receiver's viewpoints. The concept of prejudgment, or prejudice, is carefully thought about in the final lesson, giving students an opportunity to recognize uninformed behavior and its effects on others.

10

Developing Self-Acceptance

People may choose whether or not to accept themselves for who they are. This choice is based on a number of assumptions that can be discovered if they learn to pay attention to the statements they tell themselves about themselves—the self-talk that plays inside their minds like an ongoing tape.

Some people make up their own statements, but sometimes their self-talk statements are comments that others, such as peers, teachers, and family members, have made first and that the person has internalized. A person often believes these statements without checking whether they are true, assuming that if others say them, they must be true. Then, the person begins to rehearse those same statements, arriving at his or her self-talk independently. But still, the self-talk is not necessarily based on fact.

When people believe their self-talk, they help or hurt themselves depending on the nature of their self-conversation—whether positive or negative. Self-talk can be a large factor in someone's level of self-esteem. It is worthwhile to examine these statements and explore self-talk, which can help people feel good about themselves.

This lesson helps students examine their self-talk and explore nurturing ways they can talk to themselves. Activity 1 provides additional practice in cooperation. Activity 2 gives students another stress management technique. Activity 3 offers an exploration of students' levels of self-acceptance. Activity 4 builds students' positive self-talk skills. Activity 5 helps students identify and share both negative and positive self-talk.

Additional ways to encourage self-acceptance are to model positive self-talk, sharing good things about yourself as well as listening to students' self-talk; to discourage focus on negativity and weakness; and to encourage focus on positive comments and building on strengths.

▶ Activity 1: WORDS

1. Tell students that as a class, they are to create a word by using their bodies to form each letter of the word. (This activity is similar to Alphabet, Lesson 2, Activity 1.)

2. Give the students a word to form. Then ask students if the letters in the word were easier or harder to form than they were the first time they formed letters. Ask them what they think is different about how they are working together now.

▶ Activity 2: RAGS

Do the relaxation exercise as described in Lesson 5, Activity 5. Ask students if they use this activity to relax. How have they used this or other relaxation activities in their lives?

▶ Activity 3: SELF-ACCEPTANCE BAROMETER

1. Clear space for the students to stand between beginning and end points you designate. Use the examples provided or create your own opinions for the barometer.

2. Explain that the students are going to create a barometer to measure a number of different opinions. It consists of (1) an imaginary line between the beginning and end points that you point out and (2) the students as actual points on the line. Designate one end of the barometer as high, the other as low, and mark the quarter points, perhaps by using classroom furniture or equipment—for example, a chair or an eraser. This will help students find an appropriate degree between high and low where they can stand to express their opinion. Remind them that a weather barometer measures different degrees of pressure, and explain that this opinion barometer measures different degrees of opinion.

3. Explain to the students that you will make a statement, and they are to share their opinion on the statement by taking a position on the opinion barometer that represents their degree of feeling about the statement. After taking a moment to decide how they feel about what you say, students stand on the part of the barometer that reflects their opinion. Assure them that there is no right or wrong answer, so they are to take a stand based on their own personal opinion. Even if their friend or every other student is on a different part of the barometer, encourage them to stay with what they feel. Examples of statements you might make include

   "I feel good about myself." Stand on the line according to how much of the time you feel this way, for example, 0% of the time, 25% of the time, 50% of the time, 100% of the time.

   "I like myself." Stand on the line according to the degree to which you like yourself, that is, not at all, a little bit, quite a bit, a great deal.

Extension

Construct a barometer that reflects the full range of self-acceptance. Then give a "self-acceptance report," like a weather report, stating the self-acceptance readings in place of barometric pressure readings. Feel free to add questions for the barometer, and encourage students to ask them as well. Note that this barometer activity may be used to measure responses to other issues and therefore can be adapted for use in other lessons.

▶ Activity 4: INQUIRY

Make copies of the Self-Acceptance handout in Resource A, and ask students to complete the positive sentences.

▶ Activity 5: TUNING IN TO SELF-TAPES

1. Explain that in this activity students are going to tune in to the statements they think about themselves.

2. Ask them to spend a moment thinking about all the negative statements they tell themselves, then write these statements on a separate page in their journal. For example, a student might think

   I'm stupid.

   I can never do anything right.

   Nobody likes me.

3. The things people tell themselves about themselves can make them feel bad—or good. It is important for people to examine these things to see if they are true and to work toward telling themselves positive things so they can feel good more often. Ask students to spend a moment thinking about all the positive sentences they tell themselves or that they could tell themselves. Then, ask them to write them on a new page in their journals. Examples of positive thoughts that students might record include

   I'm nice.

   I do well in math.

   I'm a good friend.

4. Go around the room, and have each student read at least one positive statement he or she wrote about him- or herself. If a student has a difficult time thinking of positive statements, have the student ask a classmate to offer a suggestion. You can tape these and play them back to the class.

Extension

Ask students to examine the assumptions in the statements they wrote for both the negative and positive thoughts. Is there a difference in the assumptions; for example, are there more provable beliefs in the positive or negative statements?

Does the negative thought seem as real when it is written out as when they heard it in their head? Then, ask them to tear out that page of negative thoughts from their journal, crumple it up, and throw it in the wastebasket. Let them know that they have the power to "throw these thoughts away" whenever they come into their heads and replace them with positive statements.

A week or so after this lesson, give students the opportunity to share positive statements from their Self-Acceptance handouts and to discuss statements from their self-tapes that they were aware of during the week.

Middle School Modifications

SELF-ACCEPTANCE BAROMETER—Have students provide the items for the barometer.

TUNING IN TO SELF-TAPES—Include others' negative and positive comments as well.

ADDITIONAL ACTIVITES—Have the students come up with a list of things that people do to make themselves acceptable to themselves and others. They can present this in scene form. Students can also come up with a collage of media messages that tell people the things they must do to become acceptable.

11

Examining Self-Measurement

Some people choose not to accept themselves if they do not measure up to the standards they set for themselves. Often, they use others as their standard of measurement, and they choose not to accept themselves unless they are as talented, intelligent, good-looking, rich, athletic, or any number of other characteristics as someone else. Sometimes they do not realize that they may not be able to change or control many of their characteristics. Some characteristics are determined by genes, opportunities that occur, and other factors over which individuals have no choice. In addition, these may not be the most important characteristics with which to measure self-worth.

This lesson examines assumptions and choices made regarding the criteria that may be used to measure self-worth. Activity 1 explores the characteristics in which people have choices and those in which they do not. Activity 2 builds students' awareness of their self-measurement behavior. Activity 3 explores the assumption, "It is awful, and I must not accept myself until I measure up to everyone else" through a series of scenes.

Additional ways to encourage self-acceptance without comparison to others are modeling, providing activities where students work toward their own personal bests, and discouraging comparative comments.

▶ Activity 1: CHOICE/NO CHOICE

1. Explain that there are some personal characteristics that people can change and others that they cannot change.

2. In this activity, list a series of characteristics, and tell students that as they consider each characteristic individually, they are to raise their hand when you say *choice* if they believe that they can change that characteristic without an extreme makeover. Otherwise they raise their hand when you say *no choice* to show that they believe they cannot change that characteristic. Examples of characteristics include

Height

Weight

Color of skin

How we express our feelings

The year we were born

How we handle anxiety

The size of our families

The color of our eyes

The way our bodies are built

3. Share the information from the introduction to help students understand the nature of self-measurement.

▶ Activity 2: INQUIRY

1. Using the three-column format in Resource A, prepare the Measuring Checklist. Write the title at the top of the page. Label the columns *Day, Measured,* and *Accepted.* Add the directions: "Fill in the day and check under *Measured* if you measured yourself against someone else or under *Accepted* if you accepted yourself without measuring." Make copies of the Measuring Checklist and of the Self-Measurement handout in Resource A.

2. Ask students to complete the inquiry sentence—"I sometimes feel bad about myself because, compared to everyone else, I . . ." on the Self-Measurement handout.

3. Introduce the Measuring Checklist, and ask students to fill it out during the week.

▶ Activity 3: SCENE INVESTIGATION: SELF-ACCEPTANCE

1. Scene 1: Based on Unprovable Assumption

Explain to students that they will be acting out a scene that examines the assumption:

It is awful, and I must not accept myself until I measure up to everyone else.

Have the students choose roles and stand in front of the class. Have the assumption, thoughts, and feelings stand behind Chris as if they are a part of him. Instruct all students to express the dialogue with their bodies and voices. Remind the observers to watch for evidence of thoughts, feelings, actions, and consequences as they reflect the assumption.

Scene 1: Self-Acceptance

Narrator: Gym class is about to begin. The teacher says:

Teacher: We're going to warm up by running a few laps around the gym.

Narrator: Chris stands frozen in place. He assumes:

Assumption: It is awful, and I must not accept myself until I measure up to everyone else.

Narrator: Chris thinks:

Thoughts: This is awful. I can't run. I'm not as good as anyone else at gym. I stink.

Narrator: He feels:

Feelings: I am so frustrated and embarrassed.

Narrator: The teacher adds:

Teacher: After we run, we're going to practice shooting basketballs.

Narrator: Chris thinks: There is no way that I can ever get the ball to go into the hoop. Everyone here is better than I am. I'm worthless.

Narrator: He says to the teacher:

Chris: I'm not feeling very well. I'd like to sit off to the side.

Narrator: The teacher says:

Teacher: Chris, that's the second time this week. It can't be very much fun just to watch, and your grade is going to suffer.

Narrator: Chris says:

Chris: I know, but I just can't join in today.

---

2. Assumption Examination

Remind students that the assumption was "It is awful, and I must not accept myself until I measure up to everyone else." Have the students examine the assumption by exploring the ways in which it reflects the errors in logic, using the following questions. Provide the answers if necessary.

Was the assumption based on crystal-balling?

Choice-detectives know that it is impossible for people to predict whether or not they will ever measure up to everyone else. They also know that it is difficult for people to base their acceptance of themselves on something that may or may not happen in the future.

Was the assumption based on generalizing?

Choice-detectives know that the words *must* and *everyone* are examples of generalizing. Although people might prefer to measure up, they are exaggerating when they say that they must not accept themselves if they do not measure up. They can choose to accept themselves just because they are who they are, knowing that they have some areas in which they excel. Although they may want to measure up to others, it is an exaggeration to say that they have to or that it is even possible to measure up to every single person in every single area.

Was the assumption based on awfulizing?

Choice-detectives know that it is stretching the truth for people to believe that it is awful if they do not measure up. People might prefer to measure up to others, but they cannot prove that it is awful if they do not.

3. Scene Examination

Have students answer the following questions. Answers are provided if necessary.

Applying assumption examination:

Do you think that it is awful if you are not as good as others at some things? (No, I might like to be as good as others are at some things, but it is not awful if I am not.)

Are you worthless if you are not as good as others at some things? (No, everyone has some things that they are good at and other things that are more difficult for them.)

Do you think that Chris made good choices about gym class? (No, Chris did not talk about how he was feeling, he didn't try to improve himself, he felt bad about himself, he had no fun, and his grade suffered.)

Changing assumption to provable belief:

What would be a better belief for Chris to have about how he measures his self-worth? (I can accept myself as worthwhile without having to measure up to anyone else.)

Rewriting thoughts to reflect new belief:

What thoughts might that lead to? (I can accept what I can do in gym and improve as much as I am able. I can have fun no matter how good I am. I may not be able to run as fast as some others, but I can try to see how fast I can run today and then see if I can run a little faster tomorrow. I can be proud of my improvement and also be proud of the things at which I excel.)

Redefining feelings based on thoughts:

What feelings might that lead to? (Hopeful that he might enjoy gym, pride in his improvement.)

Predicting actions and consequences based on new belief:

How do you think the scene might have ended differently, getting Chris's needs met and allowing him to persevere? (Chris might have tried to run and shoot hoops and enjoyed himself as well as improved his skills.)

4. Scene 2: Based on Provable Belief

Tell students that they will be acting out a scene that reflects the provable belief:

I can accept myself as worthwhile without having to measure up to anyone else.

Have different students play the roles in this scene. The same instructions that were given for the first scene apply.

Scene 2: Self-Acceptance–Revised

Narrator: Gym class is about to begin. The teacher says:

Teacher: We're going to warm up by running a few laps around the gym.

Narrator: Chris now believes:

Belief: I can accept myself as worthwhile without having to measure up to anyone else.

Narrator: He now thinks:

Thoughts: I can accept what I can do in gym and improve what I can. I can have fun no matter how good I am. I may not be able to run as fast as some others, but I'll try to improve each day. I'll take pride in the things that I am good at.

Narrator: He now feels:

Feelings: I am hopeful that I may begin to enjoy gym class more.

Narrator: The teacher adds:

Teacher: After we run, we're going to practice shooting basketballs.

Narrators: Chris thinks:

Thoughts: I know that the hoop is pretty high for me, and I could chicken out and sit on the side. That doesn't sound like much fun. I think I'll try and see just how high I can get the ball to go, even if it never gets in the basket. He says to the teacher:

Chris: I'm trying something new today. I'm going to stop worrying about how good I am, and start enjoying sports just for the fun of it!

Teacher: I'm so proud of you for trying. Enjoy yourself!

Middle School Modifications

CHOICE/NO CHOICE—Talk about the time that people spend trying to change things over which they have no choice, such as their looks.

ADDITIONAL ACTIVITIES—Have the students draw a ruler and fill it with drawings or words to represent the qualities they possess that make them proud.

12

Evaluating Unrealistic Expectations

Some people refuse to be happy unless and until everything they do is perfect. Sometimes they have a difficult time dealing with limitations and accepting the necessity of making mistakes in order to learn. Rather than looking at a mistake as a positive opportunity to learn about what they need to do differently, they sometimes look at mistakes as evidence of their failure. This can lead to great anxiety in some people and an avoidance of trying altogether in others, due to an assumption that they will fail.

This lesson examines assumptions and choices around people's expectations of themselves—their perceived need to be perfect and their assumption that they will fail. Activity 1 offers an exercise designed to help students increase their ability to manage stress and anxiety. Activity 2 elicits students' experiences with perfectionism and giving up and builds their skill in setting realistic expectations and goals for themselves. Activity 3 explores the assumptions, "If I am not always perfect, it is awful" and "I will never succeed so why bother to try" through a series of scenes.

Additional ways to promote realistic self-expectations are modeling, that is, being honest and openly accepting your own imperfections; tolerating students' mistakes; praising all worthwhile attempts; and listening for and correcting language that supports perfectionism and giving up.

▶ Activity 1: TENSE/RELAX

1. Explain that the students will learn a new relaxation exercise. Tell them that they will tense and relax their bodies, starting at the top of their heads and moving slowly down to their toes. They are to tighten their muscles, a few at a time, for a few seconds, so that they are as tense as they can possibly be. Then, they are to relax those muscles completely, letting go of every last bit of the tension, so that there is no tension left.

2. Ask if this exercise helped them to relax. How is this similar to or different from other exercises they have done? In what situations might they use this exercise?

▶ Activity 2: INQUIRY

1. Using the three-column format in Resource A, prepare the Unrealistic Expectations Checklist. Write the title at the top of the page. Label columns *Day, Perfect, Gave Up,* and *Realistic.* Add the directions: "Fill in the day, then check under the appropriate box as to whether you felt you had to be perfect that day, whether you gave up without trying, or whether you had realistic expectations of yourself. Make copies of the Unrealistic Expectations Checklist and of the Unrealistic Expectations handout from Resource A.

2. Ask students to complete this sentence—"A time I felt that I had to be perfect" or "A time that I gave up without trying was . . ." on the Unrealistic Expectations handout.

3. Introduce the Unrealistic Expectations Checklist, and ask students to fill it out during the week.

▶ Activity 3: SCENE INVESTIGATION: UNREALISTIC EXPECTATIONS

1. Scene 1: Based on Unprovable Assumption

Share the information from the introduction to help students understand the nature of the expectations people have of themselves. Then explain to the students that they will be acting out a scene that examines the assumptions:

If I am not always perfect, it is awful.

I will never succeed so why bother to try.

Have the students choose roles, and have all the actors but Marvin and Mary stand in front of the class. Marvin and Mary should sit, with their assumptions, thoughts, and feelings behind them as if they are a part of them. Remind all the students to express the dialogue with their bodies and voices, and remind the observers to pay attention to evidence of errors in logic.

Scene 1: Unrealistic Expectations

Narrator: The teacher hands out an in-class assignment to be completed within 15 minutes. He says:

Teacher: Here is your assignment. I'd like you to complete it by the time we leave for recess.

Narrator: Marvin has a hard time in school because he wants to be perfect. He assumes:

Assumption: If I am not always perfect, it is awful.

Narrator: As soon as he hears about the assignment, he thinks:

Thoughts: Oh no! That's not enough time to complete the assignment to have it be exactly the way that I want it to be! It's going to be awful!

Narrator: He feels:

Feelings: I'm so stressed!

Narrator: As Marvin tries to complete the assignment, he sighs often, fidgets with his pencil and paper, and looks very upset. He then makes a mistake on the assignment and thinks:

Thoughts: I can't hand this paper in. An eraser mark will ruin the whole thing. Just forget it. I'm a failure again.

Narrator: Marvin then crumples up the paper and throws it in the garbage. Another student, Mary, also has a hard time in school because she doesn't try to do her work. She assumes:

Assumption: I will never succeed, so why bother to try.

Narrator: As soon as she hears about the assignment, she thinks:

Thoughts: There is no way that I'll get anything right so I'm not even going to waste my time and look at the assignment.

Narrator: She feels:

Feelings: It's hopeless.

Narrator: After the teacher hands out the assignment, Mary holds it in front of her and pretends to look at it until the 15 minutes are up. She then hands it to the teacher with nothing written on it. The teacher says:

Teacher: Time is up. Please hand in your assignments.

Narrator: When the teacher sees that neither Marvin or Mary have anything to turn in, he says:

Teacher: I'm very disappointed to have to give you both a zero on the assignment.

2. Assumption Examination

Remind students that the assumptions were "If I am not always perfect, it is awful" and "I will never succeed so why bother to try." Have the students examine the assumptions by exploring the ways in which they reflect the errors in logic. Ask the students the questions below and help them by providing as much of the answers as is necessary.

Were the assumptions based on crystal-balling?

Choice-detectives know that it is impossible for people to predict whether or not they will succeed. There are a range of options—failure is not the only possibility. A person might do well if he or she tried.

Were the assumptions based on generalizing?

Choice-detectives know that using the word *always* is an example of exaggeration. The belief that a person must or is able to be perfect every single minute is not based on facts and cannot be proven. Mistakes are a natural part of life. *Never* is also an example of exaggerating. A person might indeed succeed.

Were the assumptions based on awfulizing?

Choice-detectives know that using the word *awful* is an example of stretching the truth. People might prefer to be perfect, but they cannot prove that it is awful if they are not 100% perfect all the time. The worst thing that might happen if they were to make a mistake would be that they might have to correct that mistake. They cannot prove that that would be so awful.

3. Scene Examination

Have students answer the following questions. Answers are provided if necessary.

Apply assumption examination:

Do you think that either Marvin or Mary were realistic about the end result of doing the assignment? (No, Marvin was unrealistic about having to be perfect, and Mary was unrealistic about getting nothing right.)

Do you think that it's necessary or even possible to be 100% perfect all the time? (No, it's OK to make mistakes as long as we try. That is how we learn.)

What is the worst thing that might have happened if Marvin made a mistake? (He would have done the assignment again. It wouldn't have meant that he was a failure.)

Do you think it is likely that Mary would have gotten nothing at all right on her assignment? (No, if she tried, it is likely that she would have gotten some things right.)

Changing assumption to provable belief:

What do you think would be a better belief to have about one's work? (I can do the best that I can do.)

Rewriting thoughts to reflect new belief:

> What thoughts might that lead to? (I'll try my best on my assignment, and I might do well.)

Redefining feelings based on thoughts:

> What feelings might that lead to? (Calm, hope.)

Predicting actions and consequences based on new belief:

> How might the scene end differently, with Marvin and Mary getting their needs met and being allowed to persevere? (Both students might have finished their assignments and done well.)

4. Scene 2: Based on Provable Belief

Tell students that they will be acting out a scene that reflects the provable belief:

> I can do the best that I can do.

Have different students play the roles in this scene. The same instructions that were given for the first scene apply in terms of placement of actors, use of body and voice, and observers' role.

Scene 2: Unrealistic Expectations–Revised

Narrator:	The teacher hands out an in-class assignment to be completed within 15 minutes. He says:
Teacher:	Here is your assignment. I'd like you to complete it by the time we leave for recess.
Narrator:	A student, Marvin, now believes:
Belief:	I can do the best that I can do.
Narrator:	He now thinks:
Thoughts:	I might do well on this assignment. It's not awful if I make a mistake. I'll take a deep breath, try my best, and learn from what I did wrong without feeling like a failure.
Narrator:	He now feels:
Feelings:	I feel pretty calm, and I hope that I do as well as possible.
Narrator:	Marvin takes a few deep breaths and begins the assignment. He makes a mistake and takes another deep breath as a reminder not to get upset about it. He then erases the error and continues with the assignment. Another student, Mary, now believes:
Belief:	I can do the best that I can do.

Narrator:	She now thinks:
Thoughts:	I'll try to do this assignment. I might get some right. I'll take a deep breath and do my best.
Narrator:	She now feels:
Feelings:	I'm pretty calm and hopeful about this assignment.
Narrator:	Mary takes a deep breath and begins the assignment. She struggles with a problem and takes another deep breath as a reminder not to get upset and hopeless about it. Both Marvin and Mary hand in the assignment. The teacher says:
Teacher:	I'm very proud of both of you for doing your very best!

Have students choose an art form in which they feel the least proficient. Options include music, dance, and visual art. Ask them to create a brief project of their choice, for example, a song, dance, or drawing, and to work on staying relaxed and enjoying the process rather than creating a masterful product. Ask them to share their project as well as their feelings about the process with another student. A week after this lesson, give students an opportunity to share highlights from their Unrealistic Expectations Checklist and to discuss experiences that they had with perfectionism during the week.

Middle School Modifications

SCENE INVESTIGATION—Increase the tension in the situation by adding the element that the student needs to be perfect every time, for example, he or she needs to get an A+ with every single answer correct, every time.

ADDITIONAL ACTIVITIES—Have the students make a poster highlighting all their tiny successes. Have the students create an event for the school that celebrates effort, not necessarily achievement.

13

Promoting Friendship

This lesson explores choices and assumptions people make in their relationships with others. Students learn to apply self-awareness and emotional self-control to building healthy relationships. As choices and assumptions are examined and social skills built, students develop a sense of empathy and a growing ability to handle relationships effectively and to exhibit kindness.

There are many ways to behave with friends. Some people hardly ever question how they act with their friends, behaving mostly out of habit. The need for friendship is so strong that many people may be pulled to make ineffective choices to gain or keep friends. Because some of these behaviors are more helpful than others, choice-detectives want to choose those that are most helpful in becoming and having good friends.

The activities examine assumptions and choices made about friendship. Activity 1 explores students' beliefs about their choices regarding friendship. Activity 2 builds students' skills in distinguishing between positive and negative friendship behaviors. Activity 3 explores the assumption "I will never be able to do anything to be a better friend" through a series of scenes.

Additional ways to promote positive friendship choices are sharing choices you have made and discussing choices you observe students making.

▶ Activity 1: FRIENDSHIP CHOICES

1. Explain that this activity examines some behaviors toward friends.

2. Tell students that you will read descriptions of behaviors toward a friend. After you read a description, students decide whether they think that behavior

would help them to be a good friend or whether that behavior would not help them to be a good friend.

3. After each description is read, students vote by raising their hands when you say *help* if they believe that behavior would help them to be a good friend, or after you say *not help* if they believe that behavior would not help them to be a good friend. Examples of descriptions that you might use for this activity include

Accepting that not all your friends need to act exactly like you do

Believing that all your friends need to act exactly like you do

Showing off

Sharing your skills

Talking to your friends only about your problems

Sharing the good and the bad

Talking about how you feel

Taking your feelings out on your friends

Never talking to somebody new

Reaching out and saying hello

Really listening to others

Paying attention only to your own thoughts

Buying a friend

Making friends by being yourself

▶ Activity 2: INQUIRY

1. Using the three-column format in Resource A, prepare the Friendship Checklist. Write the title at the top of the page. Label the columns *Day, Positive Choice,* and *Negative Choice.* Add the direction: "Fill in the day and check under *Positive Choice* if you made a positive behavior choice that day regarding your friends or *Negative Choice* if you made a negative choice that day regarding your friends." Make copies of the Friendship Checklist and of the Friendship handout, also in Resource A.

2. Ask students to complete the inquiry sentence—"One way that I now act with my friends is that I . . ." on the Friendship handout.

3. Introduce the Friendship Checklist, and ask students to fill it out during the week.

▶ Activity 3: SCENE INVESTIGATION: BEING FRIENDS

1. Scene 1: Based on Unprovable Assumption

Share the information from the introduction about how people behave with friends. Next, explain to students that they will be acting out a scene that examines the assumption:

I will never be able to do anything to be a better friend.

Have the students choose roles and stand in front of the class. Have the assumption stand behind the nominees in the center of the group. Have each of the nominee's thoughts and feelings stand behind him or her as if they are a part of him or her. Instruct all students to express the dialogue with their voices and bodies. Tell the observers that they are to act as if they are judges for the "Friend of the Year" awards show, listening for evidence of the quality of friend each nominee is, based on his or her choices.

Scene 1: Friend of the Year

Host:	Welcome to the "Friend of the Year Awards." We are down to the final three nominees. They will tell us why they think that they deserve to be the winner and you, our judges, will cast the final vote.
Narrator:	The nominees all assume:
Assumption:	There is nothing I can do to be a better friend.
Narrator:	They all describe why they think that they deserve the "Friend of the Year" award. Cindy begins. She thinks:
Thoughts:	I am the best friend I can possibly be. Every time a friend asks me to do something, I do it, no matter what it is.
Narrator:	She feels:
Feelings:	I feel guilty about saying no and hurting someone and frustrated at having to do things I don't always want to do.
Narrator:	She says:
Cindy:	I know that I deserve to win this award. Every time my friends ask me to do something, I do it. Last week, my new friend told me that my old friend shouldn't be a part of our group any more. She told me that I should ignore her and not go to her house any more. So I don't talk to her any more.
Narrator:	Another nominee, Maria, thinks:
Thoughts:	I know that I am the best friend in the world. I am the boss of all my friends, and they count on me.
Narrator:	She feels:
Feelings:	No one knows that I am unsure of myself and that I get stressed out.
Narrator:	She says:
Maria:	I am the queen of all my friends. They count on me to keep the conversation interesting and moving by talking about myself. I'm a real leader. I tell my friends what to do so they never have to figure things out for themselves. Last week, I told my friend, for her own good, not to talk to another friend and she listened.

Narrator:	The last nominee, Hassan, thinks:
Thoughts:	There is no question that I should win this award. I give my friends anything they want.
Narrator:	He feels:
Feelings:	Inside, where nobody can see it, I feel frustrated and resentful that my friends like me for what I can give them and not for who I am.
Narrator:	He says:
Hassan:	I am going to win this award like I win all my friends. There was this kid that never talked to me before. I gave him all my candy and some money I had, and he played with me for a few minutes. When the candy was gone, he left, but he said that he'd come back when I have some more candy.
Host:	Will the nominees please go into the soundproof booth while the judges deliberate. Esteemed judges, please answer the following questions to determine who is to win the coveted "Friend of the Year" award.

2. Assumption Examination

Remind students that the assumption that was used here was "I will never be able to do anything to be a better friend." Have the students examine the assumption by exploring the ways in which it reflects the errors in logic. Ask the students the questions below with answers provided as necessary.

Was the assumption based on crystal-balling?

Choice-detectives know that it is impossible to predict what someone will or will not be able to do in the future. It might be easier to keep on acting the same way all the time, relying on habits rather than choices. However, it is not based on fact to say that a person will never be able to do anything to be a better friend in the future.

Was the assumption based on generalizing?

Choice-detectives know that it is exaggerating to use the word *never*. It might not be easy to do the things it might take to be a better friend. However, it is stretching the truth to say that a person could never do those things.

3. Scene Examination

Have students answer the following questions, and answers are provided if necessary.

Applying assumption examination:

Do you think that there is nothing anyone can do to be a better friend? (No, there are some things that you can do to be a better friend.)

Do you think that you should do everything your friends ask you to do? (No, not if you don't want to do it, if you think it's wrong or will hurt yourself or someone else.)

Do you think that you should talk only about yourself and tell your friends what to do? (No, it's important to listen, share conversations, and encourage your friends to name their own choices.)

Do you think that you should buy friends? (No, there are ways to make real friends, including listening to and asking to join in on conversations and activities.)

Do you think that any of the nominees really has the kind of friendship that he or she wants? (No, they all express feelings that prove otherwise.)

Changing assumption to provable belief:

What do you think would be a better belief to have about friendship? (There are some things I can do to be a better friend.)

What could Cindy do to be a better friend? (She could do what she feels is the right thing to do, even if a friend disagrees.)

What could Maria do to be a better friend? (She could listen, share conversation, and encourage her friends to make their own choices.)

What could Hassan do to be a better friend? (He could be himself and ask to join in activities.)

Predicting actions and consequences based on new belief:

Do you think that any of the nominees should win the award? (Only if they make some of the new choices we discussed.)

4. Scene 2: Based on Provable Belief

Tell students that they will be acting out a scene that reflects the provable belief:

There are some things I can do to be a better friend.

Have different students play the roles in this scene. The same instructions that were given for the previous scene apply to this one.

	Scene 2: Friend of the Year–Revised
Host:	Judges, I thank you for reaching the correct decision. I have read your answers to the nominees, and perhaps they have come to different conclusions themselves.
Narrator:	The nominees have come back in, and after hearing the judges' comments, they now believe:
Belief:	There are some things I can do to be a better friend.
Narrator:	Cindy now thinks:
Thoughts:	I know that I shouldn't get the award because I do things that my friends ask me to do, even if I disagree with them.

Narrator:	She feels:
Feelings:	I feel hopeful that I will have better friendships.
Narrator:	She says:
Cindy:	Judges, please do not vote for me to win this award until I try to be a better friend and have better friends by being myself and doing what I believe is right.
Narrator:	Maria now thinks:
Thoughts:	I know that I shouldn't win because I boss my friends around and completely take over all conversations.
Narrator:	She feels:
Feelings:	I feel hopeful that I will enjoy my friendships more.
Narrator:	She says:
Maria:	Judges, please do not make me "Friend of the Year" until I can support my friends in making their own decisions and have conversations where everyone gets to be heard.
Narrator:	Hassan now thinks:
Thoughts:	I should not win this award or win my friends by giving them things.
Narrator:	He now feels:
Feelings:	I feel hopeful that I will make true friends by being myself, and that those friends will like me for who I am and not for what I can give them.
Narrator:	He says:
Hassan:	Judges, I do not deserve this award until I can make friends by being myself and not by buying them.
Host:	The judges are so impressed by what the nominees have learned that they are giving all three nominees the award for "Most Improved Friend of the Year." Congratulations!

Extension

Write and perform a friendship rap, song, or jingle including all the points discussed in the friendship lesson. Assign students to groups with others who are not their close friends. Ask them to share what they learned about themselves from working with their group.

About a week after this lesson, give students the opportunity to share highlights from their Friendship Checklists and to discuss the different ways they behaved regarding friends during the week.

Middle School Modifications

FRIENDSHIP CHOICES—Add examples such as putting someone down, dressing like everyone else, taking a drink or a drug just once, and cheating or lying for someone. Also discuss how hard it is to stay true to your own ideals when the friendship stakes are so high as well as some ways to do so.

SCENE INVESTIGATION—Change the characters' choices to reflect the above choices.

14

Strengthening Family

A family is a group of people, all of whom have their own needs and have different ways of thinking, expressing feelings, and behaving, based on their own assumptions and choices. Every member of a family plays an important part, doing the tasks that need to be done and trying to get along with one another.

Sometimes family members get along easily and well with one another, and sometimes they get along with more difficulty. There are choices that can be made to help families get along better. One of these choices is to take everyone's needs in the family under consideration, rather than focusing only on personal needs.

This lesson continues building relationship skills by examining assumptions and choices made about a person's family. Activity 1 is the construction of a web to explore the nature of being a child in a family. Activity 2 consists of a guided fantasy designed to sensitize students to the needs and feelings of their parents. Activity 3 builds awareness of students' behavior as a family member. Activity 4 explores the assumption "My family must only meet my needs" through a series of scenes.

Additional ways to promote positive family choices are sharing personal experiences and discussing students' choices as they come up. Also, students can be helped to take their peer's needs under consideration when interacting with them.

▶ Activity 1: ATTRIBUTE WEB

1. Explain to students that they are to create a web that shows the attributes of a role that they have in the world.

2. Hand out paper and pencils.

3. Ask students to draw a circle and put the word *child* in the center.

4. Tell them that they are to draw lines coming from the outside of the circle, like a spider web. On the lines, they are to write as many things as they can think of that describe what it is like to be a child in a family. Include things they like about it as well as things they do not like. Examples of attributes include

Like

Having meals made for me
Having someone who makes sure that I have everything I need
Being able to play

Dislike

Being told when I have to go to bed
Having to eat things I don't like
Not being taken seriously

▶ Activity 2: GUIDED FANTASY

1. Explain that this activity asks students to imagine they are someone else. Ask students to close their eyes and listen to you. As they listen, they are to picture in their minds what you are describing.

2. Ask them to imagine that they are either their father or their mother. They should imagine the things their parent does and the way he or she feels from moment to moment. Have them imagine the first thing their parent does after waking up. Is it make the beds? Get ready for work? Get the children ready for school? Prepare breakfast for the family? Tell them to picture their parent doing his or her activities.

3. Tell students to imagine what goes through a parent's mind and pay attention to what he or she is thinking about and might be feeling. Is their parent worried about having so much to do? Calm?

4. Now ask students to picture the parent doing his or her next activity. Is it cleaning and doing laundry? Is the parent at work? What does the parent have to get done before the end of the day? Students should pay attention to what he or she is thinking and feeling. Is the washing machine broken, and is the parent frustrated? Is the parent's boss angry at him or her for something the parent did not finish on time? What is he or she thinking and feeling?

5. Now have students imagine what the parent is doing at the end of the day. What still has to be done before going to bed? What is the parent thinking and feeling?

6. Have students return to themselves and open their eyes.

7. What did the students learn about the things their parents do, think, and feel? What do they think they would like and dislike about being a parent in a family? For example, would they like making a difference in their children's lives? Would they dislike all the responsibilities?

▶ Activity 3: INQUIRY

1. Using the three-column format in Resource A, prepare the Family Checklist. Write the title at the top of the page. Label columns *Day, Positive Choice,* and *Negative Choice.* Add the direction: "Fill in the day, then mark under *Positive Choice* if you made a positive behavior choice that day regarding your family or under *Negative Choice* if you made a negative behavior choice regarding your family." Make copies of the Family Checklist and of the Family handout, which is also in Resource A.

2. Ask students to complete the inquiry sentence—"One way that I now act with my family is that I . . ." on the Family handout.

3. Introduce the Family Checklist, and ask students to fill it out during the week.

▶ Activity 4: SCENE INVESTIGATION: STRENGTHENING FAMILY

1. Scene 1: Based on Unprovable Assumption

Share information from the introduction about the nature of families. Explain to students that they will be acting out a scene that examines the assumption:

My family must meet only my needs.

Have the students choose roles, with the family members seated in front of the class, the assumption behind the family members in the center, and each family member's thoughts and feelings behind him or her. Remind students to express the dialogue in their voices and bodies. Tell the observers that they are experts on family life, watching a video of a struggling family to evaluate their assumptions, thoughts, and feelings.

Scene 1: Strengthening Family

Narrator: We are happy to have with us the nation's leading experts on developing great family relationships. We are looking forward to having you observe this family closely and help them to get along better. You may start the video now while I narrate. The family is seated at the kitchen table. They all assume:

Assumption: My family must meet only my needs.

Narrator: Mother thinks:

Thoughts: I want my child to go to bed early tonight, and I know that when I tell her, the same thing will happen that always does. I've just got to get her to bed.

(Continued)

(Continued)

Narrator:	She feels:
Feelings:	I'm worried and frustrated.
Narrator:	She says:
Mother:	You're going to bed early tonight, and I don't want to hear another word about it.
Narrator:	Father thinks:
Thoughts:	Oh, terrific, here we are again. I come home from a long day at work and have to face the same family problems every night.
Narrator:	He feels:
Feelings:	I feel tired, stressed, and frustrated.
Narrator:	He says:
Father:	Can't you control your daughter? Listen, your mother told you to go to bed, and that's the way it's going to be, young lady.
Narrator:	The daughter thinks:
Thoughts:	They always tell me what to do, and there's never any good reason why I should. They don't care about what I want to do.
Narrator:	She feels:
Feelings:	I feel hurt and frustrated.
Narrator:	She says:
Daughter:	You only care about what you want. You don't care about me.
Narrator:	Mother says:
Mother:	Here we go again. It always ends up this way. That's it young lady. Up to your room!
Narrator:	As you can see, experts, this family is struggling and could really use your help. Please help them evaluate their assumptions and thoughts and come up with some choices that will work better for all of them.

2. Assumption Examination

Remind students that the assumption was, "My family must meet only my needs." Using the following questions, have the students examine the assumption by exploring the ways in which it reflects the errors in logic. Answers are provided if necessary.

Was the assumption based on generalizing?

Choice-detectives know that it is exaggerating to use the words *must* and *only*. A family can meet a variety of needs, including those of each family member. However, it is an exaggeration to say that a person's family must meet only his or her needs.

3. Scene Examination

Have students answer the following questions. Answers are provided if necessary.

Applying assumption examination:

> Do you think that a family must meet only one family member's needs? (No, a family is made up of more than one person and more than one need. It is possible and important to come up with ways to consider each family member's needs in some way.)

> Did the family members communicate well with each other? (No, each person spoke out of frustration.)

> What do you think would have been a better way to communicate? (It would have been better if they all explained how they felt and said what they needed and why.)

Changing assumption to provable belief:

> What do you think would have been a better belief to have about families? (It is helpful if families consider every member's needs.)

Rewriting thoughts to reflect new belief:

> If the family in the video shared that belief, what thoughts might that lead to? (I don't have to react out of frustration. I can think before I speak, talk about my feelings and needs, and find a way to work this out.)

Redefining feelings based on thoughts:

> What feelings might that lead to? (Hope.)

Predicting actions and consequences based on new belief:

> How might the video have ended differently, meeting everyone's needs and allowing each family member to act with empathy and kindness? (The parents and the daughter might have come to an understanding about an early bedtime.)

4. Scene 2: Based on Provable Belief

Tell students that they will be acting out a scene that reflects the provable belief:

It is helpful if families consider every member's needs.

Have different students play the roles in this scene. The same instructions that were given for the first scene apply.

Scene 2: Strengthening Family–Revised

Narrator:	Thank you, experts, for doing such a great job. I have shared your suggestions with the family and have made another videotape after they put your ideas into practice. Watch with pride the family you have helped so much. They are again sitting at the kitchen table. They now believe:
Belief:	It is helpful if families consider every member's needs.
Narrator:	The mother now thinks:
Thoughts:	I want my child to go to bed early tonight, and I don't want the same thing to happen that usually happens when I tell her. I wonder if it might help if I tell her my concerns and explain why I want her to go to bed early.
Narrator:	She feels:
Feelings:	I am hopeful that she might listen.
Narrator:	She says:
Mother:	I know that you enjoy staying up and watching TV. But during the past few days, you seem to have had a harder and harder time concentrating on your homework. I'm also worried about that gymnastics show you have coming up tomorrow. I don't want you to hurt yourself because you're tired. I think that it would be a good idea if you got to bed a little earlier tonight.
Narrator:	The daughter looks up at the mother and thinks:
Thoughts:	This is the first time Mom told me why she wants me to do certain things. I would prefer to stay up, but she kind of makes sense, too.
Narrator:	While the daughter is thinking, the father thinks:
Thoughts:	She hasn't said anything in response to her mother, but I don't think she's ignoring her. It looks like she listened.
Narrator:	He feels:
Feelings:	I feel hopeful that we might be able to work this out.
Narrator:	He says:
Father:	We both want to make sure that everything goes well for you. I know that it's tough to go to bed when there are other things you'd rather do, but we think that it is important for tonight.
Narrator:	The daughter thinks:
Thoughts:	I could make a big fuss about this but that would only make everyone angry. Maybe I could tell them how I feel.

Narrator:	She feels:
Feelings:	I'm hopeful that they might listen and understand.
Narrator:	She says:
Daughter:	It's hard to go to bed as early as you want because that means I only have time to do my homework, eat supper, and go to bed. Could I stay up for half an hour and then go to bed?
Narrator:	The mother says:
Mother:	I'm proud of you for listening and sharing your feelings and needs. Most of the time, we can find a solution that satisfies everyone. However, since it is already late and you have that gymnastics show tomorrow, how about if we stick to the time I set for tonight, and then you can stay up for that extra half hour tomorrow?
Daughter:	That sounds fair, mom.

Extension

Students create two cartoons of their family. One cartoon shows communication between family members at its worst and the other communication at its best.

About a week after this lesson, give students the opportunity to share highlights from their Family Checklists and to discuss behavior choices they made regarding their families during the week.

Middle School Modifications

ATTRIBUTE WEB—Make a second web for parents.

GUIDED FANTASY—Follow up with a revised version of the parent web based on students' new discoveries.

SCENE INVESTIGATION—Change the first scene so that the bedtime argument focuses on getting the daughter to go to bed before midnight. Change the revised scene so that the mother is concerned over slipping grades, frequent illness, and the upcoming SAT exam. Have the daughter talk about needing time for homework, job, social life, and relaxation.

15

Learning About Put-Downs

Some people assume that to feel good about themselves, they must make others feel bad about themselves. Sometimes people put others down in an attempt to feel better about themselves, to stop others from putting them down, to get attention, to look important, to try to gain power, or just for fun. They do not always realize the negative effect that this may have on those they put down, as some of these people may choose to feel hurt, become upset, and begin to put themselves down. Also, some people have a difficult time giving or accepting compliments, a critical skill for interacting effectively with others.

This lesson examines assumptions and choices made regarding put-downs. Activity 1 reinforces the skill of anxiety management through an exercise for relaxing. Activity 2 provides an opportunity for sharing put-downs and compliments that are received and for exploring the emotional consequences of each. Activity 3 builds students' skills in recognizing and handling negative and positive interactions with others. Activity 4 explores the assumption, "In order to feel good about myself, I must try to make someone else feel bad about him- or herself," in a series of scenes.

Additional ways to discourage put-downs are modeling positive behavior, listening for and discouraging put-downs in class, and offering regular opportunities for students to give each other compliments.

▶ Activity 1: TENSE/RELAX

Do the exercise described in Lesson 12, Activity 1. Discussion can focus on asking students how much they were able to relax using the exercise this time. Have they used this or other relaxation exercises on their own? What could they be doing to help themselves stay relaxed even more?

▶ Activity 2: PUT-DOWN/COMPLIMENT CIRCLE

1. Explain that a put-down is a negative statement about someone, which is meant to make that person feel bad, and that a compliment is a positive statement made about someone, which is meant to help that person feel good.

2. Tell students that they are going to do an activity that shows the effect that put-downs and compliments can have on people.

3. Form students into a circle. Explain that each member of the circle is to state one put-down that he or she has either given or received at some point in his or her life. As each person states the put-down, the rest of the circle members are to show with their bodies what they might feel like if that put-down were directed toward them.

4. After going around the circle once for the put-downs, tell students that now each one in the circle is to state one compliment he or she has either given or received at some point in his or her life. As each person states the compliment, the rest show with their bodies what it might feel like if that compliment were directed toward them.

Extension

Ask students what they felt like when they stated a put-down. What did they feel when they heard the put-down? What did they feel when they stated a compliment? What did they feel when they heard the compliment?

▶ Activity 3: INQUIRY

1. Using the three-column format in Resource A, prepare the Put-Down Checklist. Write the title at the top of the page. Label the columns *Day, Put-Down,* and *Complimented*. Add the direction: "Fill in the day and mark under *Put-Down* if you put someone down that day or mark under *Complimented* if you helped someone to feel good that day." Make copies of the Put-Down Checklist and of the Put-Downs handout, which is also found in Resource A.

2. Ask students to complete the inquiry sentence—"A put-down I once said to someone was . . ." on the Put-Downs handout.

3. Introduce the Put-Down Checklist, and ask students to fill it out during the week.

▶ Activity 4: SCENE INVESTIGATION: RELATING TO OTHERS

1. Scene 1: Based on Unprovable Assumption

Share information about put-downs from the introduction. Explain that the students are creating a scene to investigate the effects of different ways to relate to others, particularly using put-downs and giving compliments. Remind students that they will be acting out a scene that examines the assumption:

> In order to feel good about myself, I must try to make someone else feel bad about him- or herself.

Have the students choose roles. Have Neil and Erika sit in front of the class, and have Erika's assumption, thoughts, and feelings stand behind her as if they are they are a part of her. Remind the actors to express the dialogue with their voices and bodies, and remind the observers to listen carefully for evidence of illogic in Erika's assumption and thoughts.

Scene 1: Relating to Others

Narrator: The teacher has called on a student to answer a particular math problem. He asks:

Teacher: Neil, would you please give us the answer?

Narrator: Another student, Erika, worries in class because she doesn't feel like she's very smart. However, she does know the answer to the question the teacher has asked. She notices that Neil is struggling to find the answer. She assumes:

Assumption: The only way that I can feel good about myself is if I make someone else feel bad about him- or herself.

Narrator: She thinks:

Thoughts: I can't believe that he doesn't know the answer. Everyone will laugh at him and know how smart I am if I show them how dumb he is.

Narrator: She feels:

Feelings: I'm worried about looking stupid.

Narrator: She says:

Erika: You don't know the answer, do you? Boy, are you dumb.

Narrator: Neil looks at her sadly, and the teacher says:

Teacher: Erika, I'd like to see you after class so we can talk about the choice you made.

---

2. Assumption Examination

Remind students that the assumption was, "In order to feel good about myself, I must try to make someone else feel bad about him- or herself." Have the students examine the assumption by exploring the ways it reflects the errors in logic. Answers are provided as necessary.

Was the assumption based on crystal-balling?

Choice-detectives know that it is impossible for people to predict how they will feel about themselves in the future. Even if a person succeeds in making someone else feel bad about him- or herself, it is not possible to predict that this would definitely lead to positive feelings about oneself. It might even lead to feeling bad about oneself.

Was the assumption based on generalizing?

Choice-detectives know that it is exaggerating to use the word *must*. It is not based on fact for people to think that the only way to feel good about themselves is to try to make someone else feel bad. People have control over their choices about what they can do to feel good about themselves, including empathizing with others' feelings and giving themselves or others a compliment. It is possible for them to feel good about themselves at the same time that others are feeling good about themselves.

3. Scene Examination

Have students answer the following questions. Answers are provided if necessary.

Applying assumption examination:

> Do you believe that the only way that people can feel good about themselves is to make someone else feel bad? (No, there are many ways to help ourselves feel good, including remembering to measure ourselves fairly, reminding ourselves of our strengths, and helping others feel good about themselves.)
>
> What could Erika have done to help Neil? (She could have helped him to come up with the answer.)

Changing assumption to provable belief:

> What would be a better belief for Erika to have about feeling good about herself? (I don't have to make others feel bad to feel good about myself—I have many other better choices.)

Rewriting thoughts to reflect new belief:

> What thoughts might that lead to? (I can find all kinds of ways to feel good about myself, including reminding myself to measure myself fairly, reminding myself about my strengths, and helping other people feel good about themselves. It would be an easy laugh and a way to show off if I make fun of Neil. But that would only make him feel bad, and no one will know that I know the answer. Maybe I could try to help him out. He'd feel better, and everyone would know that I'm smart, and that would feel good.)

Redefining feelings based on thoughts:

> What feelings might that lead to? (Confidence, happiness.)

Predicting actions and consequences based on new belief:

> How might the scene have ended differently so that Erika might have gotten her needs met as well as embodying empathy and kindness? (Erika might have

helped Neil come up with the answer. Neil and Erika might have both felt good, and the teacher might have been proud.)

4. Scene 2: Based on Provable Belief

Tell students that they will be acting out a scene that reflects the provable belief:

I don't have to try to make others feel bad about themselves in order to feel good about myself. I have many other better choices.

Scene 2: Relating to Others–Revised

Narrator:	The teacher has called on a student to answer a particular math problem. He asks:
Teacher:	Neil, would you please give us the answer.
Narrator:	Another student, Erika, worries in class because she doesn't feel that she's very smart. She now believes:
Belief:	I don't have to try to make others feel bad about themselves to feel good about myself. I have many better choices.
Narrator:	She now thinks:
Thoughts:	I can find all kinds of ways to feel good about myself including reminding myself to measure myself fairly, reminding myself about my strengths, and helping other people feel good about themselves. It would be an easy laugh and a way to show off if I make fun of Neil. But that would only make him feel bad, and no one will know that I know the answer. Maybe I could try to help him out. He'd feel better, and everyone would know that I'm smart, and that would feel good.
Narrator:	She feels:
Feelings:	I feel more confident and happier.
Narrator:	Erika looks over at Neil, smiles, and says:
Erika:	Come on, you can do it. You know the answer.
Narrator:	Neil smiles back, thinks hard, and still can't come up with the answer. Erika asks the teacher:
Erika:	May I help him with the answer?
Narrator:	The teacher says:
Teacher:	That would be nice of you.
Narrator:	Erika leans over and whispers a hint into Neil's ear. Neil says:
Neil:	The answer is 24!
Narrator:	Both students look smart and feel good about themselves, and their teacher is very proud.

Extension

Divide into groups and create and then perform a song in honor of the other group. Be sure to include one positive statement about each member of the group. Have each student take a turn at getting a compliment from every student in the class.

About a week following this lesson, give students the opportunity to share highlights from their Put-Down Checklists and to discuss their experiences with put-downs during the week.

Middle School Modifications

PUT-DOWN/COMPLIMENT CIRCLE—Do this activity on paper if your students would find it difficult sharing these thoughts aloud. Students can then take the paper home.

SCENE INVESTIGATION—Change the situation to that of a student, Sue, watching and commenting as a new student, Dina, comes into the room.

16

Dealing With Peer Pressure

This lesson examines two ways that peer pressure can affect a person. In one way, someone may use peer pressure to coerce someone else. Sometimes, people make the choice to try to get others to do what they would like them to do by putting pressure on them in a number of different ways, such as being bossy, teasing, bribing, or threatening. Sometimes they do this as part of a group, and sometimes they do it by themselves. They do not always realize the negative effects of their pressuring another person and how bad the person being pressured may feel.

The second way peer pressure may be viewed is from the perspective of the person being pressured. Some people might feel pressured to do things that others tell them to do, allowing others to determine choices they make. Sometimes they base their definition of "cool" on others' assumptions or on assumptions they have developed. There are a number of qualities they assume they must have and a number of actions they assume they must take in order to be cool. They might feel pressured to do these things in order to be thought cool. They do not always examine these assumptions to determine whether the assumptions are based on facts. Sometimes what seems to be cool at first glance turns out to be not cool when examined more thoroughly.

Some people might give in to pressures to act in a certain way because they are afraid that others might not like them if they do not do so. They might assume that it is important to be liked by everyone. They might assume that if they do not give in to pressuring, they will not be liked and that would be awful.

The activities explore choices and assumptions related to peer pressure. Activity 1 provides a kinesthetic understanding of the nature of pressuring. Activity 2 explores examples of pressuring through communication. Activity 3 builds students' skills in recognizing and quashing their own activities that pressure others. Activity 4 explores the assumption, "I must pressure others in order to always have my way, or it will be awful," through a series of scenes. Activity 5 explores students' definitions of cool. Activity 6 builds students' awareness and ability to resist pressuring from others. Activity 7 explores the assumption, "I must give in to pressure to be cool and be liked by everyone, or it will be awful," in a series of scenes. Note that activities for each perspective on peer pressure are arranged together (Activities 1 through 4 for pressuring a peer and Activities 5 through 7 for being pressured). At your discretion, you may choose to present the two Inquiry activities at the same time and mix the other activities as you think best, although I recommend doing the two Scene Investigations separately.

Additional ways to discourage pressuring others are personal modeling and watching for and discouraging examples of pressuring. Discourage acceptance of pressure by modeling, sharing personal stories, and watching for and discouraging acceptance of pressure while encouraging assertiveness and independent choices.

▶ Activity 1: FORTRESS

1. Single out one student, and tell the others to all join hands in a circle.

2. Ask the single student to try to join the circle while everyone in the circle tries to keep the student out. The joining student is not to use physical force to get into the circle. Take turns and let several students try to enter the circle.

3. How did each student try to get into the circle? Was pressure involved? In what ways (e.g., threatening, bribing)?

▶ Activity 2: PRESSURING CIRCLE

1. Explain that pressuring is when people try to get someone to do something they would like them to do in a way that leads the person being pressured to feel that he or she has no choice but to go along with what the person applying pressure wants.

2. With students still in the circle from Activity 1, ask each student in the circle to give an example of something that someone might be pressured to do and how that pressuring might be communicated. For example,

pressuring someone to play a game I want to play by saying that he won't be my friend any more if he doesn't play

pressuring someone to give me her lunch money by threatening to punch her

pressuring someone to give me his or her homework by promising to be his or her best friend

▶ Activity 3: INQUIRY

1. Using the three-column format in Resource A, prepare the Pressuring Checklist. Write the title at the top of the page. Label the columns *Day,*

Pressured, and *Asked.* Add the direction: "Fill in the day and mark under *Pressured* if you pressured someone to get what you wanted that day or mark under *Asked* if you asked directly for what you wanted that day." Make copies of the Pressuring Checklist and of the Pressuring handout, also in Resource A.

2. Ask students to complete the inquiry sentence—"A time I pressured someone was when . . ." on the Pressuring handout.

3. Introduce the Pressuring Checklist, and ask students to fill it out during the week.

▶ Activity 4: SCENE INVESTIGATION: PRESSURING PEERS

1. Scene 1: Based on Unprovable Assumption

Share information from the introduction about pressuring and being pressured. Explain to students that they will be acting out a scene that examines the assumption:

I must pressure others in order to always have my way, or it will be awful.

Have the students choose roles and stand in front of the class with King Cool's assumption, thoughts, and feelings standing behind him. Remind the students to express the dialogue through their bodies and voices, and remind observers to listen carefully for evidence of illogic in the king's assumption and thoughts.

	Scene 1: Pressuring Peers
Narrator:	The King of Cool is at lunch, surrounded by his royal subjects. He is very hungry and wants a brownie, but the royal chef is all out of them. He assumes:
Assumption:	I must pressure others in order to always have my way, or it will be awful.
Narrator:	He thinks:
Thoughts:	I must get what I want any way that I can. I'd better throw my weight around and show them who's king.
Narrator:	He feels:
Feelings:	I'm worried that I might lose my royal power and respect.
Narrator:	He makes a royal proclamation, saying:
King:	All royal subjects who wish to get on the good side of the king will relinquish their brownies.
Narrator:	His royal subjects continue to eat, knowing that once their brownies are gone, the king will forget all about them. King Cool thinks:

Thoughts:	I must get my way. What can I do to force them to give me what I want? Maybe I can focus on one of my weaker subjects, and he'll give in.
Narrator:	The king calls Ronald over to him and says:
King:	I bid you come to me this instant!
Narrator:	Ronald comes to him, thinking:
Thoughts:	What does the king want from me? I want the king to like me.
Narrator:	The king thinks:
Thoughts:	This will get him.
Narrator:	He says:
King:	Ronald, you will turn over your brownie to me immediately, or I will banish you from the Kingdom of Cool. Unless you do as I say, I won't like you, and you will never be cool or popular again.
Narrator:	Ronald thinks to himself:
Thoughts:	I'm really hungry, but I'd hate if the king didn't like me, and being banished from Cool would be awful.
Narrator:	He says:
Ronald:	All right, your majesty, have my brownie.
Narrator:	The other royal subjects, seeing what the king has done, speak among themselves. One royal subject says:
Royal Subject:	Our king is so sneaky. I wish he would just ask for what he wants without being so bossy. None of us like him. I wonder if he even cares.
Narrator:	Feeling bad for Ronald for giving up his brownie, the royal subject calls him over and shares his brownie with Ronald. They watch as the king finishes Ronald's brownie and sits all alone, with a look of sadness in his eyes.

2. Assumption Examination

Remind students that the assumption was "I must pressure others in order to always have my way, or it will be awful." Have the students examine the assumption by exploring the ways in which it reflects the errors in logic. Answers are provided if necessary.

Was the assumption based on crystal-balling?

Choice-detectives know that it is impossible for people to predict how it would be if they did not use pressure and did not always get their way. There are many possibilities. What happens might be not to their liking, or it might even be just fine. However, they cannot prove that it would be awful.

Was the assumption based on generalizing?

Choice-detectives know that using the words *must* and *always* are examples of generalizing. They might want to use pressure to have their way as often as possible. However, there are other options to try to get things they want, such as asking directly. It is stretching the truth to say that people must pressure others to have their way.

Was the assumption based on awfulizing?

Choice-detectives know that it is an exaggeration for people to believe that something awful will happen if they do not pressure or do not have their way. The worst that might happen is they might not get exactly what they want at that particular moment. They might prefer that this were not so, but saying that this would be awful is not based on facts.

3. Scene Examination

Have students answer the following questions. Answers are provided as necessary.

Applying assumption examination:

Do you think that you must always pressure others to get what you want? (No, *must* and *always* are exaggerations. There are all kinds of ways to get what I want.)

Do you think it is awful if you don't always have things your way? (No, I'd prefer things to be the way I want them to be, but it is not awful if they are not.)

Do you think that the king communicated well to get his brownie? (No, he was bossy and sneaky; he pressured people by ordering them around.)

Do you think that the king got everything he wanted by making the choices he did? (No, he might have gotten the brownie, but he lost the respect of his royal subjects.)

Changing assumption to provable belief:

What do you think would be a better belief to have about how to get your needs met? (There are many ways to get my needs met without using pressure.)

Rewriting thoughts to reflect new belief:

What thoughts might that lead to? (I don't have to use everything in my power to show everyone that I'm in charge and that I'm King Cool. They already know that. I don't have to pressure others to get what I want. I can ask directly. If I'm nice about it, I might get what I want and have my subjects like me, too.)

Redefining feelings based on thoughts:

What feelings might that lead to? (Hope, security, happiness.)

Predicting actions and consequences based on new belief:

How might the scene have ended differently so that the king could have gotten his needs met and acted with kindness? (The king might have asked nicely and had plenty of offers of brownies from the royal subjects who liked their king.)

4. Scene 2: Based on Provable Belief

Tell students that they will be acting out a scene that reflects the provable belief:

There are many ways to get my needs met without using pressure.

Have different students play the roles in this scene. The same instructions that were given for the first scene apply to this one.

Scene 2: Pressuring Peers–Revised

Narrator: The King of Cool is at lunch, surrounded by his royal subjects. He is very hungry and wants a brownie, but the royal chef is all out of them. He now believes:

Belief: There are many ways to get my needs met without using pressure.

Narrator: He now thinks:

Thoughts: I'm hungry, and my chef didn't pack a brownie for me. I could command that all my subjects give me one of theirs. But nobody likes a king who throws his weight around. I think I'll just ask them.

Narrator: He feels:

Feelings: I feel hopeful that someone may share a brownie.

Narrator: He says:

King: Royal subjects, I, the king, am hungry. My chef didn't pack a brownie for me. I would be very grateful if one of you would share your brownie with me.

Narrator: The king looks around, wondering how the subjects feel about his direct approach. Within moments, a large group of his subjects go up to the throne, gladly offering to share their brownies. And all was well in the Kingdom of Cool.

Design and share a scientific experiment or perform a pantomime or dance demonstrating pressure.

▶ Activity 5: COOL FORMULA

1. Explain that each student is going to write a formula for what it takes to be cool. The formula should include personal qualities and behaviors that they believe contribute to someone being thought of as cool, as well as behaviors and qualities that detract from someone's coolness.

2. When the students have finished writing, ask them to share their formula with another student or with the class.

3. Did everyone define cool in the same way? Who decides what is cool and what is not cool? On what is that decision based? Can one become cool? How?

► Activity 6: INQUIRY

1. Using the three-column format from Resource A, prepare the Being Pressured Checklist. Write the title at the top of the page. Label columns *Day, Gave In,* and *Own Choice.* Add directions: "Fill in the day and mark under *Gave In* if you felt you made a choice by giving in to pressure that day or mark *Own Choice* if you acted on your own choice that day." Make copies of the Being Pressured Checklist and of the Being Pressured handout, also in Resource A.

2. Ask students to complete the Inquiry sentence—"A time I gave in to pressure was . . ." on the Being Pressured handout.

3. Introduce the Being Pressured Checklist, and ask students to fill it out during the week.

► Activity 7: SCENE INVESTIGATION: BEING PRESSURED BY PEERS

1. Scene 1: Based on Unprovable Assumption

Explain to students that they will be acting out a scene based on the assumption:

I must give in to pressure to be cool and to be liked by everyone, or it will be awful.

Have the students choose roles, and have Lisa and the group of girls sit in front of the class while the assumption, thoughts, and feelings stand behind Lisa. Remind the actors to reflect the dialogue in their bodies and voices, and the observers to listen closely to the assumption and thoughts for evidence of errors in logic.

	Scene 1: Being Pressured by Peers
Narrator:	A group of girls is sitting on the floor of their friend's bedroom, talking and eating potato chips. One of the girls, Akiya, says to Lisa, the girl who is hosting the slumber party:
Akiya:	Is there anything to drink?
Narrator:	Lisa says:
Lisa:	I don't know. I'll go check.
Narrator:	Lisa goes into the kitchen to search the fridge for something to drink. She finds half a carton of milk, a little orange juice, and a few cans of coke. She decides to bring in the cokes. As she is reaching for the last can, she notices a can of beer toward the back of the fridge. She wondered what it would taste like and figured her mom wouldn't notice that one can of beer was missing. She decides to tell her friend, Akiya, to come into the kitchen to try it with her. She says:

Lisa:	Akiya, come in here for a second.
Narrator:	Akiya walks into the kitchen to join her friend. Lisa points to the can of beer and says:
Lisa:	Hey, Akiya, look what I found. I think we should try some. My mom's upstairs so she'll never know.
Narrator:	Akiya often does what her friends tell her to do. She assumes:
Assumption:	I must give in to pressure to be cool and be liked by everyone, or it would be awful.
Narrator:	She thinks:
Thoughts:	I really don't want to try it, but she'd probably think I wasn't cool and would stop being my friend if I didn't.
Narrator:	She feels:
Feelings:	I'm worried she won't like me, and I'm confused about what to do.
Narrator:	She thinks:
Thoughts:	Maybe I can get out of having to drink it and still have her think I'm cool.
Narrator:	She says:
Akiya:	You know what? I'm not really thirsty any more. Besides, there isn't a lot there. Why don't you have it all?
Narrator:	Lisa says:
Lisa:	It won't be as much fun if we don't taste it together. You're my best friend, and we do everything together. You're not afraid to try it, are you?
Narrator:	Akiya thinks:
Thoughts:	I don't want the beer, but I don't want to lose her as a friend. That would be awful.
Narrator:	She says:
Akiya:	All right, I'll try a little.
Narrator:	Lisa gives her the can of beer, and Akiya takes a sip. Lisa says:
Lisa:	Come on, you can drink more than that.
Narrator:	By this time, the other girls have made their way to the kitchen. One girl says:
Girl:	Oh, she's not cool enough to drink the whole thing.
Narrator:	With that, Akiya quickly drinks the whole beer. The girls gather around her asking questions about what it tastes like. Akiya starts feeling worse and worse, upset that she did something she didn't believe was right and beginning to feel sick to her stomach. In the middle of being asked one of the questions, Akiya runs to the bathroom, where she spends the rest of the night. Her friend, Lisa, is nowhere to be found.

2. Assumption Examination

Remind students that the assumption was, "I must give in to pressure to be cool and to be liked by everyone, or it will be awful." Have the students examine the assumption by exploring the ways in which it reflects the errors in logic. Answers are provided if necessary.

Was the assumption based on crystal-balling?

Choice-detectives know that it is impossible for people to predict how it would be if they did not give in to pressure. They do not know for a fact that it would be awful not to give in. Nor can they prove that giving in to pressure would cause them to be cool or result in having others like them.

Was the assumption based on generalizing?

Choice-detectives know that using the word *must* is an example of generalizing. People might find it easier to give in to pressure, but they cannot prove that this is their only choice regarding how to be cool and have friends, and that they must do so. It is possible to find friends who would like them and find them cool when they do not give in to pressure.

Was the assumption based on awfulizing?

Choice-detectives know that it is an exaggeration for people to believe that something awful would happen if they did not give in to pressure. The worst thing that might happen if they did not give in to someone's pressure might be that a particular person would not be their friend. They may prefer that the person were their friend, but they cannot prove that it would be awful if the person did not become a friend.

3. Scene Examination

Have students answer the following questions. Answers are provided if necessary.

Applying assumption examination:

Do you think that you must give in to pressure to have friends? (No, *must* is an exaggeration. I can stand up for my own choices. True friends will respect my decisions even if they don't agree with them.)

Do you think it would be awful if not every single person liked you? (No, I would prefer if people liked me, but it would not be awful if some did not.)

Do you think that you must do certain things in order to be cool? (No, I can trust that I am cool and know that the coolest people are strong people who stick up for what they believe in.)

Do you think that Akiya got what she wanted by making the choice to drink the beer? (No, she lost self-respect, got sick, and learned that Lisa was not really a friend.)

Changing assumption to provable belief:

What do you think would have been a better belief to have about friends and being cool? (I can trust that I am cool, make my own choices, and know that true friends will respect them.)

Rewriting thoughts to reflect new belief:

What thoughts might that lead to? (I can be cool and not give in to pressure. If this friend will only like me if I give in to her pressuring or do what she is doing, then maybe she is not a real friend. I can find a friend who will not pressure me.)

Redefining feelings based on thoughts:

What feelings might that lead to? (Confidence, strength.)

Predicting actions and consequences based on new belief:

How might the scene end differently, getting Akiya's needs met and allowing her to live according to her values? (Akiya might have stuck with her choice to refuse the beer, left the kitchen, and found a real friend to talk to.)

4. Scene 2: Based on Provable Belief

Tell students that they will be acting out a scene that reflects the provable belief:

I can trust that I am cool, make my own choices and know that true friends will respect them.

Have different students play the roles in this scene. The same instructions that were given for the first scene apply to this one.

Scene 2: Being Pressured by Peers–Revised

Narrator:	A group of girls is sitting on the floor of their friend's bedroom, talking and eating potato chips. One of the girls, Akiya, says to Lisa, the girl who is hosting the slumber party:
Akiya:	Is there anything to drink?
Narrator:	Lisa says:
Lisa:	I don't know. I'll go check.
Narrator:	The hostess goes into the kitchen to search the fridge for something to drink. She finds a half carton of milk, a little orange juice, and a few cans of coke. She decides to bring in the cokes. As she is reaching for the last can, she notices a can of beer toward the back of the fridge. She wonders what it would taste like and figures that her mother wouldn't notice if one can of beer was gone. She decides to tell her friend, Akiya, to come into the kitchen to try it with her. She says:
Lisa:	Akiya, come in here for a second.
Narrator:	Akiya walks into the kitchen to join her friend. Lisa points to the can of beer and says:

(Continued)

(Continued)

Lisa:	Hey, Akiya, look what I found. I think we should try some. My mother's upstairs so she'd never know.
Narrator:	Akiya now believes:
Belief:	I can trust that I am cool, make my own choices, and know that true friends will respect them.
Narrator:	She now thinks:
Thoughts:	It would be a lot easier to go along with what Lisa wants, but I really don't want to drink this beer. She may not like it, but I'm going to tell her that I don't want it.
Narrator:	She now feels:
Feelings:	I feel sure of myself and very strong.
Narrator:	She says:
Akiya:	Thanks, but I really don't want any.
Narrator:	Lisa says:
Lisa:	It won't be as much fun if we don't taste it together. You're my best friend, and we do everything together. You're not afraid to try it, are you?
Narrator:	Akiya thinks:
Thoughts:	I really don't want to lose her as a friend. But if that happens because I won't give in to her pressure and do what she wants to do, then maybe she's not the true friend I thought she was.
Narrator:	She says:
Akiya:	You are my friend, but there are some things we aren't going to do together. I don't want the beer.
Narrator:	By this time, other girls have made their way into the kitchen. One girl says:
Girl:	Oh, she's not cool enough to drink it.
Narrator;	Akiya thinks:
Thoughts:	If she doesn't think I'm cool because of this, that wouldn't be so awful. I know I'm cool.
Narrator:	She says:
Akiya:	I know I'm cool so I don't have to prove it to you by doing something I don't want to do.
Narrator:	And with that, Akiya leaves the kitchen with another friend of hers who supports her in her choice.

Extension

Design a collage using ads that try to show what should be bought and used in order to be cool, as well as pictures and statements from this lesson.

About a week after this lesson, give students the opportunity to share highlights from their Being Pressured Checklist and to discuss their experiences with peer pressure during the week of the lesson.

Middle School Modifications

FORTRESS—Discuss other situations where physical force might be used, such as in sports activities, sexual encounters, and instances of abuse.

PRESSURING CIRCLE—Use examples such as pressure to use drugs or drink alcohol, pressure to have sex, pressure to do favors. Demonstrate and discuss the variety of ways that some people pressure someone, such as teasing, bribing, being bossy, and threatening.

SCENE INVESTIGATION: PRESSURING PEERS—Use the story as a fairy tale. Have the students enact their own variations of the story, replacing the brownie with situations from their own lives, such as pressure to lend money. Have students write and share a moral to their stories.

COOL FORMULA—Follow up with a discussion of how the requirements for and importance of being cool change in different places and times. Also discuss the connection between coolness and popularity as well as the difficulty with individuality amid the pressure to conform.

SCENE INVESTIGATION: BEING PRESSURED BY PEERS—You can modify the scene to take place at a party where others are drinking or change the situation to one in which a boy tries to pressure a girl into a sexual encounter.

17

Examining Prejudice

Some people may look at certain qualities or characteristics of a person or group of people and choose to make assumptions about them based only on those qualities or characteristics, overlooking other qualities and characteristics. This is particularly true when that person or group of people is different than them in some way.

Some people choose to gossip about people who are different than themselves, spreading rumors without checking the facts. They may be afraid of those who are different, or they may even believe that people who are different than them are not as good as they are.

And some people feel that everyone should be exactly like them because it is the only good and right way to be. They do not see that people are all different from each other in certain ways and that these differences can be enjoyed.

This lesson examines assumptions and choices relating to prejudice. Activity 1 presents a story exploring the assumption, "If someone is different from me, he or she is not as good a person as I am." Activity 2 gives students the opportunity to explore their reactions to new people and to build their ability to accept a new person who is different. Activity 3 provides an opportunity to explore the story presented in Activity 1 through role-playing.

Additional ways to discourage prejudice are modeling, sharing, discouraging prejudicial comments, and supporting open, positive discussion among all students.

▶ **Activity 1: READ "NEW FRIENDS"**

1. Explain to students that you want them to hear a story so that, in a later activity, they can use it to think about an important concept called prejudice.

2. Read the story, titled "New Friends," aloud, have students read it aloud, or have them read it to themselves.

New Friends

Part One

Once upon a time, there was a farm that was home to a community of horses. There were no cows, dogs, chickens, or rabbits, just horses. They liked it that way. All the horses lived, ate, worked, and played together happily. They did things in the same way, spoke the same language, and looked a lot alike. Every horse knew what to expect of every other horse. The farm was running smoothly, and the horses were very content. Until one day, when everything changed.

It was a quiet, sunny afternoon, and the horses were nibbling lazily on some hay just outside their stalls. One of the horses heard an unusual sound coming from behind the barn and trotted around to see what was happening. He couldn't believe what his eyes beheld! Standing in front of him were creatures the likes of which he had never seen! They looked a little like him and the other horses, except that jutting out of the middle of each of their foreheads was a long, pointed, shiny horn!

"How strange," he thought. "What are they? They're so different than we are." He ran around the back of the barn to tell the other horses what he had seen. "You won't believe what I just saw. There are strange creatures on the other side of the barn with long, pointed, shiny horns coming out of their heads. I've never seen anything like it!" he said. The parents gathered their colts and fillies close to them, saying, "Don't get too near those creatures. They are not like us. We do not know what kind of harm they may cause us. We must stay with our own kind."

The horses went about their business, watching the strange creatures with a mixture of curiosity and fear. Several of the horses gathered in groups, whispering. "They talk strangely, they look odd. I wonder if they eat what we eat, sleep like we sleep, feel the same things that we feel," said one horse. "Oh, probably not," another whispered. "I'm sure they have their own strange ways of doing everything." A third exclaimed, "I don't trust them! They might bring us problems or be dangerous. We should stick to our own kind. Work, eat, and play with our own kind. After all, we're probably better than they are, and we just wouldn't mix."

The horned animals gathered in a group of their own behind the barn. "We must stay together," said one. "I don't like being away from the rest of our kind. I don't feel safe here. Who knows what harm may come to us?" "I don't know what these creatures are like," said another. "They talk strangely, they look odd. No horn. Imagine!"

As several of the horned animals continued to talk behind the barn, one of the young animals drifted around to the side of the barn watching the horses with great curiosity. She wanted to find out for

(Continued)

(Continued)

herself just what these creatures were like. They didn't seem all that fearsome to her, but it was hard not to be frightened by what everybody told her. As she watched, she couldn't help but notice how very much the horses looked like she did. She watched them eating. They ate a slightly different brand of hay, but it was still hay, nonetheless. They even played similar kinds of games, except the horses didn't have horns to help them pick things up.

As the young animal continued to watch the horses, she noticed that one of the little ones was looking in her direction. She didn't know whether to run away out of fear or move closer out of curiosity. Both animals thought, "Mom and Dad and everyone else has told me over and over again to stay away from those creatures, but I don't know. She just doesn't seem fearsome to me. I want to find out what she's like."

Both animals moved closer and closer to each other until they were just a few feet apart. Neither knew what to say. They stood that way for a few moments, each looking closely at the other, ready to gallop away if need be. Then, both at the same time blurted out a timid "hello." This made them both break out into a big smile and a giggle. They both knew, right then and there, that no creature that could smile like that could be all that bad.

They spent the next half hour speaking without stopping, asking questions of each other and answering each other, until curiosity was satisfied. "What do you eat? How do you sleep? Where do you come from? What is it like to have a horn? What is it like without one? How do you wash it?" As they talked, they slowly walked around the farm, barely noticing how far into the apple orchard they had drifted.

Part Two

Meanwhile, back at the farm, dinner time was fast approaching. As one of the horses was preparing the hay for the evening meal, she noticed that she hadn't seen her little filly in some time. She called to her but received no reply. Concerned, she called the other horses around. "My little one is missing. I've been very worried with those strange creatures around. Who knows what might have happened to her!" A similar scene was taking place in the horned animals' stalls. "I knew we should have stayed where we were, with our own kind. I was afraid something like this was going to happen. We must go look for our little girl before it's too late! I say that we check the horses' stalls."

And with that, the horned animals took off around the barn at exactly the same time that the horses were coming toward them. A chorus of voices was heard: "I knew you shouldn't be trusted. What did you do with my little one? Where is she?" All of a sudden, the animals realized that there were two creatures missing. "You mean, one of your own is missing, too?" "Yes, indeed," replied one of the horses. "Then you had nothing to do with our baby being missing," said a horned one, and the horse said, "and you had nothing to do with our little one being gone." "What are we going to do?" asked another horse. "We have to find our little one." "We have to find our little one as well," replied the horned creature. "I believe that two heads and a horn are better than one. We may have better luck if we search together. We always have our horns to dig or to poke holes with, should we need them." "Yes, we must put our differences aside for the sake of the missing children."

And with that, the horses and the horned creatures set out to find the missing youngsters. Little did they know that at that very moment, the two young animals were making their way back toward the barn, talking nonstop. "I've really had fun with you," said the filly. "So did I," said the horned animal, which the filly now knew was called a unicorn. "Why is it that horses want to stay with horses and unicorns want to stay with unicorns?" asked the filly. "We make up all kinds of horrible things about each other, but we almost never talk to find out the truth. I'm so glad I've found a new friend and learned all kinds of things that I didn't know before." "I'm glad too. I think we should let everyone know what we've found . . ." But before the little unicorn could finish her last sentence, she and the filly realized that they were horn to horn and head to head with the entire community of horses and unicorns!

Every parent, unicorn and horse alike, began to talk at once. "Where were you? We were so worried. Don't you know you're not to wander off alone like that? Are you OK?" Just as quickly as it began, all the talking stopped as the horses and unicorns looked at each other with big smiles on their faces. "Do you realize that we sound exactly alike? We say the same things to our children, feel the same way about their safety. It doesn't seem to matter if we are horse or unicorn. The important things stay the same."

The pony and young unicorn looked at each other knowingly and eagerly began sharing with the rest of the community all they had learned about each other. That evening, for the first time on the farm, a new community was formed, of horses and unicorns together. Hay was shared, conversation was lively, and in the air was the wonderful excitement that comes from knowing that you have found new friends.

► Activity 2: INQUIRY

1. Using the three-column format in Resource A, prepare the Prejudice Checklist. Write the title at the top of the page. Label the columns *Day, Differences,* and *Whole Person*. Add the direction: "Fill in the day and mark under *Differences* if you paid closest attention to another person's differences that day, or mark under *Whole Person* if you paid closest attention to *all* the qualities of another person that day." Make copies of the Prejudice Checklist and of the Prejudice handout, also in Resource A.

2. Ask students to complete the inquiry sentence—"A time I believed I was better than someone else was . . ." on the Prejudice handout.

3. Introduce the Prejudice Checklist, and ask students to fill it out during the week.

▶ Activity 3: STORY INVESTIGATION: NEW FRIENDS

Share the information about prejudice from the introduction. Explain that the story, "New Friends," from Activity 1, will be the basis of an investigation of the assumption:

If someone is different than me, he or she is not as good a person as I am.

1. Enact Part One

The students act out Part One of the story. It can be enacted in any way that they find most comfortable. For example, the story can be read aloud while students act out the movements. Or one student can narrate the story, stopping at key points to allow other students to act out those parts of the story. Or you can have the students enact the story using their own dialogue and gestures.

2. Reflect on the Enactment

Ask students the following questions. Answers are provided if necessary.

When the horses first saw the unicorns, what were some of their thoughts about them? (They may cause us harm, we're better than they are.)

When the unicorns first saw the horses, what were some of their thoughts about them? (It's not safe, they're strange.)

What do you think the horses and unicorns felt when they were near one another? (Fear, mistrust, curiosity.)

How did the assumption, and the thoughts and feelings that followed, lead the animals to behave? (Whispering, gossiping, staying away from one another.)

When the two young animals met, what did they find out about one another? (That they were both friendly, that they were more alike than they thought.)

When the older animals found their youngsters, what did they find out about one another? (That neither was at fault for the youngsters' disappearance, that they all cared about their youngsters, that they were more alike than they thought.)

How, at the end of the story, might the animals have changed their initial assumption? (They might think, "If someone is different than me, he or she is just as good a person as I am.")

3. Enact Part Two

Have students act out Part Two of the story, using their own dialogue if possible. The story used was about animals and prejudice. Ask students to think about these questions:

In what ways do people make the same assumptions?

What kinds of differences among people make them uncomfortable?

What kinds of things to people feel when someone is different than them?

What kinds of things do people do?

What can people do to act based on the provable belief rather than the assumption?

How can people embody the values of tolerance and acceptance?

Another good follow-up activity is to have students create and illustrate a story of their own that shows the coming together of two different kinds of creatures or people.

About a week after the lesson, give students the opportunity to share highlights from their Prejudice Checklists and to discuss their experiences with prejudice during the week.

Middle School Modifications

READ "NEW FRIENDS"—Inform students that the story is the basis of a later activity. Have them read it silently.

SCENE INVESTIGATION—Divide students into groups. Have each group create a lesson for younger students based on the story. Have groups develop an introduction, make a choice as to whether they will enact the story or have the younger students do the acting, decide on which assumption the story is based and how to change that to a provable belief, and make analogies between the story and real-life situations. Feel free to fill in the gaps for them with the material provided in the lesson. As a closing activity, either have them lead a lesson in your class or with a lower grade.

Section 3

Developing Life Skills

The first part of the final section will focus on the development of the life skills necessary to execute increasingly effective choices rather than merely understanding how to make them. People may know that they can choose to be effective friends or family members, but if they do not have the skills to execute their choices, it becomes merely a cognitive exercise.

Researchers have outlined the importance of exposing youths to a comprehensive repertoire of life skills, fundamental to making increasingly effective life choices (Cowan & Clover, 1991; Deline, 1991; Erin et al., 1991; Jones et al., 1990; Rolan, 1991; Rotheram, 1982).

The World Health Organization (2001) connects the building of life skills with the prevention of health and social problems and the promotion of personal and social development. According to the National Institute on Drug Abuse, effective prevention programs should use methods that focus on skill training in areas such as assertiveness and communication (Sloboda & David, 1997).

The second part of this section will help students to build the skill of values clarification, exploring the ways in which the choices they make are in accordance with their values. As discussed earlier, our aim, supported by other researchers, has been to provide students with the knowledge and skills they need to make choices based on their deepest values, rather than on emotional reactions, and then to follow these choices with actions (Belvel & Jordan, 2002).

Once students have built emotional, social, and life skills, they can truly begin to consciously and consistently explore their values and determine whether or not their choices are in line with these values. They can examine more complex choices, such as whether or not to use illegal substances or to bully others, and bring all their knowledge and skills to bear on these choices. Not only will they be able to talk about and define their values, but also they will have experienced using the knowledge and skills that it takes to live in accordance with them.

Up to this point in the curriculum, students have been exposed to a variety of life skill-building activities in the areas of stress and anger management, effective uses of body and voice, and cooperation. The first five lessons in this section offer opportunities for building additional life skills in the areas of direct communication, active listening, giving feedback, assertiveness, negotiation, and study skills. The next five lessons build values clarification skills and explore choices in the areas of cheating, stealing, bullying, and alcohol and drug use. The final sessions explore situations where it might be necessary to seek adult assistance, and the final lesson explores risk taking and goal setting.

18

Looking at Manipulation

Sometimes people choose to try to get people's attention and other things they want in indirect ways. This is known as manipulation. Some examples of manipulation, such as whining and threatening, were explored in earlier activities. When manipulating, people try to get what they want by using their bodies and voices and choosing certain kinds of behaviors. But using manipulative behavior does not guarantee success. In addition, manipulating others often leads to misunderstanding and conflicts. Certain skills, such as stating one's feelings and asking directly for what one wants, can help to let others know more clearly what is desired. This increases the likelihood of achieving a goal, decreases the likelihood of misunderstanding and conflicts, and supports values such as empathy and kindness.

This lesson addresses the issue of manipulation, helping students to look at helpful and less helpful methods of communication. Activity 1 provides an opportunity to reinforce cooperation. Activity 2 offers practice in the students' choice of relaxation techniques. Activity 3 builds students' awareness and understanding of manipulating actions. Activity 4 offers a kinesthetic exploration into a variety of methods of manipulation. Activity 5 offers an opportunity to rehearse effective communication techniques.

Additional ways to promote effective communication are modeling, reinforcing positive examples, and offering students a chance to reword ineffective communication techniques as they are observed.

▶ Activity 1: PULSE

1. Have the students sit in a circle, and join them.

2. Explain that you want them to hold hands with the people to either side of them. Tell them that when their left hand is squeezed, they should use their

right hand to squeeze the hand of the next person in the circle. Begin by gently squeezing the hand of the person to your right. This should create a "pulse" that continues all the way around the circle. The purpose is to see how quickly the circle can pass the pulse around the room.

3. Ask students what helped to pass the pulse quickly. What stopped the pulse? What could they do to pass the pulse around the room with more speed?

▶ Activity 2: RELAXATION OF CHOICE

Have the students take a vote to determine which relaxation exercise to do, and do the exercise. Consider asking one of the students to lead the class in the exercise, with your guidance if it is needed. Remind students of the different relaxation exercises: rags, slow breathing, and tense/relax.

▶ Activity 3: INQUIRY

Give students the Manipulation Check from Resource A, and ask them to fill it out during the week.

▶ Activity 4: MANIPULATION CIRCLE

1. Share information about manipulation from the introduction. Explain that most people use their bodies and voices in certain ways and choose certain kinds of behaviors to try to get others to pay attention to them and to get other things they want.

2. Tell students that you are going to describe a certain kind of behavior and give an example of that behavior. After each description, they are to come up with another example of that behavior and then show that behavior with their bodies and voices. As you go through the list of behaviors, students may add other manipulating behaviors that they or others choose to try. See Figure 18.1 for suggestions of manipulating behaviors to use for this activity.

Figure 18.1   Manipulation Behaviors

Whining	Nobody ever listens to me.
Acting out	I'll run around the room until somebody pays attention to me.
Commanding	Give me that now!
Threatening	You'd better give me that, or else!
Accusing	You never give me anything.
Labeling	You're so mean.

3. Ask students how they feel when someone is whining, acting out, threatening, commanding, accusing, labeling, or lying. Are they more or less likely to give that person what he or she wants? Do they use any of these behaviors to try to get what they want? How do others react when they do this?

▶ Activity 5: "I" MESSAGES

1. Divide the students into groups of three. If students have difficulties working on their own, consider having several groups of three take turns demonstrating the skills for the rest of the class.

2. Tell students that they are going to practice the skills of stating their feelings and asking directly for what they want. When they state their feeling, they are to use a feeling word to help the other person understand how they feel. An example of stating their feeling would be, "I feel frustrated when I can't get anyone's attention." When stating their feeling, they should not accuse the other person of causing them to feel that way. They are merely explaining how they feel.

3. Tell them that when they ask directly for what they want, they simply ask specifically. An example of asking directly would be "I'd like you to pay attention to me." When people ask directly, they do not demand that the other person give them what they want but merely ask. Give students the "I" Messages handout from Resource A (on page 194), and ask them to complete the assertive statements on the form.

4. Tell them that they are going to practice these skills in groups of three. One student, the asker, asks for something; the partner is the person receiving the request; and the third student, the observer, observes the interaction.

5. The asker chooses something he or she wants from the partner. For example, he or she might want attention, a compliment, or some help with homework. The asker states his or her feeling about what is wanted and asks directly for it.

6. The partner lets the asker know how he or she felt about being asked for something in this way and lets the asker know that the partner would be likely to give the asker what was wanted, based on being asked in this way.

7. The observer closely watches the conversation, paying attention to use of body and voice and to the words being spoken by both participants. The observer shares his or her observations with the other two, letting them know how the new skills worked.

Extension

Have students add lined or unlined paper to the back of their notebooks. Ask them to begin keeping a journal, writing down their observations, assumptions, beliefs, feelings, skills, and behaviors. Students may keep their journals using one or a variety of methods: stories, poetry, recipes, formulas, survival guides, drawings, songs, or any other ideas they may have.

About one week after this lesson, give students the opportunity to share highlights from their Manipulation Check handouts and to discuss their experiences with asking directly for what they want.

19

Strengthening Active Listening and Feedback Skills

As shown in the previous lesson, people spend a great deal of time communicating with others around them. They use words and body language to get their ideas across, share feelings, and ask for what they want.

When communicating with someone, most people like to be listened to. Sometimes people may think they have listened to another person and understand what that person is saying, but this is not always true. At times, when someone else is talking, people become lost in their own thoughts and are not paying close attention to what is being said. Their thoughts may have nothing to do with what the speaker is saying. The listener may be thinking of a response to the speaker. Although trying to listen, if the listener disagrees with what is being said, he or she does not really hear what the speaker is trying to convey.

Certain skills, such as active listening and giving feedback, can help most people listen and communicate more effectively. In active listening, people use their bodies to show another that they are paying attention. Repeating back what someone has said, called giving feedback, shows the speaker that the listener was listening.

When giving feedback, it is important that listeners repeat as closely as possible what was said and that they do not give their opinion about what was said or their advice about what to do about what was said; they simply restate the facts told to them.

The activities in this lesson address the skills of listening and giving feedback. Activity 1 provides an opportunity to brainstorm and rehearse examples of listening body language. Activity 2 builds students' recognition and skill in listening and giving feedback through monitoring of their own activities. Activity 3 provides rehearsal in active listening. Activity 4 provides rehearsal in giving feedback.

Additional opportunities for promoting active listening and giving feedback are modeling, reinforcing these skills as observed, and providing remedial opportunities for rehearsing these skills when necessary.

▶ Activity 1: BRAINSTORM

1. Explain that people communicate to get their ideas across, share their feelings, and get their needs met. When they communicate, most people appreciate knowing that they have been listened to and heard.

2. Explain to the students that they are going to brainstorm as many ways as possible in which their bodies can show another person that they are listening. As they come up with an example, they all use their bodies to demonstrate that example. Some examples of behavior that show a person is listening—leaning forward, making eye contact, nodding.

▶ Activity 2: LISTENING AND GIVING FEEDBACK CHECK

1. Using the two-column format in Resource A, prepare the Listening and Giving Feedback Checklist. Write the title at the top of the page. Label the columns *Day* and *Example*. Add the direction: "Fill in the day and describe a brief example of something you listened to someone say during that day."

2. Introduce the Listening and Giving Feedback Checklist, and ask students to complete it during the week.

▶ Activity 3: LISTENING PRACTICE

1. Divide the class into groups of three. If students have a difficult time working in small groups, choose three students to demonstrate this activity for the rest of the class. One student is the speaker; one, the listener; and one, the observer.

2. Explain to students that they are going to practice the skill of active listening, using their bodies to show that they are listening. Figure 19.1 defines the behaviors of active listening and giving feedback.

3. The speakers speak briefly about something that happened to them that week.

4. Listeners use their bodies to let the speakers know that they are being listened to. Listeners can refer back to the brainstorm activity to remind themselves about the ways in which bodies can show that a person is listening.

Figure 19.1   Listening and Giving Feedback: Definitions

Active Listening	Using your body and face to let others know you are listening
Giving Feedback	Briefly repeating the facts of what others say without giving your own opinions or advice

5. Observers watch the listeners, looking to see the ways in which they are using their bodies to show that they are listening. Observers watch the speakers to see if they are reacting in any way to being listened to in this manner.

6. Have the groups discuss among themselves what each person observed and felt. What did students observe? How was the body used to show that they were listening? What was it like to listen in this way? Was it easier to pay attention to what was being said? What was it like to be listened to in this way? Did it make speakers more eager to tell their story?

▶ Activity 4: FEEDBACK PRACTICE

1. Have the students stay in the same groups that they were in for Activity 3.

2. Explain that they are going to continue to use their listening skills but that they are going to add to them by learning to giving feedback. When giving feedback, people restate the facts that they have been given by the speaker, to let the speaker know that he or she has been heard (see Figure 19.1). For example, if the speaker said, "Last week, I forgot my tennis shoes for gym class," feedback from the listener might be, "You didn't have your tennis shoes in gym last week."

3. Explain that feedback does not give an opinion, such as, "You really shouldn't have forgotten your shoes," or give advice, such as, "Next time, you should leave your shoes by the front door." Feedback simply restates the facts as given.

4. As a warm-up, give students the Feedback Practice form from Resource A, and have them read the situation and choose the statement that is feedback.

5. Speakers talk about the same situation as in Activity 3. Listeners actively listen to the brief story and then give the speaker feedback about what was heard. Observers listen to hear if the listener is giving feedback or giving opinion or advice. The observer also watches the speaker to observe reactions to the feedback. The group then discusses what each person observed and felt.

6. Ask students what they observed. Was it difficult or easy to give feedback about the facts and not give advice or opinions? Were they able to understand more or less of what was being said? What was it like to hear the feedback about what they said? Did they feel that they were heard?

Extension

A good follow-up activity is to have students continue their journals. If they have been using one medium, add another as their method of journalizing. Remind them to add experiences from their most recent lessons on manipulating, asking for things directly, listening, and giving feedback. About a week after this lesson, give students the opportunity to share highlights from their Listening and Giving Feedback Checklist and to discuss their experiences with listening and giving feedback during the week.

20

Developing Assertiveness

People sometimes choose not to ask for what they want because they do not feel that they have a right to do so. Or they may ask for what they want, but they do so using very little energy. By acting passively, they are telling others by what they say and how they say it that they really do not have a right to be asking and that they do not expect to receive what they are asking for. At other times, people choose to demand what they want, using more energy than they need and imposing on others' rights, that is, acting aggressively.

There is a way to use just the right amount of energy to ask for what is wanted and to refuse what is not wanted. People can ask for things assertively, which acknowledges their rights but does not impose on others' rights. Acting in this way can help get what is wanted but avoid conflicts.

When someone is trying to get a person to do something that the person does not want to do, or if a person is being physically threatened, an initial response might be to assertively deny the request. However, if pressure continues, a person may sometimes have to behave more aggressively to get the initiator to stop.

This lesson explores and offers rehearsal in assertiveness, comparing it to passivity and aggression. Activity 1 offers a kinesthetic exploration of passivity, assertiveness, and aggressiveness. Activity 2 builds students' awareness of response choices that they can make. Activity 3 offers rehearsal in clear communication through tone of voice. Activity 4 provides an opportunity to practice and distinguish passive, aggressive, and assertive behaviors through brief scenes.

Additional ways to promote assertiveness are through modeling, rewarding assertive behaviors, and offering in-class opportunities to replay problematic situations using assertive behaviors.

▶ Activity 1: PASSIVE/ASSERTIVE/ AGGRESSIVE GREETINGS

1. Share the information from the introduction about passivity, assertiveness, and aggression. Explain that this activity gives students the opportunity to practice using just the right amount of energy to say something.

2. Tell students that they will do this activity three times. In each case, after a count of three, they say the word *hello:* The first time, they say it passively, using too little energy and space; the second, assertively, taking just enough energy and space; and the third, aggressively, taking too much energy and space. Each time, they are to use both their bodies and voices to express the kind of greeting they are giving.

3. Ask them to think about some of the differences in the ways they used their bodies and voices in each of the greetings. How did they feel as they experienced each greeting? Which kind of greeting made them the most comfortable?

▶ Activity 2: ASSERTIVENESS CHECK

1. Using the four-column format in Resource A, prepare the Assertiveness Checklist. Write the title at the top of the page. Label columns *Day, Passive, Aggressive,* and *Assertive.* Add the directions: "Fill in the day and mark under *Passive* if you were mostly passive that day, *Aggressive* if you were mostly aggressive that day, or *Assertive* if you were mostly assertive that day." Make copies of the Checklist and of the Assertiveness handout, which is also in Resource A.

2. Ask students to complete the assertive statements on the Assertiveness handout.

3. Introduce the Assertiveness Checklist to students, and ask them to complete it during the week.

▶ Activity 3: YES/NO

1. Explain that the class is going to practice saying the words *yes* and *no* assertively and aggressively, using their voices and facial expressions to communicate their feeling. On the count of three, all say the word *yes.* First, students say the word assertively, pretending, for example, that they are saying the word as if their teacher had asked them if they wanted to try to solve the problem on the board, and they wanted to try it.

2. The next time they say the word aggressively, that is, they are to say the word as if a classmate were trying over and over again to get them to smoke a cigarette and has now asked if they are sure they do not want to try just a puff. They are sure they do not want to try it and say *yes* aggressively.

3. This time, on the count of three, all say the word *no.* First, they say the word assertively, as if they are being asked if they will show a classmate the answers to a test. Second, they say the word aggressively, as if a classmate is trying to force them to take a taste of beer, and they are sure they do not want

to try it. They can try other words such as *stop* and can brainstorm additional words as well.

4. Ask students in what specific ways their voice and facial expressions reflect the way they say the words. In what kinds of situations would it be most helpful to speak assertively? In what kinds of situations would it be most helpful to speak aggressively?

▶ Activity 4: ASSERTIVENESS PRACTICE

1. Explain that students are going to enact several brief scenes to practice assertive behaviors. First, they enact the scene behaving passively and a second time behaving aggressively. Then, they use their investigative know-how to change the scene so that they are behaving assertively. You can ask students for situations to enact and for behaviors and consequences resulting from each scenario.

2. Enact the first scene (for passive behavior): A book bag is taken by a classmate at recess. The student says nothing and stands there whimpering as the contents of his or her book bag are thrown around the playground.

3. Enact the second scene (for aggressive behavior): When the book bag is taken, the student yells and gets close to his or her classmate as if he or she was about to get into a fight. Both students are blamed and punished, and the book bag is kept by the teacher.

4. Enact the third scene (for assertive behavior): When the book bag is taken, the student asks directly and firmly for his classmate to return it. The classmate tries to upset the bag's owner by teasing and threatening, but the student does not respond to this and asks the classmate to return the book bag. Seeing that he or she is not going to upset the student, the classmate returns the book bag and walks away, grumbling.

Extension

Students continue writing in their journals, adding media and experiences relating to the current lesson.

About a week after this lesson, give students the opportunity to share highlights from their Assertiveness Checklists and to discuss their experiences with assertiveness during the past week.

Middle School Modifications

YES/NO—Use different examples.

Yes: For assertive, try "Say the word as if you are being asked if you think you are a good person." For aggressive, try "Say *yes* as if someone was pushing you into a sexual relationship, and asking you if you were sure that you didn't want to get involved that way."

No: For assertive, try "Say *no* as if you were being asked if you wanted a beer, and you didn't want one." For aggressive, try "Say *no* as if someone was trying to harm you."

ASSERTIVENESS PRACTICE—Use different examples, such as being teased.

21

Learning Communication and Negotiation

As discussed, when people communicate with each other, sometimes one person wants one thing and the other person wants something else. In situations like this, the participants may choose to use methods of communication that lead to misunderstanding and arguments and result in neither person getting what is wanted.

To avoid arguments and please all participants, some people use a method of communication called negotiating, in which people work together to come up with a solution that is agreeable to everyone, so everyone wins in some way. The steps to successful negotiating are shown in brief form in Figure 21.1.

Figure 21.1   Steps to Successful Negotiating

State desires directly.

Give feedback.

Brainstorm possible solutions.

Agree on a solution and follow it through.

To negotiate means doing the following:

1. Each person in turn states directly what he or she wants without manipulating and without being interrupted.

2. After a person states what he or she wants, the other person gives feedback to the requester, thus confirming that he or she has been heard. The feedback given is a restatement of facts and is not advice or opinions.

3. Both people brainstorm to come up with solution alternatives. These solutions must take the desires of both people into consideration. Neither person may get exactly what is wanted, and each might have to give up something so that both people can be satisfied. For example, if both wanted to play with the one ball left on the playground, one solution might be that they would play with the ball together. Each gives up the ability to play alone with the ball, but both are able to play with the ball. Another solution might be that each person plays with the ball for half of recess. Each person gives up half of the time with the ball, but both are able to play with it alone.

4. Both people agree on a solution and follow it through.

This lesson explores and rehearses the art and skill of negotiation. Activity 1 offers an opportunity to examine effective and ineffective communication methods. Activity 2 offers rehearsal in negotiation. Activity 3 builds negotiating awareness and skill by focusing on students' personal efforts.

Additional ways to support negotiation are to model it, to try to work together with students to make joint choices, and to offer students opportunities to work out conflicts through negotiation.

▶ Activity 1: BRAINSTORMING ABOUT COMMUNICATING AND NEGOTIATING

1. Share the information about communication and negotiating from the introduction. Explain that when someone wants one thing and another person wants something else, the two may either behave in ways that lead to problems or use positive methods of communicating that help them to figure out what to do.

2. The students are going to brainstorm a list of behaviors that might lead to problems in such situations and a list of behaviors that might help them to work out a solution.

3. First, have students develop a list of problems in communicating. Examples of problems include not listening, yelling, not being willing to compromise, and leaving.

4. Next, have students develop examples of solutions that might help them, including listening, talking calmly, being willing to compromise, and going over alternatives to arrive at a solution together.

▶ Activity 2: NEGOTIATING PRACTICE

1. Divide the class into groups of three. If students have a difficult time working in small groups, choose three students to demonstrate this activity for the rest of the class.

2. Explain that they are going to practice negotiating, following the four steps of the negotiating process. Introduce the four steps, using the material outlined in the lesson introduction. Also, use Figure 21.1—you might want to make copies for distribution.

3. When you are comfortable that the students understand the idea of negotiating, ask two students in each group to be negotiators and one to be an observer.

4. The negotiators decide on something they will negotiate about. For example, both might want the same piece of cake, or one friend might want to play house but the other wants to watch television. Following the four-step process, they are to negotiate a solution they both agree on.

5. The observer watches the negotiators, checking to see how the steps are followed. The observer checks how each person stated what he or she wanted, what the feedback was like, and how the solution was determined.

6. The group discusses what each person observed and felt.

   Did either negotiator use manipulation to get across what he or she wanted, or were desires stated directly?

   Was the feedback based on the facts of what each person said, or did it include advice or opinions?

   Were the brainstormed solutions fair to both people, or did they reflect the needs of just one person?

   Was a decision reached by both people?

   What could have made the negotiating work even better?

   In what situations could students use this skill?

▶ Activity 3: NEGOTIATING CHECK

1. Using the two-column format from Resource A, prepare the Negotiating Checklist. Write the title at the top of the page. Label columns *Day* and *Example*. Add the directions: "Fill in the day, and describe a brief example of a situation in which you negotiated to arrive at a solution."

2. Introduce the Negotiating Checklist to students and ask them to fill it out during the week.

Extension

An additional activity to encourage effective communication is the use of the Friendship Circle to resolve conflicts that have occurred in the class. Students sit in a circle, and each one shares the choices he or she made in the situation being discussed. Students examine the assumptions on which their choices were based and the outcome of their choices. They then determine other choices that could have been made and the way that the conflict could have been resolved differently.

Have students continue writing in their journals, adding media and experiences relating to this lesson.

About one week after this lesson, give students the opportunity to share highlights from their Negotiating Checklist and to discuss their experiences with negotiating during the week.

Middle School Modifications

NEGOTIATING PRACTICE—Offer a different example, such as two friends who want to do two different things on a Saturday night.

22

Building Study Skills

In this lesson, success and pride are discussed with the students, and skills are suggested with which to achieve both. Most people like to succeed, to take pride in what they do, and to feel good about themselves. School work is one area in which students can all succeed and take pride. The more effort that they put into work, the more they can achieve. As students begin to believe that they may be able to succeed, certain skills, when learned, can help them succeed at a higher level.

Organizing desks and materials helps many people get needed objects with greater ease and speed, which frees more time for work. Directions help those who follow them to know exactly what to do and in what order to do it. Making an outline of what has been said in class helps many listeners identify the most important parts of what is being said. Making a summary of what is read helps many readers attend to the most important parts of the reading. Finding a special place and time for doing homework and rewarding themselves when they have done it helps many successful learners complete their homework regularly.

The activities provide practice in study skills critical to students' success in school. Activity 1 provides practice with relaxation techniques. Activity 2 offers an opportunity to brainstorm effective school behaviors. Activity 3 provides practice in the study skills previously mentioned. Activity 4 builds students' awareness of the value of study skills by self-monitoring their study efforts and results.

Additional opportunities for rehearsing skills such as following directions, outlining, and summarizing can be incorporated in daily activities. Desk organizing can also be encouraged. In addition, talk to students about their study habits at home, and help them become more efficient.

▶ Activity 1: RELAXATION EXERCISE

1. Have the students vote on a relaxation exercise of their choice and do the exercise. Ask one of the students to lead the class in the exercise.

2. Ask students what their level of relaxation is now as compared with the beginning of the choice-making training. What has helped them most to relax? What effect does their level of relaxation have on their thoughts, feelings, and behaviors? What effect does their level of relaxation have on their ability to do well in school? Is it helpful to relax before doing an assignment or taking a test? How is it helpful?

▶ Activity 2: SCHOOL SUCCESS ASSUMPTIONS

1. Explain that assumptions can get in the way of success in school. Have the students brainstorm a list of assumptions previously examined as well as explore other possible assumptions that might stop them from working hard to achieve their best in school. For example, the following might be included

I will never succeed so why bother to try.

I can get by on luck.

I know everything already.

2. Discuss the illogic behind these statements, and help students arrive at beliefs that can help them achieve success. For example

School is a place where I can take pride and build success.

The more effort I put into my work, the more I can achieve.

▶ Activity 3: BRAINSTORMING ABOUT STUDYING

Ask students to brainstorm activities they think they could do that might help them perform better in school. These may be in-class as well as at-home activities. For example, the following might be included

Following directions

Finding a special place and time for doing homework.

▶ Activity 4: STUDY PRACTICE

1. Tell students that they are going to practice each study skill individually.

2. Explain that you are going to tell them exactly what they are going to do and in what order they are going to do it. Following these directions is their first study skill to practice! After hearing the directions, students are to begin acting on the first direction given.

3. The first direction is to make a list of the directions that you give them. In the list, they are to number the directions in the order they are to be done. After each number, they are to write one or two words that would describe each particular direction, for example "1. Organize desk. "

4. The second direction is to organize their desks and materials. They are to look at what they have in and on their desks and to throw out what they do not need. Then, they are to find specific places for the things that they use and put their things in those places, where they will always be put.

5. The third direction is to ask each student to choose a brief story and read it quietly. They are to write a brief summary of what they read. The summary is to describe the main points of the story in a few sentences.

6. The fourth direction is to do a brief assignment at home. (Give the students an assignment of your choice.) They are to choose a specific place to complete the assignment. The place is to be one in which they find it best to do their homework. A quiet place without distractions might be helpful. They are to choose a specific time to do their assignment. The time is one that they find best for doing their homework. It might be helpful to do the assignment not too long after they get home, before other activities get in the way. If they need to, they can give themselves some short breaks. They are to choose a specific reward for themselves, to be enjoyed after they complete the assignment. An example of a reward might be an hour of watching television or a special snack.

▶ Activity 5: INQUIRY

1. Ask students to complete the sentence—"One skill that could help me do better in school is . . ." on the Study Skills handout in Resource A.

2. Give students the Study Skills Check from Resource A, and ask them to fill it out during the week.

Extension

Students continue writing in their journals, adding media and experiences relating to the current lesson.

About one week after this lesson, ask students to share highlights from their Study Skills handouts and discuss their experiences in using study skills with each other.

23

Clarifying Values and Consequences

When people make choices, they are deciding what is best between two or more alternatives. When choosing, they need to consider the things that are truly most important to them, in other words, their values. In this way, they can choose in accordance with those values.

It is helpful to consider values not only when choosing between alternatives but also when considering what may happen as a result of those choices, in other words, the consequences of choosing. When people consider the possible consequences of their choices, they can choose whether they are willing to accept those consequences. They can then choose whether they truly want to make that choice.

Making choices based on values is not always easy. People may have to develop the patience to wait for what they really want or give up something they want if they are unwilling to accept the consequences of their choice.

At times, choices between values must be made as well. For example, let's say that someone values being a nice person and also values doing well in school. This person is using the classroom computer for an important assignment during his or her turn, but a classmate, who is behind in his or her work, asks to use the computer. Now the student must decide between continuing on the computer or letting the classmate use it, which is really making a choice between working on school success or working on being nice to someone.

This lesson offers an opportunity to examine the values underlying choices and the consequences of basing choices on those values. Activity 1 offers an additional experience in cooperation. Activity 2 provides an opportunity for students to rank values in order of their importance. Activity 3 provides an opportunity for students to closely examine the consequences they would be willing to accept for a choice they might make. Activity 4 builds awareness of personal values and behavior, including a look at consequences of a choice.

Additional ways to help students examine their values and the consequences of their choices would be to discuss the values on which students' observed choices are based as well as pointing out and examining possible and real consequences of choices.

▶ Activity 1: GROUP ACTIVITY

1. Have the students vote on a group exercise of their choice, such as Alphabet or Pulse, and do the exercise.

2. Ask students to consider how they chose to complete the exercise. Did they choose to use what they know about what makes cooperation work? Was the exercise easier than at the beginning of the choice-making training or more difficult? How do their choices about cooperation affect them in their daily lives? What new choices are they now making regarding cooperation? What values does choosing to cooperate express?

▶ Activity 2: VALUES RANKING

1. Explain that students are going to identify and rank values in this activity.

2. Tell them that you are going to list a number of values. As each value is listed, they are to write it on their paper. There are no right or wrong answers, only their own answers. Examples of values that might be used are success, popularity, money, happiness, family harmony, feeling good about yourself, and being the kind of person you want to be.

3. After students have listed all the values, have them put the No. 1 next to the value that is most important to them and continue numbering each of the values in the order of declining importance.

4. Ask students if it was easy to order their values. What made it difficult? Did everyone find the same values to be of equal importance? Where do values come from? Do people ever change values? When might they do so?

▶ Activity 3: ACTION-CONSEQUENCE CONTINUUM

1. Explain that students are going to examine several values. They will look at several consequences that might occur as a result of making a variety of choices in accordance with those values. They are to determine which consequences they would be willing to accept, and therefore, which choice they would be more likely to make.

2. Tell them that you will announce a value, identify actions that a person might take to act in accordance with that particular value, and describe the possible consequences of taking that action. Explain that you are going to describe a number of action-consequence pairs that are related but become increasingly different from each other. Remind students to listen carefully to each action-consequence pair and be thinking if they would vote for it. These action-consequence pairs can also be role-played by students if you so desire.

3. First, read all the action-consequence pairs for one value. Then give students the opportunity to vote for their choices by calling out each pair. Examples of values, actions, and consequences include

Value: Success

Action-consequence pair 1: To achieve success, students might choose to pick a particular place and time to do their homework and do it at that time and place every day. They would do this at the same time even when there was a program on television that they wanted to watch or a friend they wanted to visit. As a consequence, they would miss good television shows and some fun times with their friends, but they would get better and better grades.

Action-consequence pair 2: Students might choose a place and time to do their homework and do it sometimes at that time and place. However, if a friend called and wanted to go somewhere, they would leave and not do their homework that day. As a consequence, they would enjoy more time with their friend, but their grades would go up and down.

Action-consequence pair 3: Students might choose never to do homework and to rely on luck to get by. On a day when they were not sure of their good luck, they might choose, just this once, to look on someone else's test for the answers. As a consequence, on this particular day, they might get an A on that one test. They might also wonder if they could ever get good grades on their own. They might also have a difficult time achieving the value of feeling good about themselves, believing that cheating is not right. They might be torn between the values of achieving success and feeling good about themselves.

Action-consequence pair 4: Students may choose to look on someone else's paper all the time. Because they have not done the work in the past, they doubt their capabilities. As a consequence, they would find it more and more difficult not to get caught. They might feel worse and worse about themselves and their achievements, and they might understand less and less in class.

Value: Happiness

Action-consequence pair 1: To be happier, students may choose to think positive thoughts and get involved with things that they enjoy. As a consequence, they would have to work hard to change old emotional habits, but they would be able to be happier whenever they chose to be happier.

Action-consequence pair 2: To be happier, students may choose to do nothing. As a consequence, they would not have to work hard to change old emotional habits, and they could do what they have always done, but they would remain unhappy a lot of the time.

Action-consequence pair 3: To be happier, students may choose, just one time, to drink alcohol or use another drug. As a consequence, they would feel good at first, but then they would become sick, and they would feel unhappy again. Or they might find that they begin to want more and more alcohol or drug to help them feel happier.

Action-consequence pair 4: To be happier, students may choose always to drink alcohol or take drugs. As a consequence, they might feel happier at first, but soon they would feel unhappy, and they might no longer have a choice about whether to take drugs or alcohol. Their bodies would have a physical urge for the drugs, and they would hurt if they stopped taking them. Also, they might find it harder and harder to do their schoolwork, making it more difficult for them to achieve the value of success.

Value: Money

Action-consequence pair 1: To have money, students might choose to do what they could to earn it, such as working on a paper route, baby-sitting, or doing odd jobs for their neighbors. As a consequence, they would have less time for recreation, but they would feel a sense of achievement and enjoy having their own money to do with what they liked.

Action-consequence pair 2: To have money, they might choose to ask their parents for money all the time. As a consequence, they would have more time for recreation, but they would not always be able to count on having money, and they might run into difficulties with their parents.

Action-consequence pair 3: To have money, they might choose to take just a little money from their parents' wallets, just one time, promising themselves that they will return it as soon as they can. As a consequence, they would have some money without giving up any recreation time, but they would feel bad, worry about getting caught, or actually get into trouble.

Action-consequence pair 4: To have money, they might choose to steal from others all the time. As a consequence, they would have some money without having to work, but they would eventually be sent to jail. Even if they tried to make money a different way, if they got out of jail, they would have no skills with which to earn money, so they might have to go back to prison.

▶ Activity 4: CLARIFYING VALUES AND CONSEQUENCES PRACTICE

1. Using the four-column format in Resource A, prepare the Values and Consequences Checklist. Write the title at the top of the page. Label columns *Day, Choice, Value,* and *Consequence.* Add directions: "Fill in the day, a choice you made, the value it was based on, and the consequences of that choice." Make copies of the Checklist and of the Clarifying Values and Consequences handout, which is also in Resource A.

2. Ask students to complete the matching exercise on the Clarifying Values and Consequences handout.

3. Give students the Values and Consequences Checklist, and ask them to complete it during the week.

4. Discuss the rewards and difficulties of living in accordance with one's values. Discuss the ways to continue to develop the strength and patience to do so.

Extension

Students continue adding media and experiences relating to the current lesson to their journals.

About one week after this lesson, give students the opportunity to share highlights from their Values and Consequences Checklist and to discuss the choices they made that week, the values on which the choices were based, and the consequences that occurred as a result of their choices.

Middle School Modifications

REFLECTIVE DETECTIVE—Discuss the particular difficulty with acting according to one's own values when those values are in conflict with those of the majority. Discuss situations in which students have done this, and brainstorm additional methods of doing so. Create a group mural to express these ideas.

24

Investigating Cheating

Cheating, defined as "to fool by trickery," is seen as behavior that seems to be based, at least partly, on several assumptions, including, "I don't have to work hard at school. I'll be lucky and win the lottery or become famous," and "I will never succeed so why bother to try," and "It is awful, and I must not accept myself until I measure up to everyone else." But the facts show that cheating does not solve all problems and that the consequences of being caught are long lasting. See Figure 24.1 for information about cheating.

This lesson helps students examine the choice of cheating. Activity 1 has students exploring personal experiences with cheating. Activity 2 explores the choice of cheating through the development, enactment, and

Figure 24.1 Facts About Cheating

- Definition—Cheat: to fool by trickery.

- One of five adults cannot read or write.

- Many people cannot read warning labels, order from a menu, or fill out job applications.

- The difference in lifetime earnings between someone who has stayed in school and someone who has dropped out of school is hundreds of thousands of dollars.

analysis of three brief scenes. The first scene, based on the assumptions, depicts the effect of cheating on the present life of the individual making this choice. The second depicts the effect that this choice might have on that person's future. This will be followed by an analysis of the scenes and a discussion of how to arrive at a better belief regarding doing work. The students will then develop and enact a scene that will reflect the thoughts, feelings, actions, and immediate and far-reaching consequences stemming from the provable belief.

Should a student be observed making the choice to cheat, it might be helpful to have him or her examine his or her choice, values, assumptions, and future consequences of his or her actions.

▶ Activity 1: INQUIRY

Ask students to complete the sentence "An experience I had with cheating or observing cheating was when . . ." (There is no handout.)

▶ Activity 2: SCENE INVESTIGATION: CHEATING CONSEQUENCES

1. Tell students that they are to develop and enact two brief scenes. The choice to be enacted is the choice of cheating. Explain to the students that cheating, defined as "to fool by trickery," is seen as behavior that seems to be based, at least partly, on several assumptions, including "I don't have to work hard at school. I'll be lucky and win the lottery or become famous," "I will never succeed so why bother to try," and "It is awful, and I must not accept myself until I measure up to everyone else." But the facts show that cheating does not solve all problems and that the consequences of cheating are long-lasting. Share the Facts About Cheating sheet with the students as well.

2. Tell the students that the first scene they will enact depicts the choice being made and the effect that this has on the present life of the individual making this choice. The second scene depicts the effect that this choice has on the future life of this individual. For convenience, two possible scenes are outlined briefly. Feel free to embellish these outlines or develop an original scene based on ideas from students. Different sets of students can act out the two separate scenes.

3. Share the two scene outlines with the students. Encourage them to create their own dialogue and actions to go with the scene. Encourage them to include the assumptions, thoughts, and feelings as characters in the scenes.

Scene Idea 1

As a young person, Pam often pretends that she is sick so that she can miss school. She assumes that she will never succeed so she shouldn't even bother to try. When she is in school, she feels nervous and sad, and she rarely listens or pays attention. As an older student, Pam never does homework because she feels that she would not do the work as well as she would like. She assumes that it is awful because in her mind, she doesn't measure up to other students. She begins to convince herself that she doesn't have to work hard in school because she'll be lucky and win the lottery or become famous. She gets by for a while on luck. A difficult test is given for which she has not studied, and Pam looks on a neighbor's paper for the answers. The teacher catches her and sends her to the office to discuss the matter with the principal. Pam tells the principal that she will never do it again. When the next test is given out, Pam does not trust her own knowledge and copies from a classmate again. Her grades become worse and worse. Pam has lost her self-respect, her parent's and teacher's respect, and the trust and respect of her peers.

Scene Idea 2

Pam, now in her twenties, dropped out of high school having found it more and more difficult. She has been applying for jobs and has not been hired for any of them. She is now applying for a job at McDonald's and cannot fill out the application because she does not understand some of the questions. Pam goes into the office to be interviewed. When asked why she did not finish filling out the application, she tries to bluff her way through it. However, the manager tells her that she is not McDonald's material and sends her out the door without a job.

4. Have students discuss the choices made. They are to use all of their choice-making skills to determine whether these were the best possible choices. Have them answer a series of questions related to making the choices. (Brief possible responses are shown.)

   Were these choices based on assumptions or facts? (Assumptions.)

   On which assumptions were the choices based? (I will never succeed so why bother to try. It is awful, and I must not accept myself until I measure up to everyone else. I don't have to work hard at school. I'll be lucky and win the lottery or become famous. Have students explore other possible assumptions.)

   How could the assumptions be changed into provable beliefs? (I can do the best that I can do. I can accept myself as worthwhile without having to measure myself against anyone else. It is important to work hard at school. I do not have to be perfect.)

   What were the consequences of Pam's choices? (Being called into the principal's office, losing self-trust and developing a pattern of cheating, dropping out of school, having trouble finding a job.)

   Would these consequences be acceptable to them? (No.)

   Were the choices based on their highest value? (No.)

   What might have been better choices that would have allowed Pam to get her needs met and live by her values? (Doing the schoolwork as well as possible even though it might be a struggle and asking for help when having difficulties.)

5. Divide the students into small groups. Ask students to rewrite the scenes to reflect what they feel would be the best possible choice, showing the effect of that choice on the present and future life of that individual. Ask them to

include the new beliefs and the accompanying thoughts, feelings, actions, and consequences, both immediate and long term. Examples may include having studied hard, graduating near the top of her class, going to a good college, and becoming a lawyer.

Extension

Students continue adding comments and thoughts to their journals, using different media and experiences relating to the current lesson.

25

Investigating Stealing

This lesson examines the choice of stealing, defined as "to take the property of another without right or permission." See Figure 25.1 for the facts associated with stealing. The assumption that "I can take something from someone just once and that does not mean that I am a thief" is coupled with the assumptions: "The only way that I can get what I want is by lying," "I can never be happy and life will be awful unless certain things are a certain way," and "I am responsible for nothing" to create a dilemma that has affected many children under the age of 18.

Activity 1 has students exploring personal experiences with stealing. Activity 2 explores the choice of stealing through the development, enactment, and analysis of two scenes. The first scene depicts the effect of stealing on the present life of the individual making this choice. The second scene depicts the effect that this choice might have on the future of the person making this choice. This will be followed by an analysis of the scenes and a discussion of how to arrive at a better belief regarding getting

Figure 25.1   Facts About Stealing

- Definition—Steal: to take the property of another without right or permission.

- Many children under the age of 18 will commit some kind of crime for which they could be arrested.

- Juvenile criminals can be sent to jail as well as other public and private institutions.

the things one wants. The students will then develop and enact a scene that reflects the thoughts, feelings, actions, and immediate and far-reaching consequences stemming from the provable belief.

Should a student be observed making the choice to steal, it might be helpful to have him or her examine his or her choice, values, assumptions, and future consequences of his or her actions.

▶ Activity 1: INQUIRY

Ask students to write about "An experience I had with stealing or witnessing stealing was when . . ." (There is no handout.)

▶ Activity 2: SCENE INVESTIGATION: STEALING CONSEQUENCES

1. Explain that students are to investigate two scenes about the choice and consequences of stealing. Explain to them that the assumption that "I can take something from someone just once and that does not mean that I am a thief" is coupled with the assumptions "The only way that I can get what I want is by lying," "I can never be happy, and life will be awful unless certain things are a certain way," and "I am responsible for nothing" to create a dilemma that has affected many children under the age of 18. Share the Facts About Stealing sheet with them as well.

2. Share the following scenes with them to use as the basis of the investigation, or develop appropriate scenes of your own. Different sets of students can act out the two separate scenes. Encourage the students to include the assumptions, thoughts, and feelings as characters in the scenes.

Scene Idea 1

A youngster, Mark, is at a toy store with a friend. He sees a toy car that he really wants, but he doesn't have enough money to buy it. He knows that he would be so happy if he could only have the car that he really wants. His friend suggests that he just take it because the store has a lot of them and would never miss the one that he took. Mark takes the car because he believes that he can't be happy unless he has it right away. Because he believes he is responsible for nothing but his own happiness, he doesn't think about whether it is a right or wrong thing to do. He is stopped by the store manager before he gets to the exit. The store manager calls Mark's parents. When his parents ask what he has done, he tells them that he has done nothing. He doesn't consider telling the truth because he assumes that lying is his only choice. The store manager tells Mark's parents that he has taken the toy. Mark's parents bring him to the store and make their son return the item and promise to never steal anything again. The next time Mark is at a store, he takes a chocolate bar without paying for it. As a teenager, he sees money on his parents' dresser when they are not home. He wants to go to a movie and doesn't have his own money. Believing that his parents will never know and never miss the money, he takes it. His parents trust him less and less, and the other students in the school know that Mark is not someone that they can believe or trust.

Scene Idea 2

Mark is now in his forties and is in jail. He is in an office, trying to convince a panel of officials that he should be let out of jail on parole. He tells them that he promises never to steal another thing and that he will work very hard to be a model citizen. He leaves the room as the panel discusses whether to grant his parole. When he returns, the panel tells him that his parole is not going to be granted. Even though he may want to make different choices and change his ways, he has not shown that he is able to make this choice. Every time he has been released on parole, he has stolen again and been brought back to jail. Therefore, he will serve his entire sentence with no parole.

3. Have students discuss the choices made. They are to use all of their choice-making skills to determine whether they were the best possible choices. Have them answer a series of questions relating to making these choices. (Brief responses are shown.)

Were Mark's choices based on assumptions or facts? (Assumptions.)

On which assumptions was the choice based? (I can take something from someone just once, and that does not mean I am a thief. I can never be happy, and life will be awful unless certain things are a certain way. The only way that I can get what I want is by lying. I am responsible for nothing.)

How could they rewrite the assumptions into provable beliefs? (If I take something from someone, I am acting as a thief. I can choose to be happy even if things aren't exactly the way I want them to be. I have many choices about how I can get the things that I want. There are some things for which I am responsible and some things for which I am not responsible.)

What were the consequences of Mark's choices? (Getting into trouble with parents, developing a pattern of stealing, going to jail, staying in jail for life.)

Would these consequences be acceptable to them? (No.)

Was Mark's choice based on their highest value? (No.)

What might have been a better choice that would have allowed Mark to get his needs met and to live by his values? (Doing without the toy even though he might want it and enjoying other things, asking parents to buy him the toy for his birthday even though it might be hard to wait for it, trying to get a job to save money to buy it himself, playing with toys he already owns, asking his parents to borrow some money.)

4. Divide the students into small groups. Ask the students to rewrite the scenes to reflect what they feel would be the best possible choice, showing the effects of that choice on the present and future life of that individual. Ask them to include the new beliefs and the accompanying thoughts, feelings, actions, and consequences, both immediate and long-term. Examples might be that he held jobs while going to school, saved money for college, and graduated with a degree in business, and that he is now a wealthy businessman who contributes much of his earnings to deserving boys and girls.

Extension

Students continue adding comments and thoughts to their journals, using different media and experiences relating to the current lesson.

About one week after this lesson, give students the opportunity to discuss experiences—past, present, and future—with stealing.

26

Investigating Bullying

Bullying—defined as an act of physical, verbal, or emotional violence that is meant to hurt someone—is partly based on the assumptions, "In order to feel good about myself, I must make someone else feel bad about him- or herself," "I must give in to pressure to be cool and to be liked by everyone or it will be awful," and "I must pressure others in order to always have my way, or it will be awful." However, bullying is harmful not only to the victim but to the perpetrator as well. See Figure 26.1 for information about bullying.

This lesson helps students examine the choice of bullying. Activity 1 has students examine their personal experiences with bullying. Activity 2 explores bullying through the development, enactment, and analysis of three brief scenes. The first scene, based on assumptions, depicts the effects of bullying in the present life of the individual making that choice. The second scene depicts the effect this choice might have on that person's future. This will be followed by an analysis of the scene and a discussion of how to arrive at a better belief regarding dealing with others. The students will then develop and enact a third scene, which will reflect the thoughts,

Figure 26.1   Facts About Bullying

- Definition—Bully: an act of physical, verbal, or emotional violence that is meant to hurt someone

- Those who bully are at the greatest risk for being lonely, having a hard time making friends and doing poorly in school

feelings, actions, and immediate and far- reaching consequences stemming from the provable belief.

Should students be observed making the choice to bully, it might be helpful to have them examine their choice, values, and assumptions, as well as the consequences of their actions.

▶ Activity 1: INQUIRY

Ask students to complete the sentence, "An experience I had with bullying or observing bullying was when . . ." (There is no handout.)

▶ Activity 2: SCENE INVESTIGATION: BULLYING CONSEQUENCES

1. Tell students that they are to develop and enact two brief scenes. The choice to be enacted is the choice of bullying. Explain to the students that bullying—defined as an act of physical, verbal, or emotional violence that is meant to hurt someone—is partly based on the assumptions, "In order to feel good about myself, I must make someone else feel bad him- or herself," "I must give in to pressure to be cool and to be liked by everyone, or it will be awful," and "I must pressure others in order to always have my way, or it will be awful." However, bullying is harmful not only to the victim but to the perpetrator as well. Share the fact sheet with the students.

2. Tell students that the first scene they will enact depicts the choice being made and the effect that this has on the present life of the individual making the choice. The second scene depicts the effect that this choice has on the future life of the individual. For convenience, two possible scenes are outlined briefly. Feel free to embellish these or to develop an original scene based on ideas from students. Different sets of students may act out the two separate scenes.

3. Share the two scenes outlined with the students. Encourage them to create their own dialogue and actions to go with the scene. Encourage them to include the bully's assumption, thoughts, and feelings as characters in the scenes.

Scene Idea 1

Danita is in the cafeteria with some other students and a girl named Jasmine, who is one of the popular girls in class. Danita wants to impress Jasmine because she assumes that it is very important to be cool and liked by everyone. Danita sees an old friend, Monica, walking toward the group, and Danita starts to move toward her. Jasmine sees this and tells Danita that if she wants to be with the popular girls, there are certain people she can't talk to anymore, and Monica is one of them. Danita turns away from Monica.

As Monica turns to walk away, she tells Danita that she can't trust her and doesn't want to be her friend anymore. When Danita walks back to talk to Jasmine, she is told that she is busy with her other friends. Danita struggles to make other friends, but the students know what she did to Monica; Danita develops a reputation at school as a person who cannot be trusted as a friend. Feeling bad about herself and believing that she has no power, Danita operates under the assumption that she will have to pressure others into spending time with her. She does so and makes friends with one other girl, Jodi.

Still feeling insecure about herself with only one friend, and operating under the assumption that she can only feel good about herself if she makes someone else feel bad about him- or herself, she spreads rumors throughout the school about some of the other girls in school. She convinces Jodi to ignore these girls. Her reputation as someone not to be trusted continues to grow. Once she gets into high school, she gets into more and more fights. She spends much of her time in detention and does worse and worse in school. Eventually, after her parents and the school have run out of options, she ends up in a juvenile detention home.

Scene Idea 2

In her twenties, Danita is very lonely and confused. She has no friends or relationships she can count on. She didn't finish high school, never went to college, and has few choices about what to do with her life.

3. Have students discuss the choices Danita made. They are to use all of their choice-making skills to determine whether these were the best possible choices. Have them answer a series of questions related to making the choices. (Brief responses are provided.)

    Were these choices based on assumptions or facts? (Assumptions.)

    On which assumptions were the choices made? (In order to feel good about myself, I must make someone else feel bad about him- or herself. I must give in to pressure to be cool and to be liked by everyone, or it will be awful. I must pressure others in order to always have my way, or it will be awful.)

    Have students explore other possible assumptions.

    How could the assumptions be changed to provable beliefs? (I can trust that I am cool, make my own choices, and know that true friends will respect them. I do not have to pressure others to have my way. I don't have to try to make others feel bad about themselves in order to feel good about myself. I have many other better choices.)

    What were the consequences of Danita's choices? (Losing a friend; having a hard time making other friends; spending time in detention; doing poorly in school; going to juvenile detention; having few options for the future.)

    Would these consequences be acceptable to them? (No.)

    Were these choices based on Danita's highest values? (No.)

    What might have been a better choice that would have allowed Danita to get her need met and to live by her values? (Sticking by her old friend and realizing that she was already cool.)

4. Divide the students into small groups. Ask students to rewrite the scenes to reflect what they feel would be the best possible choice, showing the effect of that choice on the present and future life of that individual. Ask them to include the new beliefs and the accompanying thoughts, feelings, actions, and consequences, both immediate and long term. (Examples include staying true to Monica; becoming class president, homecoming queen, and head of sorority in college.)

5. Students continue adding comments and thoughts to their journals, using different media and experiences relating to bullying.

27

Investigating Abuse of Alcohol and Other Drugs

This lesson examines the choice of using alcohol, defined as a drug found in drinks such as beer, wine, or liquor, and taking drugs, defined as chemicals that change the way the body and mind work. Figure 27.1 presents some of the assumptions and facts associated with alcohol and other drug use. Assumptions such as, "I can take as much alcohol or other drugs as I want—they won't hurt me, and I can stop when I want to" and "I must give in to pressure to be cool and to be liked by everyone, or it would be awful" combine to produce a dangerous choice for some students. Young people may use substances for a wide range of misguided reasons, such as to lower stress, to become happier, or to try to deal with feelings of low self-worth. Therefore, it might be helpful to go back to other lessons and reexamine the assumptions associated with these issues as well.

Students need to know that some drugs are safe—they are prescribed when people are ill—but other drugs are harmful to minds and bodies. Dangerous drugs can make people unable to stand or walk; make them pass out; cause damage to parts of their bodies, such as their liver, stomach, or brain; and cause many problems for themselves, their family, and their friends. Some people may become dependent on, or addicted to, a drug, taking it more and more and having difficulty in stopping.

The process of addiction is has several stages. At first, drugs are used because people believe using drugs will take away their scary or sad feelings. They may learn that although the drug does not take away the feeling for good, it may help them forget those feelings for a while. Later, they may begin to look forward to using the drug and will actively look for it. Until this point, people are still able to choose other ways to make themselves feel better, besides using the drug. However, they are likely to choose the drug over any other method. Next, they have no choice except to take the drug because they need it to survive. Their body needs the chemicals, and they ache if drugs are not taken. They use the drug on a regular basis because they have to do so. The final stage is one of three results: recovery, where very hard work with lots of help enables the person to stop taking the drug; serious illness; or death.

Figure 27.1   Facts About Alcohol and Other Drugs

Definitions

- Alcohol—A drug found in drinks such as beer, wine, or liquor.

- Drug—A chemical that changes the way the body and mind work.

  Some drugs are safe—they help us when we are sick.

  Many drugs harm our minds and bodies. These drugs may make us unable to stand or walk; cause us to pass out; cause damage to parts of our bodies, such as our liver, stomach, and brain; and cause many problems for us, our friends, and our families.

  When youngsters use drugs, drugs interfere with their growth; slow their learning; change their moods causing stress, sadness, or anger; cause problems with school, friends, and family; and leave them open to the process of addiction.

Addiction Process

- People can become dependent on or addicted to a drug, so that it becomes more and more difficult to stop using the drug.

- At first, people may use a drug to take away scary or sad feelings. They may learn that although the drug doesn't take the feelings away for good, it may help them forget those feelings for a while.

- Next, people may begin looking forward to using the drug and will actively look for the drug. Until this point, people can still choose other ways to feel better, besides using the drug. However, they may choose the drug over any other method.

- Next, people have no choice except to take the drug because they need it to survive. Their body needs the chemicals, and it hurts their body if the drug is not taken. The drug is used on a regular basis because people have to do so.

- The final stage is either recovery, where people work very hard with lots of help to stop taking the drug; serious illness; or death.

When youngsters use drugs, the drugs interfere with their growth; slow their learning; change their moods, causing anxiety, sadness, or anger; cause them problems in school and with friends and family; and leave them open to the process of addiction.

Activity 1 in this lesson has students exploring personal experiences with alcohol and other drug use. Activity 2 explores the choice of alcohol and other drug use through the development, enactment, and analysis of three scenes. The first scene depicts the effect of alcohol and other drug use on the present life of the individual making this choice. The second scene depicts the effect that this choice might have on the future of the person making this choice. This will be followed by an analysis of the scene and a discussion of how to arrive at a better belief regarding drug use. The students will then develop and enact a third scene, which will reflect the thoughts, feelings, actions, and immediate and far-reaching consequences stemming from the provable belief.

Should students be observed making a choice to use alcohol and other drugs, it might be helpful to have them examine their choice, values, and assumptions, as well as the future consequences of their actions.

▶ Activity 1: INQUIRY

Ask students to complete this sentence: "An experience I had with alcohol or other drugs or observing use of alcohol or other drugs was when . . ." (There is no handout.)

▶ Activity 2: SCENE INVESTIGATION: CONSEQUENCES OF ABUSING ALCOHOL AND OTHER DRUGS

1. Tell students that they are to develop and enact two brief scenes. The choice to be enacted is the choice of using alcohol and other drugs. Present the information to them that is found in the introduction to this lesson, including the definitions, assumptions, and facts.

2. Tell students that the first scene they will enact depicts the choice being made and the effect that this has on the present life of the individual. The second scene depicts the effect that this choice has on the future life of this individual. Have students suggest scenes or use the two that are shown. Different sets of students can act out the two separate scenes.

3. Share the two scene outlines with the students. Encourage them to create their own dialogue and actions to go with the scenes. Encourage them to include Rashid's assumptions, thoughts, and feelings as characters in the scenes.

Scene Idea 1

Rashid has just moved to a new city. He is stressed because he struggles in school and is worried that this new school will be harder. He is sad because he misses his old friends. Rashid is at a party and is sitting off by himself because he doesn't know anybody. Another youngster approaches Rashid and tells him that some of the people at the party are going into the kitchen to have some of the beer they found in the refrigerator. If he wants to be one of the cool people and feel a lot happier, he can join them. Rashid starts to say no, but the other youngster accuses him of being uncool, so Rashid joins them in the kitchen. He drinks two beers, and although his stomach feels a little funny, he enjoys being with the group and finds that the drinks have helped him to forget about how sad, stressed, and insecure he was.

Rashid continues to drink every time he is with his friends and sometimes when he is alone. As a teenager, he remains friends with people who often drink and use drugs. He drinks more and more, gets worse and worse grades, argues often with his family, and is sick a great deal of the time.

Scene Idea 2

Rashid is now in his thirties and is surrounded by friends, family, and coworkers as they tell him about how they know he is addicted to alcohol and how that is affecting him, his family, friends, and work. Rashid's boss tells him that he has been doing worse and worse at work, coming in late, sleeping at work, and causing several accidents as a result of coming to work drunk. His friends tell him that he has been losing more and more weight and getting sick more and more often; he has not been a friend to himself, let alone a friend to them. His wife tells him that he has been a different person, yelling all the time or not being there at all. His boss tells him that he will be fired unless he gets help, and his wife says that she will divorce him unless he gets help for his addiction.

4. Have the students discuss the choices made. They are to use all of their choice-making skills to determine whether these were the best possible choices. Use these questions or create some of your own. (Brief possible responses are shown.)

Were these choices based on assumptions or facts? (Assumptions.)

On which assumptions were the choices based? (I can take as much alcohol or other drugs as I want and they won't hurt me, and I can stop when I want to. I must give in to pressure to be cool and to be liked by everyone, or it would be awful.)

How could you rewrite the assumptions into provable beliefs? (I will be harmed by alcohol and other drugs, and eventually, I may not be able to stop when I want to stop. I can trust that I am cool, make my own choices and know that true friends will respect them.)

You can also discuss the assumptions related to stress, happiness, and self-measurement as they apply to Rashid's choices. In addition, you can have students explore other possible assumptions that might have led to the choices made by Rashid.

What were the consequences of Rashid's choices? (Drinking more and more often, becoming thin and ill, doing a poor job at school and work, not being a good family member or friend, not being a good husband, job is threatened, marriage is threatened.)

Would these consequences be acceptable to them? (No.)

Were Rashid's choices based on his highest value? (No.)

What might have been a better choice that would have allowed Rashid to get his needs met and to live by his values? (Refusing the drink and assertively sticking with this choice; trying to make friends with someone at the party who wasn't drinking; talking about his feelings regarding moving and school; finding healthy ways to deal with his stress such as changing his thoughts and doing relaxation exercises; finding things to do and ways to think that make him happy; finding non–drug-using friends.)

5. Divide the students into two small groups. Ask students to rewrite the scenes to reflect what they feel would be the best possible choice, showing the effects of that choice on the present and future life of that individual. Ask them to include the new beliefs and the accompanying thoughts, feelings, actions, and consequences, both immediate and long-term. (Examples may include being known in school as someone with strong convictions, becoming class president, doing well in college, being promoted at work, and being happily married for 25 years.)

6. Ask students to write about the lesson in their journals.

7. About one week after this lesson, give students the opportunity to discuss experiences—past, present, and future—with alcohol and other drug use.

28

Getting Help

Sometimes, people find themselves in unsafe situations that they have a difficult time handling on their own. First, they must try to get out of the situation themselves, as quickly as possible. If they are unable to do this alone, rather than staying in an unsafe situation, they can choose to get help from someone whom they trust.

Examples of situations for which people may need to ask for help are situations that make them unhappy, uncomfortable, or at risk. Figure 28.1 shows examples of times when it is important to ask for help.

In any of these situations, it is important for students to realize that they are not at fault. Also, it helps if they realize that others have experienced what they are experiencing and know how to help. It is important,

Figure 28.1   Ask for Help When . . .

- You are very sad for a long time, you don't know why, and nothing you do helps you to feel happier.

- You are so sad or upset that you want to hurt yourself or try to end your life.

- You are not being taken care of so that you don't have enough food to eat or warm enough clothes to wear.

- You are constantly told that you are not a good person, called names, and yelled at.

- You are physically hurt by someone.

- You are being touched in places where you don't want to be touched or are being asked to touch others in places where you don't want to touch them.

as soon as they can, to find someone they trust, preferably an adult, and tell that person exactly what is happening in as much detail as possible. Examples of people they might talk to would be a parent, another adult relative, an adult friend of the family, a neighbor, a teacher or another adult at school, or a trusted friend. Emphasize that if the first person they talk to is not able to help them leave the harmful situation, they *must* keep talking to people until they get the help they need and are able to leave the negative situation.

This lesson examines the concept of asking for help in unsafe situations. Activity 1 has students determine specific situations in which they would get help. Activity 2 has students determine specific people they would ask to help them. Activity 3 offers rehearsal in asking for help through scene development and enactment.

You can support your students by offering to be available should they want to talk about situations in their lives. You can then access the necessary resources with which to help them.

▶ Activity 1: HELP VOTE

1. Explain that you are going to describe a variety of situations.

2. Tell students that, after you describe each situation, they are to raise their hand if they believe they would ask for help in that situation. Examples of situations that you might use include:

   Your parent hits you every day and leaves bruises on your body.

   Your parent yells at you for making a mess in the kitchen.

   You have been very sad all week and don't understand why, and you have been thinking a lot about what it might be like to die.

   You are sad because you have just moved to a new city.

   Your next-door neighbor asks you to touch him or her in a place where you do not want to touch him or her.

3. Give students the Getting Help form in Resource A to add to their personal journals. Have students come up with other situations of their own. Have them discuss the kinds of situations in which they would ask for help and from whom. Also, discuss the things that get in the way of asking for help, such as fear and shame, and how to overcome them.

▶ Activity 2: BRAINSTORM

Tell students that they are going to brainstorm as many people as they can think of from whom they would be able to ask for help. Examples of people that students might ask for help include uncle, principal, and big brother. Ask them to write these in their journals.

► Activity 3: SCENE INVESTIGATION: ASKING FOR HELP

1. Have the students enact a scene in which they are asking for help to get out of a negative situation. Ask them to decide on the situation, to choose the person from whom they are requesting help, and to describe the situation in as much detail as possible. You may play the role of the adult helper, assuring the youngster that help will be available to get out of the situation. An example scene outline is shown below for your reference. You are encouraged to solicit scene ideas from students.

Scene Idea

Teresa is talking to her mother. She tells her mother that when her uncle was at their house and they were alone in the den, he asked her if she would touch him in a place she did not want to touch him. When Teresa said that she didn't want to touch him there, he told her that she should be a good little niece and do what her uncle asked her to do. She left the room, feeling frightened and uncomfortable. Mother responds by assuring her daughter that she will protect her and make sure that this never happens again. She commends her for doing the right thing and coming to her for help.

2. Ask students to think about the scene and write a personal promise about finding help, if they need it.

3. Some time after this lesson, give students the opportunity to discuss past and present experiences with seeking and receiving help. Offer privacy and confidentiality for personal disclosures according to the applicable school policy.

Middle School Modifications

SCENE INVESTIGATION—Change the scene to consider a girl talking to her friend about her problems and her hopelessness in changing them. The friend takes her to the school counselor for help.

29

Taking Risks and Setting Goals

As discussed in the very first lesson, every choice made in the present creates a chain reaction. Therefore, the choices people make now determine the choices that they will be able to make in the future.

Figure 29.1 Risk Taking and Goal Setting

Avoid Harmful Risks

- Choices based not on your beliefs but on others' beliefs
- Choices that are not based on your highest values
- Choices that will make you uncomfortable or unhappy
- Choices that will be followed by immediate or future negative consequences
- Choices that will hurt you or others emotionally or physically

Take Safe Risks

- Try positive, new choices about thinking
- Try positive, new choices about feeling
- Try positive, new choices about behaving

People can choose to make their present choices with their future in mind. In this way, they can choose the kind of people they want to become and use their choice-making know-how to help them choose actions that will lead toward this goal. Rather than making choices just because everyone else makes those choices or letting their choices just happen, people can take the future into their hands by shaping it with every choice that they make.

To reach their goals, most people have to work hard, make sacrifices, and take risks. It is helpful to understand which risks are safe, which will not hurt, and which will help to achieve goals. People can then look at ways to help avoid unsafe risks and take safe risks, despite their fears and their tendency to want to retain their old, comfortable ways of feeling, thinking, and behaving.

People are taking unsafe risks when they do something that may hurt themselves or others physically; that make them very uncomfortable or unhappy, either immediately or in the future; or that they believe are wrong or not truly based on their own values. An example of an unsafe risk would be trying beer at a party.

People are taking safe risks when they make new choices that will not hurt themselves or others, that will make them happier, and that are based on their own beliefs. An example of a safe risk would be trying to negotiate to resolve a conflict rather than making an old choice of yelling and getting angry. (See Figure 29.1 for an overview of this discussion.)

This lesson helps students become part of the process of determining the kind of people they would like to be and focuses on the concepts of risk taking and goal setting. Activity 1 gives students opportunities to consider a particular risk and whether they would consider it safe or unsafe to take it. Activity 2 builds students' awareness of their own risk-taking and goal-setting behavior. Activity 3 gives students the opportunity to choose for themselves goals and behaviors that they would want as part of their characters.

▶ Activity 1: RISK VOTE

1. Explain that you are going to describe a variety of risks. Define taking a risk as doing something out of the ordinary without knowing exactly what will happen.

2. After each risk, you say *safe* and *unsafe*. If the students believe that the risk would be safe to take, they are to raise their hand after you say *safe*. If they believe the risk would be unsafe to take, they raise their hand after you say *unsafe*.

Examples of risks include

   Looking at someone else's test paper during a test

   Jumping off a moving train

   Acting assertively even though you are more comfortable being passive

   Taking a candy bar from a store without paying for it

Changing your self-talk so that you begin to believe that you do not have to be perfect, even though you always thought you did

Taking some time away from watching television to do homework at a regular time even though it's hard to put off doing what you enjoy

Saying no to a boyfriend or girlfriend who wants you to do something you do not want to do

Trying activities such as rock-climbing or completing a ropes course

3. Discuss with the students what makes a risk safe or unsafe. Discuss how the potential consequences of choices affect decisions made.

▶ Activity 2: GOAL SETTING

1. Using the two-column format in Resource A, prepare the Goal Setting and Risking Taking Checklist. Write the title at the top of the page. Label columns *Day* and *Actions*. Add directions: "Fill in the day, and describe two actions you took to begin reaching your goal."

2. Give the Goal Setting and Risking Taking Checklist to students and ask them to fill it out during the week.

▶ Activity 3: DESIGN CONTRACT

1. Explain to students that you are going to trace each of their bodies on a large piece of paper (or have pairs of students trace each other) and that each of them will prepare a contract called "The Person I Want to Be." Give each person a large piece of paper for the outline and a copy of The Person I Want to Be Contract in Resource A. On this contract, there are several areas for them to fill out. Completing these areas will help them to design the person they would like to be in the future.

2. The first area to be filled out on the contract is called, "How I Choose to Feel, Think, and Act." They should use the space to describe the ways in which they would like to feel, think, and act. The second area, labeled "Assumptions, Thoughts, Feelings, and Behaviors I Want to Change," asks them to describe assumptions they would have to change to feel, think, and act in the ways they have described. The third area, called "Risks and New Skills," asks them to describe risks they will take and new skills they will use to act in new ways. The final area, "My First Two Steps," asks them to describe the first two actions they will take immediately to begin reaching their goals. Examples of answers in these areas include

How I Choose to Feel, Think, and Act: feeling less anxious, being happier when I choose to be happy, using positive self-talk, negotiating instead of yelling, studying instead of cheating

Assumptions, Thoughts, Feelings, and Behaviors I Want to Change: I must be perfect; if something seems fearsome, I must get terribly upset.

Risks and New Skills—Use listening skills, assertive statements

My First Two Steps—I will listen to my sister and give her feedback about what she says to me; I will spend a half hour doing homework tonight

3. After students complete their contracts, ask them to share them with a friend or with the class. Then connect each of the contracts to the student's body outline and display all of the images on classroom walls.

4. About a week after this lesson, ask students to share in pairs how they are doing on their contracts, with attention to the parts they are having trouble with.

Middle School Modifications

RISK VOTE—Instead of the vote, have your students develop a list of safe risks and a list of unsafe risks. Discuss the allure of risk-taking behaviors for adolescents and some ways to address this.

DESIGN CONTRACT—Have students decide on a way to share or display their contracts.

Epilogue

A Teacher Rejoices

Wow, I feel like I'm able to make an even greater impact on my students than I ever thought possible!

The students seems happier, the class is getting along better, there are fewer problems, I seem to have more time for teaching and they seem to be doing better academically.

Look—she has a smile on her face! It seems like she's finally able to stop her stress headaches.

I am amazed that he just told his friend that he was angry rather than pushing him.

I can't believe that I actually have in my hand an assignment that she turned in with eraser marks rather than throwing it away because it was less than perfect.

These quotes describe just a few of the success stories this author has observed. I have fond recollections of the second grader who, upon seeing my sad face as I walked down the hall, asked me "Adina, what are you assuming and thinking to make you so sad?" Or when, after a fifth grader answered a question about his behavior with "I had no choice," the entire rest of the class said, "Yes, you did."

I remember the student who said that he puts people down because that's just the way he does things. Struggling with the impending lesson about put-downs, he was told that he did not have to change his ways, merely listen to some options. Following the lesson, he went up to the teacher and asked her to help him learn to stop putting others down.

I recall the students who struggled with lying. After being questioned about their values and determining that they believed lying was wrong, they discovered that they lied because they assumed that this was the only way to get their needs met. After learning that they had other options and developing skills in communication and negotiation, their behavior changed dramatically; they were able to make choices in accordance with their values.

I would love to hear your stories. I am excited about the impact that I know you will have on your students, your classroom, your school, and—ultimately—the world in which we all live.

Resource A

REPRODUCIBLE MASTERS

Contents

Two-Column With Scale	174
Two-Column	175
Three-Column	176
Four-Column	177
The Cooperation Rules We Choose by Majority	178
Anxiety	179
Uncovering Feelings	180
Anger	181
Responsibility	182
Happiness	183
Self-Acceptance	184
Self-Measurement	185
Unrealistic Expectations	186
Friendship	187
Family	188
Put-Downs	189
Pressuring	190
Being Pressured	191
Prejudice	192
Manipulation Check	193
Asking Directly	194
Feedback Practice	195
Assertiveness	196
Study Skills	197
Study Skills Check	198
Clarifying Values and Consequences	199
Getting Help	200
The Person I Want to Be Contract	201

Title:

Directions:

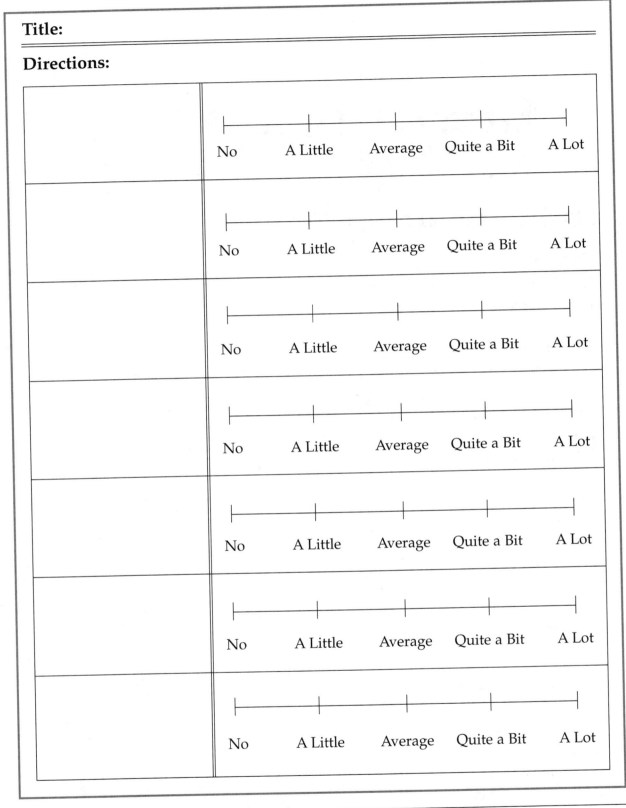

Title:

Directions:

Title:

Directions:

Title:

Directions:

The Cooperation Rules We Choose by Majority

Anxiety

INQUIRY   I am anxious when

_____

_____

_____

ASSUMPTION

If something seems scary, I must get terribly upset.

Investigating Procedures

☑ Rewrite assumption into a provable belief
☑ Change thoughts
☑ Change behaviors

PROVABLE BELIEF

If something seems scary, I can look closely to figure out what the risks are.

SELF-TALK

Statements I make to myself that make me feel relaxed:

Statements I make to myself that make me feel stressed:

Relax your body!

Uncovering Feelings

INQUIRY   A time when I kept my feelings inside was

_____

_____

_____

ASSUMPTION

I must never let out my feelings, or it would be awful.

Investigating Procedures

☑ Rewrite assumption into a provable belief
☑ Change thoughts
☑ Change behaviors

PROVABLE BELIEF

It will not hurt, and it might even help to let out my feelings.

SELF-TALK

Statements I make to myself that lead me to cover my feelings:

Statements I make to myself that lead me to share my feelings:

Talk about your feelings!

Anger

INQUIRY   A time I got angry was

_____

_____

_____

_____

ASSUMPTION

It is awful, and I must get angry when things don't go
the way I want them to go.

Investigating
Procedures

☑ Rewrite assumption into a
   provable belief
☑ Change thoughts
☑ Change behaviors

PROVABLE BELIEF

Sometimes I would like
situations to be different, but
I can deal with them calmly
or let them go.

SELF-TALK

Statements I make to myself that influence me to get angry:	Statements I make to myself that influence me to want to seek solutions:

Look for a positive solution!

Responsibility

INQUIRY   A time I felt totally responsible or not responsible was

_____

_____

_____

ASSUMPTION

I am responsible for everything. I am responsible for nothing.

Investigating Procedures

☑ Rewrite assumption into a provable belief
☑ Change thoughts
☑ Change behaviors

PROVABLE BELIEF

There are certain things for which I am responsible and certain things for which I am not responsible.

SELF-TALK

Statements I make to myself that influence me to feel that I am responsible:	Statements I make to myself that influence me to feel that I am not responsible:

Examine the facts!

Happiness

INQUIRY   A time when I felt unhappy was

_____

_____

_____

_____

ASSUMPTION

I can never be happy, and life will be awful unless certain things are a certain way.

Inv)estigating Procedures

☑ Rewrite assumption into a provable belief
☑ Change thoughts
☑ Change behaviors

PROVABLE BELIEF

I can choose to be happy even if things aren't exactly the way I want them to be.

SELF-TALK

Statements I make to myself that influence me to feel unhappy:

Statements I make to myself that influence me to feel happy:

Think about what makes you happy!

Self-Acceptance

❑ I choose whether to accept myself because I am me.

❑ I choose to believe negative or positive statements others tell me and I tell myself.

❑ I can choose to tell myself positive statements.

Positive Statements: Fill in these statements.

Something I like about myself is

_____

_____

_____

I'm really good at

_____

_____

_____

I choose to accept myself because

_____

_____

_____

Self-Measurement

INQUIRY

I sometimes feel bad about myself because, compared to everyone else, I

_____

_____

ASSUMPTION

It is awful, and I must not accept myself unless
I measure up to everyone else.

Investigating Procedures

☑ Rewrite assumption into a provable belief
☑ Change thoughts
☑ Change behaviors

PROVABLE BELIEF

I can accept myself as worthwhile without having to measure up to anyone else.

SELF-TALK

Statements I make to myself that influence me to measure myself against others:	Statements I make to myself that influence me to accept myself:

Set realistic goals for yourself!

Unrealistic Expectations

INQUIRY

A time I felt that I had to be perfect was

_____

_____

_____

ASSUMPTION

If I am not always perfect, it is awful. I will never succeed so
why bother to try.

Investigating Procedures

☑ Rewrite assumption into a
   provable belief
☑ Change thoughts
☑ Change behaviors

PROVABLE BELIEF

I can do the best that I can do.

SELF-TALK

Statements I make to myself that influence me to want to be perfect:	Statements I make to myself that influence me to want to learn from mistakes:

Do what you can do!

Friendship

INQUIRY   One way that I now act with my friends is that I

_____

_____

_____

_____

ASSUMPTION

I will never be able to do anything to be a better friend.

Investigating Procedures

☑ Rewrite assumption into a provable belief
☑ Change thoughts
☑ Change behaviors

PROVABLE BELIEF

There are some things I can do to be a better friend.

SELF-TALK

Statements I make to myself that influence me to want to make negative friendship choices:

Statements I make to myself that influence me to want to make positive friendship choices:

Try better friendship choices!

Family

INQUIRY   One way that I now act with my family is that I

_____

_____

_____

ASSUMPTION

My family must meet only my needs.

Investigating Procedures

☑ Rewrite assumption into a provable belief
☑ Change thoughts
☑ Change behaviors

PROVABLE BELIEF

It is helpful if families consider every member's needs.

SELF-TALK

Statements I make to myself that influence me to make negative family choices:

Statements I make to myself that influence me to make positive family choices:

Consider everyone's needs!

Put-Downs

INQUIRY   A put-down I once said to someone was

_____

_____

_____

ASSUMPTION

To feel good about myself, I must try to make other people
feel bad about themselves.

 **Investigating Procedures**

☑ Rewrite assumption into a
  provable belief
☑ Change thoughts
☑ Change behaviors

PROVABLE BELIEF

I don't have to try to make
others feel bad about
themselves in order to feel
good about myself. I have
many other better choices.

SELF-TALK

Statements I make to myself that influence me to put down others:	Statements I make to myself that influence me to build up others:

Help others to feel good!

Pressuring

INQUIRY   A time I pressured someone was when

_____

_____

_____

ASSUMPTION

I must pressure others in order to always have my way, or it will be awful.

Investigating Procedures

☑ Rewrite assumption into a provable belief
☑ Change thoughts
☑ Change behaviors

PROVABLE BELIEF

There are many ways to get my needs met without using pressure.

SELF-TALK

Statements I make to myself that influence me to pressure others:	Statements I make to myself that influence me to directly ask for what I want:

Ask for what you want!

Being Pressured

INQUIRY   A time I gave in to pressure was

_____

_____

_____

_____

ASSUMPTION

I must give in to pressure to be cool and to be liked by everyone,
or it will be awful.

Investigating Procedures

☑ Rewrite assumption into a provable belief
☑ Change thoughts
☑ Change behaviors

PROVABLE BELIEF

I can trust that I am cool. I can make my own choices and know that true friends will respect them.

SELF-TALK

Statements I make to myself that influence me to give in to pressure:

Statements I make to myself that influence me to take pride in my own choices:

Take pride in your choices!

Prejudice

INQUIRY   A time I believed I was better than someone else was

_____

_____

_____

ASSUMPTION

If someone is different from me, he or she is not as good a person as I am.

Investigating Procedures

- ☑ Rewrite assumption into a provable belief
- ☑ Change thoughts
- ☑ Change behaviors

PROVABLE BELIEF

If someone is different from me, he or she is just as good a person as I am.

SELF-TALK

Statements I make to myself that influence me to be prejudiced toward others:	Statements I make to myself that influence me to be accepting of others:

Look at the whole person!

Manipulation Check

Fill in the day, then put a check mark in the appropriate box depending on how you tried to get what you wanted that day.

DAY	Whine	Act Out	Command	Threaten	Accuse	Label	Lie	Ask Directly

"I" Messages

❏ "I'd like it if you would pay more attention to me."

❏ "Could I have some of your popcorn?"

❏ "I would really like a lick of your ice cream."

Assertive Statements: Please complete the following sentences with a statement that asks directly for what you want.

If the teacher is paying attention to other students and doesn't see that I want attention, I could say:

_____

_____

_____

If my friend has a new game that I want to play, I could say,

_____

_____

_____

Feedback Practice

Jim is going to tell you about something that happened to him yesterday. After you read the story, check off the sentence that you believe would be feedback based on just the hard facts of what he said.

"In school yesterday, the teacher announced that we were going to have a test. When she said that, I realized that I could have gotten nervous about it, and my stomach might have started hurting. Instead, I took deep breaths and told myself that I would probably do well on the test. I told myself that the worst thing that could happen would be that I might have to take the test again, and that wouldn't be so awful. I took the test and got 100."

❑ "You got smart and stopped being chicken about the test."

❑ "You talked to yourself and took deep breaths and did well on the test."

❑ "You should have done the rag exercise also."

Assertiveness

Pay attention to
me or else!

Aggressive:
I must impose on
others' rights.

I don't mind if
you ignore me.

Passive:
I have no rights.

I'd like your
attention.

Assertive:
I can assert my
rights.

Assertive Statements: Please complete the following sentences with a statement that asserts your rights without imposing on anyone else's rights.

If somebody took something that belonged to me, I could say,

_____

_____

_____

_____

If I wanted to have some of my friend's popcorn, I could ask,

_____

_____

_____

_____

Study Skills

PROVABLE BELIEF

I can achieve success in school!

Study Skills

☑ Organize desk and materials.
☑ Follow directions.
☑ Make an outline.
☑ Write a summary.
☑ Do homework . . .
   in a special place
   at a special time
   give yourself a reward.

A STUDY SKILL FOR ME

Please complete the following sentence.

One skill that could help me do better in school is

_____

_____

_____

_____

_____

_____

SELF-TALK

Statements I make to myself that influence me to feel I can be successful:

Study Skills Check

Fill in the day, and check off the study skill you practiced that day.

Day	Organized	Directions	Outline	Summary	Homework

Clarifying Values and Consequences

Consequences: what happens as a result of our choices

Draw a line between the choice and the consequence that might result because of that choice. An example has been provided.

Cheating one time ○   ○ Going to jail

Stealing money ○   ○ Liking yourself less and less

Taking a drink of alcohol ○   ○ Worrying about success without cheating

Putting yourself down ○   ○ Family getting along well

Trying to listen to family members ○   ○ Drinking more and more alcohol

Choosing without thinking ○   ○ Having lots of friends

Being friendly to others ○   ○ Making poor choices

Getting Help

Ask for Help When . . .

- You are very sad for a long time and don't know why, and nothing you do helps you feel happier.

- You are so sad or upset that you want to hurt yourself or try to end your life.

- You are not being taken care of so that you don't have enough food to eat or warm enough clothes to wear.

- You are constantly being told that you are not a good person, being called names, and being yelled at.

- You are physically hurt by someone.

- You are being touched by others in places where you don't want to be touched or are being asked by others to touch them in places where you don't want to touch them.

Get out of the situation if you can.

Find an adult you trust and tell him or her exactly what happened.

Adults you can ask for help include a(n)

- Parent or guardian

- Aunt or uncle

- Adult friend of the family

- Neighbor

- Teacher

- Principal

The Person I Want to Be Contract

How I Choose to Feel, Think, and Act

_____

_____

_____

_____

Assumptions, Thoughts, Feelings, and Behaviors I Want to Change

_____

_____

_____

_____

Risks and New Skills

_____

_____

_____

_____

My First Two Steps

_____

_____

_____

_____

Resource B

SUMMARY ACTIVITIES

The first two summary activities in this section are keyed to the first two parts of the curriculum. The third summary activity covers all the lessons in the book. These summary activities pull together the lessons and provide an opportunity for students to summarize and revisit the different choice-making skills and competencies that they worked on in the activities.

EMOTIONAL SKILLS ■

Individual Activity

Ask students to complete these sentences in their journals:

> When it comes to anxiety, now I . . .
>
> When it comes to uncovering feelings, now I . . .
>
> When it comes to anger, now I . . .
>
> When it comes to responsibility, now I . . .
>
> When it comes to happiness, now I . . .

Group Activity

1. Announce that students are to do group projects. Each project covers one of the five assumptions that were important to developing emotional skills.

2. Divide the class into five groups. Assign one of the five assumptions in the unit to each group:

   Anxiety: If something seems fearsome, I must get terribly upset.

   Feelings: I must never let my feelings out, or it would be awful.

   Anger: It is awful, and I must get angry when things do not go the way I want them to go.

   Responsibility: I am responsible for everything. I am responsible for nothing.

Happiness: I can never be happy, and life will be awful unless certain things are a certain way.

3. Each group is responsible for developing its assigned project, based on the assumption students have been given. The project may be a scene to be acted out; a poem or story to be read; a drawing to be described and displayed; a song, dance, or scientific experiment; or any other form that they choose.

4. Their project centers on a famous person of their choice who, at first, believes in the assumption they are treating. They will share this person's thoughts, feelings, and behaviors as a result of believing in the assumption. Their famous person discovers clues that help him or her to change the assumption to a provable belief. Students let us know how the clues were discovered and how they were used. Students also let us know the person's new thoughts, feelings, and behaviors as a result of believing in the new, provable belief.

5. Each group shares its project with the rest of the class. This can take any form the project demands. Students may choose to videotape these and play them back at a later date.

■ SOCIAL SKILLS

Individual Activity

Ask students to complete these sentences in their journals:

When it comes to self-acceptance, now I . . .

When it comes to self-measurement, now I . . .

When it comes to unrealistic expectations, now I . . .

When it comes to friendship, now I . . .

When it comes to family, now I . . .

When it comes to put-downs, now I . . .

When it comes to pressuring peers, now I . . .

When it comes to being pressured, now I . . .

When it comes to being prejudiced, now I . . .

Group Activity

1. Students do a group project that covers the material and skills transmitted in the Developing Social Skills section.

2. Divide the class into seven groups. Assign one of the following concepts to each group—self-measurement, realistic expectations, friendship, family, put-downs, peer pressure, and prejudice.

3. Each group is responsible for writing and illustrating an entry for a book about positive choices. Each group's entry talks about the best

possible choices to make with regard to its concept. The entry can be in any form. Some examples might be a letter to and response from Dear Abby, a recipe of how to make a good choice in that area, a step-by-step list of directions, a "chemical" formula, a mathematical equation, "ten commandments" of making the choice, a poem, or a story.

4. Remind students that their entry covers the provable belief associated with their concept and deals with thoughts, feelings, and behaviors.

5. Have the students read their entries aloud.

Middle School Modifications

GROUP ACTIVITY—Give students the choice to use media other than writing. Additional project options can include a piece created on computer, a video, a class lesson, a song, or a dance.

FINALE ■

This is a summary for all the choice-making lessons.

Individual Activity

Ask students to complete the following sentences in their journals:

The person I want to be:

The values I want to live by:

Assumptions I want to change:

New ways I want to think:

New ways I want to feel:

New ways I want to behave:

Safe risks I will take:

Skills I will use:

Two actions I will take immediately:

Group Activity

1. Form small groups of five or six students.

2. Ask each group to develop a story that portrays what the group members have learned from the choice-making lessons, using their personal handouts and their journals. One possible story structure is a class reunion 15 years in the future where students gather to talk about the choices they have made that have led them to their goals. Or students might create a fairy tale that describes a world

based on assumptions, where many negative choices were made, that somehow developed into a world based on beliefs, where positive choices are made. Students are encouraged to create their own story structures.

3. After creating the story, each group develops and presents it as a short scene. Each student is to take some part in this dramatization. Remind them of the steps involved in preparing a scene. They may present the scene in whatever form they choose: taped, sung, danced, drawn, performed, painted, and so on.

4. Whichever form the project takes, sharing reinforces for students what they have developed with others. This allows students to make a statement about the positive choices they want to make and be rewarded for doing so. Rather than focusing on the quality of the format of the story, focus on content. This reinforces lessons taught and encourages your students to take responsibility for new choices.

5. Each group presents its scene to the class, another class, their parents, the school, or some other suitable audience.

References

Belvel, P. S., & Jordan, M. M. (2002). *Rethinking classroom management. Strategies for prevention, intervention, and problem-solving.* Thousand Oaks, CA: Corwin Press.

Benson, P. L., Scales, P. C., Leffert, N., & Rehlkepartain, E. L. (1997). *A fragile foundation: The state of developmental assets among American youth.* Minneapolis, MN: Search Institute.

Blatner, A. (1988). *Acting-in. Practical applications of psychodramatic method* (3rd ed.). New York: Springer.

Branden, N. (1994). *Six pillars of self-esteem.* New York: Bantam Books.

Cowan, M. M., & Clover, F. M. (1991). Enhancement of self-concept through discipline-based art education. *Art Education, 44,* 41–49.

Deline, J. (1991). Why can't they get along? *Journal of Physical Education, Recreation and Dance, 62,* 21–28.

Dewhurst. D. W. (1991). Should teachers enhance their pupils' self-esteem? *Journal of Moral Education, 20,* 10–15.

Elias, M. J. (1997, December). Missing pieces: Making the case for greater attention to social-emotional learning. *Education World,* pp. 36–37.

Elias, M. J., Zins, J. E., Weisberg, R. P., Frey, K. S., Greenberg, M. T., & Haynes, N. M. (1997). *Promoting social and emotional learning: Guidelines for educators.* Alexandria, VA: Association for Supervision and Curriculum Development.

Ellis, A. (1990). *How to stubbornly refuse to make yourself miserable about anything, yes anything.* New York: First Carol.

Ellis, A. (2001). *Overcoming destructive beliefs, feelings and behaviors.* New York: Prometheus Books.

Erin, J. N., Dignan, K., & Brown, P. A. (1991). Are social skills teachable? A review of the literature. *Journal of Visual Impairment and Blindness, 85,* 60–72.

Evertson, C. M., Emmer, E. T., & Worsham, M. E. (2005). *Classroom management for elementary teachers.* Boston: Allyn & Bacon.

Frey, K. S., Nolan, S. B., Estrom, C. V., & Hirschstein, M. K. (2005). Effects of a school-based social-emotional competence program: Linking children's goals, attributes, and behaviors. *Journal of Applied Developmental Psychology, 26*(2), 171–200.

Gardner, H. (1983). *Frames of mind.* New York: Bantam Books.

Glasser, W. (1998). *Choice theory. A new philosophy of personal freedom.* New York: HarperCollins.

Goleman, D. (1995). *Emotional intelligence.* New York: Bantam Books.

Greenberg, M. T., Weissberg, R. P., O'Brian, M. U., Zins, J. E., Fredericks, L., Resnick, H., & Elias, M. J. (2003, June/July). Enhancing school-based prevention and youth development through coordinated social, emotional, and academic learning. *American Psychologist,* pp. 461–473.

Jones, R. M., Kline, K., Habkirk, S. A., & Saler, A. (1990). Teacher characteristics and competencies related to substance abuse prevention. *Journal of Drug Education, 20,* 182–198.

Lickona, T. (2004). *Character matters: How to help our children develop good judgement, integrity, and other essential values.* New York: Touchstone.

Mayer, J. D., Caruso, D. R., & Salovey, P. (2000). Emotional standards meet traditional standards for an intelligence. *Intelligence, 27*(4), 267–298.

Mayer, M. (1990). The play's the thing. *Momentum, 15,* 65–72.

McCaslin, N. (2006). *Creative drama in the classroom and beyond* (8th ed.). Boston: Allyn & Bacon.

McCullough, L. E. (2000). *Now I get it! 12 ten minute classroom drama skits for science, math, language and social studies: Vol. 1. Grades K–3.* Lyme, NH: Smith and Krauss.

Raths, L., Harmin, M., & Simon, S. (1978). *Values and teaching. Working with values in the classroom* (2nd ed.). Columbus, OH: Charles Emerill.

Rolan, A. J. (1991). Personal and social education: Citizenship and biography. *Journal of Moral Education, 20,* 27–36.

Rotheram, M. J. (1982). Social skills training with underachievers, disruptive and exceptional children. *Psychology in the Schools, 19,* 532–539.

Sloboda, Z., & David, S. L. (1997). *Preventing drug abuse among children and adolescents: A research based guide.* Washington, DC: NIDA National Institute on Drug Abuse

Tobler, N. S., & Stratton, H. H. (1997). Effectiveness of school-based drug prevention programs: A metaanalysis of the research. *Journal of Primary Prevention, 18,* 77–128.

Weissberg, R. P, Wahlberg, H. J., O'Brian, M. V., & Kuster, C. B. (2003). *Long-term trends in the well-being of children and youth.* Washington, DC: Child Welfare League of American Press.

Wilhelm, J. D., & Edmiston, B. (1998). *Imagining to learn: Inquiry, ethics, and integrity through drama.* Portsmouth, NH: Heinemann.

World Health Organization. (2001, November). *Mental health: Strengthening mental health promotion.* Geneva: Author.

Zins, J. E., Elias, M. J., Greenberg, M. T., & Weissberg, R. P. (2000). Promoting social and emotional competence in children. In K. Minke & G. Bear (Eds.), *Preventing school problems and promoting school success: Strategies and programs that work.* Baltimore, MD: National Association of School Psychologists.

Zins, J. E. , Weissberg, R. P., Wang, M. L., & Wahlberg, H. (2004). *Building academic success on social and emotional learning: What does the research say?* New York: Teachers College Press.

Index

Acceptance. *See* Self-acceptance, developing

Action-consequence continuum and clarifying values/consequences, 143–145

Alcohol abuse, investigating
facts about alcohol, 159
overview, 158–160
scene investigation: consequences, 160–162
sentence completion activity, 160

Alphabet activity
assumptions, understanding, 27
choice-making, developing group, 18
feelings, identifying, 22

Anger, dealing with
breathing, slow, 47
handout, resource, 181
letting go, 47–48
middle school modifications, 52
mirror activity, 47
overview, 46
scale, prepare an anger assessment, 47
scene investigation: controlling anger, 48–52

Anxiety, examining/lowering
handout, resource, 179
middle school modifications, 38–39
overview, 32–33
rag activity, 34
scale, prepare an anxiety assessment, 33
scene investigation: stressing out, 35–38
self-talk, 33–34
stress indicators, brainstorming, 33

Assertiveness, developing
checklist, prepare a, 133
greetings, passive/aggressive, 133
handout, resource, 196
middle school modifications, 134
overview, 132
practice, assertiveness, 134
yes/no activity, 133–134

Assumptions, understanding
alphabet, using the, 27
anger, dealing with, 48–50

anxiety, examining/lowering, 35–37
belief vote, 28–29
examining assumptions, 29–30
feelings, being aware of, 41–44
logic leading to assumptions, errors in, 5, 25–26
middle school modifications, 30–31
overview, 25
sit/stand activity, 27
study skills, building, 140
voice inflections, 28
walk, assumption, 29, 30
See also Awfulizing; Crystal-balling; Generalizing; scene investigation *under individual subject headings*

Attribute web and strengthening family, 91–92

Awfulizing
anger, dealing with, 49
anxiety, examining/lowering, 36
expectations, evaluating unrealistic, 81
happiness, choosing, 64
overview, 5, 26, 29
peer pressure, dealing with, 107, 112
self-measurement, examining, 76

Beliefs and understanding assumptions, 28–29
See also scene investigation *under individual subject headings*

Body language/movement
anxiety, examining/lowering, 34
assertiveness, developing, 133
expectations, evaluating unrealistic, 79
feelings, being aware of, 40
feelings, identifying, 23–24
happiness, choosing, 61
listening skills, strengthening, 129
manipulation, looking at, 126
put-downs, learning about, 98
self-acceptance, developing, 70
study skills, building, 140

Breathing slow and dealing with anger, 47

Bullying, investigating
facts about bullying, 155

overview, 155–157
scene investigation: consequences, 156–157
sentence completion activity, 156
See also Peer pressure, dealing with

Cheating, investigating
facts about cheating, 147
overview, 147–148
scene investigation: consequences, 148–150
sentence completion activity, 148
Choice-making, developing group
alphabet, using the, 18
middle school modifications, 19–20
overview, 16–17
rules, brainstorming, 18–19
rules vote, 19
values/consequences, clarifying, 143
Choice-making, understanding
brainstorming daily choices, 13
friendship, promoting, 84–85
informed choice makers, becoming, 14
middle school modifications, 14–15
overview, 10–11
standing up for choices, 12–13
walk, the choice, 13–14
Cognitive-behavioral approach, 3
Communication. *See* Listening skills, strengthening; Manipulation, looking at; Negotiation
Conflict management. *See* Listening skills, strengthening; Negotiation
Control theory, 3
Cool formula and dealing with peer pressure, 109
Crystal-balling
anger, dealing with, 49
anxiety, examining/lowering, 36
expectations, evaluating unrealistic, 81
friendship, promoting, 87
happiness, choosing, 64
overview, 5, 25–26, 29
peer pressure, dealing with, 107, 112
self-measurement, examining, 75

Detective metaphor, 7
Drama as a teaching strategy, 4–6
See also individual subject headings
Drug abuse, investigating
facts about drugs, 159
overview, 158–160
scene investigation: consequences, 160–162
sentence completion activity, 160

Ellis, Albert, 3
Emotional Intelligence (Goleman), 6
Emotional/social/life skills, 1–4, 203–204
See also individual subject headings

Expectations, evaluating unrealistic
checklist, prepare a, 79
handout, resource, 186
middle school modifications, 83
overview, 78
scene investigation, 79–83
tense/relax activity, 79

Family, strengthening
attribute web, 91–92
checklist, prepare a, 93
fantasy, guided, 92
handout, resource, 188
middle school modifications, 97
overview, 91
scene investigation, 93–97
Fantasy, guided
family, strengthening, 92
happiness, choosing, 61–62
Feedback skills, strengthening
checklist, prepare a, 129
defining terms, 130
handout, resource, 195
journalizing, 131
overview, 128–129
practice, feedback, 130
Feelings, being aware of
checklist, prepare a feelings, 41
idea tree, 41
masks, 40–41
middle school modifications, 45
mirror activity, 40
overview, 39–40
scene investigation: sharing feelings, 41–45
Feelings, identifying
alphabet, using the, 22
body language and messages, 23–24
gauge, feelings, 23
handout, resource, 180
middle school modifications, 24
overview, 21–22
sentence completion activity, 22–23
Fortress activity and dealing with peer pressure, 105
Frames of Mind (Gardner), 2
Friendship, promoting
checklist, prepare a, 85
choices, friendship, 84–85
handout, resource, 187
middle school modifications, 90
negotiation, 137–138
overview, 84
scene investigation: being friends, 85–89

Gardner, Howard, 2
Generalizing
anger, dealing with, 49
anxiety, examining/lowering, 36

expectations, evaluating unrealistic, 81
friendship, promoting, 87
happiness, choosing, 64
overview, 5, 26, 29
peer pressure, dealing with, 107, 112
put-downs, learning about, 101
responsibility, examining/accepting, 56
self-measurement, examining, 76
Glasser, William, 3
Goal setting, 168–169
Goleman, Daniel, 2, 3
Gratitude and choosing happiness, 62–63
Greetings, assertiveness and
    passive/aggressive, 133
Group activity and clarifying
    values/consequences, 143
    See also Choice-making, developing
        group

Happiness, choosing
    checklist, prepare a, 61
    fantasy, guided, 61–62
    gratitude, attitude of, 62–63
    handout, resource, 183
    middle school modifications, 66
    overview, 60
    scene investigation, 63–66
    sculpture, moving, 61
    values/consequences, clarifying,
        144–145
    Venn diagrams, 62
Help, getting, 163–165, 200

Idea tree and being aware of feelings, 41
"I" messages and looking at
    manipulation, 127, 194
Inter/intrapersonal intelligence, 2

Journalizing and listening/feedback
    skills, 131

Life skills, developing, 123–124, 205–206
    See also individual subject headings
Listening skills, strengthening
    brainstorming, 129
    checklist, prepare a, 129
    defining terms, 130
    journalizing, 131
    overview, 128–129
    practice, listening, 129–130
Logic leading to assumptions, errors in, 5,
    25–26

Manipulation, looking at
    behaviors, manipulation, 126–127
    circle, manipulation, 126–127
    handout, resource, 126, 193–194
    "I" messages, 127, 194
    pulse activity, 125–126
    relaxation exercises, 126

Masks and being aware of feelings, 40–41
Measurement. *See* Self-measurement,
    examining
Mirror activity
    anger, dealing with, 47
    feelings, being aware of, 40
Money and clarifying
    values/consequences, 145

National Institute on Drug Abuse, 123
Negotiation
    brainstorming, 136
    checklist, prepare a, 137
    friendship circle, 137–138
    middle school modifications, 138
    overview, 135
    practicing, 137
    successful, steps to, 135–136

Peer pressure, dealing with
    checklist, prepare a, 105–106, 110
    cool formula, 109
    fortress activity, 105
    handout, resource, 190–191
    middle school modifications, 115
    overview, 104–105
    pressuring circle, 105
    scene investigation: being pressured by
        peers, 110–115
    scene investigation: pressuring
        peers, 106–109
    See also Bullying, investigating
Personal characteristics and examining
    self-measurement, 73–74
Person I Want to Be Contract, 201
Prejudice, examining
    checklist, prepare a, 119
    handout, resource, 192
    middle school modifications, 121
    "New Friends" story, 116–119
    overview, 116
    story investigation: "New Friends,"
        120–121
Pressure. *See* Peer pressure,
    dealing with
Psychodrama, 5
Pulse activity and looking at
    manipulation, 125–126
Put-downs, learning about
    handout, resource, 189
    middle school modifications, 103
    overview, 98
    scene investigation: relating to
        others, 99–103
    tense/relax activity, 98

Rag activity. *See* Body
    language/movement
Relaxation exercises. *See* Body
    language/movement

Resource handouts, 174–178
   See also handout, resource *under
      individual subject headings*
Responsibility, examining/accepting
   checklist, prepare a, 54
   handout, resource, 182
   middle school modifications, 59
   overview, 53
   scene investigation: determining
      responsibility, 55–59
   vote, responsibility, 54
Risk taking, 166–169
Rules and developing group
      choice-making, 18–19

Self-acceptance, developing
   barometer, self-acceptance, 70–71
   handout, resource, 71, 72, 184
   middle school modifications, 72
   overview, 69
   rag activity, 70
   self-measurement, examining, 74–77
   self-tapes, 71–72
   word activity, 70
Self-esteem. *See* Expectations, evaluating
      unrealistic; Self-acceptance,
      developing; Self-measurement,
      examining
Self-measurement, examining
   checklist, prepare a, 74
   choice/no choice activity, 73–74
   handout, resource, 185
   middle school modifications, 77
   overview, 73
   scene investigation: self-acceptance,
      74–77
Self-talk and examining/lowering anxiety,
      33–34
   See also handout, resource *under
      individual subject headings*
Sentence completion activity
   alcohol/drug abuse, investigating, 160
   bullying, 156
   cheating, investigating, 148
   feelings, identifying, 22–23
   stealing, investigating, 152
   study skills, building, 141
Sit/stand activity and understanding
      assumptions, 27
Skill development, inter/intrapersonal, 6,
      203–206

Social-emotional learning and academic
      performance, linking, 2, 67–68,
      204–205
   See also individual subject headings
Stealing, investigating
   facts about stealing, 151
   overview, 151–152
   scene investigation: consequences,
      152–154
   sentence completion activity, 152
Stress. *See* Anxiety, examining/lowering
Study skills, building
   assumptions, school success, 140
   brainstorming, 140
   handout, resource, 197–198
   overview, 139
   practice, 141–142
   relaxation exercise, 140
   sentence completion activity, 141
Success and clarifying
      values/consequences, 144
Summary activities, 203–206

Teacher rejoices, a, 170–171

Values and consequences, clarifying
   action-consequence
      continuum, 143–145
   checklist, prepare a, 145–146
   group activity, 143
   handout, resource, 145, 199
   happiness, 144–145
   middle school modifications, 146
   money, 145
   overview, 123, 142–143
   rankings, values, 143
   success, 144
Venn diagrams and choosing happiness,
      62
Voice inflections and understanding
      assumptions, 28

Walking activities
   assumptions, understanding, 29, 30
   choice-making, understanding, 13–14
Word activity and developing
      self-acceptance, 70
World Health Organization (WHO), 123

Yes/no activity and developing
      assertiveness, 133–134

CORWIN PRESS

DECORATING YOUR FIRST APARTMENT

EDITOR:
PAIGE GILCHRIST

ART DIRECTOR:
CHRIS BRYANT

COVER DESIGN:
BARBARA ZARETSKY

PHOTOGRAPHER:
WRIGHT CREATIVE
PHOTOGRAPHY & DESIGN

ASSISTANT EDITORS:
VERONIKA ALICE GUNTER
HEATHER SMITH

EDITORIAL ASSISTANT:
RAIN NEWCOMB

EDITORIAL INTERNS:
ANNE WOLFF HOLLYFIELD
NATHALIE MORNU

ILLUSTRATOR:
BERNADETTE WOLF

PRODUCTION ASSISTANT:
HANNES CHAREN

SPECIAL PHOTOGRAPHY:
SANOMA SYNDICATION

Alexander van Berge
Dennis Brandsma
John Dummer
Hotze Eisma
Rene Gonkel
John van Groenedaal
Paul Grootes
Peter Kooijman
Louis Lemaire
Otto Polman
Dolf Straatemeier
Carel Verduin

Library of Congress Cataloging-in-Publication Data

Gilchrist, Paige.
    Decorating your first apartment : from moving in to making your own /
by Paige Gilchrist.—1st ed.
        p.   cm.
    ISBN 1-57990-513-7
    1. Apartments. 2. Interior decoration. I. Title.

NK2195.A6 G55 2002
747'.88314—dc21   2002020206

10 9 8 7 6 5 4 3 2 1

Published by Lark Books,
a division of Sterling Publishing Co., Inc.
387 Park Avenue South, New York, N.Y. 10016

First Paperback Edition 2003
© 2002, Lark Books

 Distributed in Canada by Sterling Publishing,
c/o Canadian Manda Group, One Atlantic Ave., Suite 105
Toronto, Ontario, Canada M6K 3E7

Distributed in the U.K. by Guild of Master Craftsman Publications Ltd.,
Castle Place, 166 High Street, Lewes, East Sussex, England BN7 1XU
Tel: (+ 44) 1273 477374, Fax: (+ 44) 1273 478606
Email: pubs@thegmcgroup.com, Web: www.gmcpublications.com

Distributed in Australia by Capricorn Link (Australia) Pty Ltd.,
P.O. Box 704, Windsor, NSW 2756 Australia

If you have questions or comments about this book, please contact:
Lark Books • 67 Broadway, Asheville, NC 28801 • (828) 253-0467

Manufactured in China

ISBN 1-57990-513-7

DECORATING YOUR FIRST APARTMENT

from moving in to making it your own

paige gilchrist

LARK BOOKS

A DIVISION OF STERLING PUBLISHING CO., INC.
NEW YORK, NY

8 introduction

BASICS

11 the hunt

14 the red tape

18 the layout

PROJECTS & IDEAS

52 walls

PAINT JUST ONE, *53*

CLIP CORD, *54*

PLOTTING WHERE
PICTURES GO, *55*

quick fix:
PROPPING PICS, *57*

COVER-UP MESSAGE
CENTER, *59*

HANGING WALLS, *62*

WALL COVER TWO WAYS, *68*

72 floors

CANVAS FLOOR COVER, *73*

MOD MODULES, *74*

RUBBER MAT KITCHEN
FLOOR, *76*

CHECKERBOARD FLOOR, *78*

quick fix:
STEPPING STONES, *82*

84 windows

WORD CURTAINS, *85*

quick fix:
RODS & FINIALS, *87*

STANDING SHEERS, *88*

PICTURE WINDOW, *90*

NO-SEW EXOTICA CURTAIN, *92*

quick fix:
MOCK STAINED GLASS, *94*

DECORATIVE PULL, *95*

156 painted file cabinet patterns

157 acknowledgments

158 contributors

160 index

contents

21 sprucing up

38 settling in

46 keeping clean

96 lighting

BEADED LAMPSHADE, 97

WASTEBASKET GLOW LAMPS, 98

quick fix:
FLOOR LIGHTS, 100

PLUMBING PARTS CANDLESTICKS, 101

MINI-LIGHTS, 104

quick fix:
CLIP-ON LIGHTS, 106

WIRE MESH BULB COVER, 107

110 furniture & accessories

PAINTED FILE CABINET, 110

NATHALIE'S CHAIR, 113

quick fix:
SARONG TABLE COVER, 117

COMPOSITION IN CANVAS, 118

BOTANICALS UNDER GLASS, 120

PILLOW TALK, 122

quick fix:
WALL OF BLACK-AND-WHITE PICS, 124

FURNITURE ON THE MOVE, 125

REINCARNATED TABLE, 126

ARTIFICIAL TURF TRAYS, 128

quick fix:
HANDLES & KNOBS, 130

URBAN JUNGLE, 131

WILD SIDE TABLE, 138

NESTING TABLES MAKEOVER, 140

142 storage

SHELVING FIVE WAYS, 142

THE INDISPENSABLE (AND AMAZINGLY EASY TO BUILD) CUBE, 146

quick fix:
STORAGE & DISPLAY IN ONE, 147

STORAGE IN DISGUISE, 149

LATTICE ORGANIZER, 150

quick fix:
UNDER-BED STORAGE, 152

COFFEEHOUSE MAGAZINE RACKS, 153

WHEN ALL ELSE FAILS: SHOP, 154

introduction

YOUR REFUGE. YOUR SHOWPLACE. YOUR ALTER EGO. Your party palace. Regardless of how you see it, the point is, your first apartment is *yours*. How you transform it into the kind of place you want to live in is totally up to you.

Trouble is, if you give it awhile, that empowering little phrase—*totally up to you*—starts running as a haunting continuous loop inside your head. Pretty soon you're feeling like the main character in a bad sitcom, stuck in an episode that does not end well. You can hear the canned laughter swell and see the credits roll as you picture yourself, chin in hands, sitting on a plastic crate in the middle of a room that features nothing but a tacked-up concert poster and the desk lamp you took to college.

This book is here to help you snap out of it. Our goal is not to pressure you into thinking your apartment must spring to life, intact, from the pages of a trendy interior decorating magazine. It's also not to encourage you to clutter your space with a bunch of junk you don't really care about or need. Instead, we're here to help you realize that you're busy, you're on a budget, you're pretty new to this, and yet it's still possible to create a place that has character and style—not to mention furniture, curtains, and a few accents on the walls.

Decorating your first apartment is essentially about making yourself at home. That means it's a pursuit that's part practical *(How do I hang a shelf?)* and part creative *(Wonder how this chair would look painted chartreuse.)*. We appeal to both sides of your brain with sensible how-to advice, imaginative yet doable projects, and page after page of inspiring, full-color ideas and examples.

the BASICS

The book's opening chapter is one of those mini-handbooks for life you always thought someone should research and write for you. It's divided into six handy sections. The Hunt is for those still in search of the right place. It covers everything from spotting potential problems with apartments to sizing up landlords. The Red Tape walks you through all the paperwork of renting. The Layout shows you how to make yourself a simple floor plan and figure out what goes where, Sprucing Up gives you the handy-person basics of everything from painting walls to refinishing furniture, Settling In is a series of cheat sheets to remind you of all those essentials (corkscrews to bath mats), and Keeping Clean is a section you'll eventually be glad you have as a reference. If you're not in the mood for these nuts and bolts right now, feel free to flip right to the heart of the book.

the DECORATING PROJECTS & IDEAS

Realizing that first apartments, like first kisses and first jobs, are often not perfect, in the book's main chapters we break apartments down into their surface elements: walls, floors, and windows. We show you step-by-step approaches for turning whatever surrounds you, perfect or not, into design features that work *for* you, rather than problems that sabotage your look. Then we move on to chapters full of dozens of inventive ways to use lighting, furniture, accessories, and clever storage tactics to turn your apartment's bare rooms into a place you're proud to call home. Oh, and don't worry. We don't suddenly forget those irritating little details—money and time. You don't need a trust fund and several personal assistants who happen to have attended design school to pull these projects off.

the DISCLAIMER

You also don't need an apartment that looks just like one of the ones we've photographed or the exact same chair, lamp, paint color, or potted plant we've used. Though we give you detailed instructions so you can replicate any project in the book, we also give you plenty of permission—along with hints, tips, idea starters, and loads of helpful sidebars—for adapting everything to suit your own setting and style.

Whether you already have a clear idea what that style is (maybe you're committed to retro kitsch) or you're just starting to experiment (a little Zen minimalism here, a touch of ethnic flair there), *Decorating Your First Apartment* can help you sort out what you want and then pull it all together. Which brings you right back to where you started. How your apartment looks *is* totally up to you—you just don't have to think of everything yourself.

BASICS

Before we launch right into the specifics of stitching beaded fringe onto throw pillows and turning Asian-print fabric into no-sew curtains, we thought we'd offer this handy overview of the basics of apartment dwelling and decorating. How can you worry about fringe and fabric, after all, when you still don't have a clue where you're going to put every-thing (we show you how to mark out a simple floor plan) or have any idea what tools you need to hang your pictures and put your shelves together (easy; see the chart on page 37). If you're a true plan-ahead type—meaning you picked up this book before you even have an apartment—you're in luck. We also offer tips on finding the right place for you and on muddling through the paperwork it takes to make it yours.

the hunt

Apartments come in the form of spacious lofts carved out of old industrial buildings, homey efficiencies in converted Victorian houses, modern flats in complexes with swimming pools and fitness centers, and plenty of low-ceilinged shoe boxes in run-of-the-mill high-rises. Much of your decision about which apartment is the right one for you will be based on what's available where you need it, when you need it, at a price you can afford. Part of it will also be based on personal priorities; maybe you're willing to sacrifice closet space if the apartment comes with a patio, or you'll settle for a smaller place if it has hardwood floors. Once you've narrowed your options using your individual criteria, here are some more general measures you can use to make your final decision.

FIRST 10 QUESTIONS TO ASK ABOUT ANY APARTMENT

It's easy to come up with a short list of potential apartments simply by working your way down the classifieds over the phone. Here's a list of 10 basic questions that'll help you narrow the possibilities.

1. How much is rent, and when is it due? (Is there a grace period? Is there a penalty for late payment?)

2. How much is the deposit? (Under what conditions is it held?)

3. Is the apartment furnished or unfurnished?

4. Are all the appliances, the plumbing, the heat, and the air conditioning in good working order?

5. Who do I contact for repairs when they're necessary? (Are maintenance hours restricted? How is emergency service handled?)

6. Are utilities furnished? (What about parking, extra storage, or garbage and recycling services?)

7. What can you tell me about the neighbors and the neighborhood?

8. Am I allowed to have pets? (Overnight guests?)

9. Can I sublease or get roommates?

10. When could I move in?

evaluating an apartment

Some landlords disguise problems with their property. Others are honest but oblivious. Sizing up an apartment with a sharp eye before you're locked into a year-long lease can help you avoid—or negotiate solutions to—problems that could cost you money, peace of mind, or your well-being later on.

■ Take a pencil and paper with you. We're aware of the fact that if this tip were coming from your mother, you'd roll your eyes. Don't worry; she never needs to know you're following our practical advice for taking stock of your potential new place. As you visit each room of the apartment you're considering, jot down any concerns or questions.

■ Move furniture so you can see every inch of wall, floor, and ceiling. If the linoleum has been peeled up on part of the bathroom floor or there's a gouge in the wall behind the current resident's couch, you want to know it now.

■ Get on your hands and knees or stand on a chair to explore questionable areas, if necessary. Forget whether this makes you feel silly; now is the time to investigate where that strange smell is coming from or how much storage space really exists above the bedroom closet.

■ Stand still and listen. Keep an ear out for problems in the apartment (loud heating or cooling systems, drips) as well as noisy neighbors and traffic. Open and close windows and doors.

■ Test the appliances.

■ Note if the apartment or the building it's housed in feature any of the signs of trouble listed below.

TELLTALE TROUBLES

1. Exposed wires, faulty electrical appliances, scorch marks, smoke damage

2. Lack of emergency exits or smoke alarms, or blocked exits

3. Pet odors or damage on carpets, floors, or walls

4. Water stains near toilets, tubs, or sinks, or temporary fixes on drains (all suggest faulty plumbing)

5. Discolored floors, ceilings, or windowsills (they probably mean water damage)

6. Holes in the walls

7. Mouse droppings, cockroaches, flies, ants, or other indications of pests

8. Leaky or broken windows, or windows that don't open smoothly

9. Cluttered or damaged entryways, halls, or stairs in a multi-unit building

10. Loud, unruly, or generally unneighborly neighbors

When you're finished looking over the apartment, if you're interested, discuss your list of questions and concerns with the landlord—and don't rent the space until you're satisfied with the explanations and/or improvement plans.

landlords:

they come with the lease

In days of yore, landlords didn't just own land—they ruled it. Anyone inhabiting the area was a tenant, subject to the landlord's whims and expected to show unwavering gratitude. (This arrangement still exists today. It's known as living at home.)

Now, customs and laws grant tenants rights when inhabiting a rented home sweet home. But the landlord remains a person you'll interact with throughout the time of your lease, whether your hot water heater is acting up or your upstairs neighbors are. Use the following suggestions to find one you'll like leasing from.

POTENTIAL LANDLORDS AND THEIR POSITIVE SIGNS

THEY'RE FORTHRIGHT AND WELCOMING.

This doesn't mean they must be super friendly or socially skilled. It does mean they provide all relevant details and stipulations for living in the property and respond thoroughly to your questions when you're checking it out (if you need some help figuring out what those questions should be, look back at First 10 Questions, page 11). Their candor and command of the facts at this early stage suggest that there won't be many surprises—such as newly imposed rules — during the term of your lease.

THEY'RE REASONABLE.

They understand that tenants will be living full and varied lives in their apartments. In your case, that could mean pet canaries, daily drum practice, a bike that needs storing—or all of the above. They discuss your specific needs and any concerns you have about the terms of the lease or condition of the apartment. When you explain your needs, they're willing to compromise a bit.

THEY CARE ABOUT THE PROPERTY.

A landlord who, while showing you around, suggests the sunniest spot for your kitchen table or is sincerely enthusiastic about the new paint job in the bathroom is someone who has thought about what it's like to live in the space he's renting. This is good. He wants you to enjoy living there—either because he's proud of the apartment or because his income is based primarily on your rent check, or both. Landlords who see their property as an investment to be cared for tend to work with tenants to avoid problems and alleviate turnover.

THEY'RE COMPATIBLE WITH YOU.

A landlord's style is usually obvious: she's firm or lenient, prompt or leisurely, etc. What's yours? Do you pay your bills like clockwork and expect others to honor their obligations? Choose a like-minded landlord, and she'll likely reward your reliability with good service when it comes to a leaking roof or clogged drain. Are you typically late paying your bills and unfazed by minor inconveniences? A lenient landlord might better suit you, but understand that if she's cutting you slack, she'll probably expect you to be patient when it comes to repairs or other requests.

THEY'RE JUST PLAIN NICE.

Nobody's perfect. But you won't feel confident interacting with a landlord who makes you feel unsafe or disrespected. And that means you won't enjoy your new home. Get a sense of a prospective landlord's temperament by talking with current or previous tenants, if you can, and by speaking or meeting with the landlord a few times, if possible. Does he complain excessively about the previous tenants? Is he intimidating? Does he ask intrusive questions or make offensive comments? Does he fail to listen to what you have to say or answer your questions directly? Remember that a landlord is probably on his best, most professional behavior when interviewing prospective tenants. If the behavior seems neither good nor professional, it's not likely to get much better.

the red tape

Yes, we know. All you really want to do is start holding up paint chips to the walls and shopping for a shag pile throw rug for the bedroom. No one actually likes all the shuffling of papers and crunching of numbers that come first, but everyone has to trudge through the process. With this simple overview of what's involved, at least it'll loom less large.

anatomy of a lease

A lease outlines a contract between a tenant and a landlord. It can be a few lines long or fill several pages. You should read every word of it before adding your signature at the end. It's a legally binding document, and your signature indicates your voluntary agreement to its terms.

A standard apartment lease includes the tenant's name, length of stay (starting and ending dates), the payments involved and when and how they're to be made, and the responsibilities of tenant and landlord. Leases typically also note what utilities are available, eviction clauses, whether or not the space can be sublet (rented to another party by the tenant), rules concerning pets and guests, and liabilities. The address of the residence should also appear, along with contact information for the manager. A lease should always be signed by each tenant and the landlord.

If you don't agree with any of the terms of the lease, discuss them with the landlord. He or she may be willing to waive or alter a policy that makes you uncomfortable. Ink in a note on the lease indicating the waiver or spelling out the new rule, then be sure both you and the landlord initial beside it. Oral contracts are legal in many places, but written leases are preferable, so everyone has a record.

UNDER THE TERMS...

Once you've read the lease carefully and signed on the dotted line, stash it in a safe place. You're responsible for following through on your part of all its terms. Likewise, there are several things your landlord is responsible for and entitled to do.

■ A landlord is responsible for providing a livable and safe home for the tenant. This includes, but is not limited to, ensuring the space passes building, health, and safety codes; installing locks and security devices; and making utility service available.

■ A landlord should have adequate insurance, because he or she can be held liable for crimes, fires, and health risks at the rental property. Renter's insurance purchased by the tenant may cover losses the landlord's policy does not.

■ A landlord may enter a rental to handle repairs, to show the space to potential renters, or, in some cases, if the renter has left for more than seven days. But a landlord must give a tenant notice in advance. Though terms vary, the tenant's permission is always required for non-emergency visits by a landlord.

security deposits
(AND GETTING THEM BACK)

When a landlord asks for a security deposit, don't take it personally. It's a standard way landlords protect themselves financially against tenants who are destructive or irresponsible. If you're neither, you'll get your deposit back when you move out. If, instead, the landlord proposes to withhold part or all of your deposit, he or she has to provide an itemized list of reasons why.

There are two general instances in which a landlord can legally retain a security deposit. One is if a tenant moves out before the lease is up. A landlord can then keep the deposit to cover the unexpected loss of rental income. (Often, however, if you have a new renter lined up, you can move out early and still take your deposit with you.) The other is in the case of damage, which is different from normal wear and tear. Fading and minor dirt or spots on a carpet are normal wear. Cigarette burns, rips, and pet stains are damage. Pinholes in walls are normal wear. Those that require patching and repainting are typically considered damage. Leaving personal property in a rental after you've moved out is even a form of damage, and a landlord can use your deposit money to have it hauled away.

If you and your landlord find yourselves quibbling over the damage issue, you may need to go to a local housing resource agency to find out about your area's ordinances. They'll spell out specifics, such as what qualifies as leaving an apartment unreasonably unclean. They'll also have guidelines that say water damage from plants, open windows, or stopped-up toilets is the tenant's responsibility, but leaks from roofs are the landlord's, and so on.

The best way to protect yourself from false or mistaken damage claims by your landlord is to tour the rental together prior to your moving in (that's where the pencil and paper we mentioned earlier come in handy) and again when you're moving out. Some landlords even have a checklist they use as a part of these tours. Before moving in, make a list of all existing damage on surfaces and appliances within the rental and throughout any exterior area you'll be using (porch, garage, etc.). Be thorough. Both you and the landlord should date and sign the document and keep a copy, then refer back to it during your moving-out tour.

renter's insurance

If you can't afford to replace your belongings if your apartment is struck by a tornado, fire, hurricane, flood, or a burglary, you might want to consider a renter's insurance policy. Your landlord should maintain insurance on the property, but if he or she doesn't—or if your losses don't exceed the deductible—you'll have to sue (and win) to be compensated for them.

A good insurance agent can answer your questions about renter's insurance (start with the person who already handles your auto insurance, if you have it, or any other coverage you have). The agent will ask you for a list of your valuables, from audiovisual equipment to furniture and jewelry, then give you an estimate on what it would cost to insure them, list your choices on deductible amounts, and tell you what documentation would be required to collect on the policy. The agent can also tell you whether you might qualify for any type of discount. Then, it's up to you to get quotes from another agent or two, check you own finances, factor in any advice you might decide to seek from savvy friends or relatives, and decide whether renter's insurance is for you.

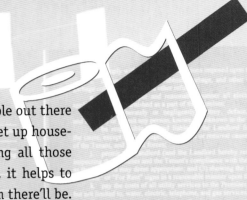

budgeting for basics

As you may have noticed, there are all kinds of people out there making a living off the fact that you've decided to set up house-keeping. While you can't do much to avoid writing all those checks to landlords, power companies, and others, it helps to have a general idea ahead of time how many of them there'll be.

RENT

Expect rent to eat up a third of your monthly income. Yes, one-third. Housing is the most costly routine expense for people in developed nations. (The upside is that we residents of developed nations also have leisure time for activities such as reading books about decorating first apartments.)

Most landlords will ask for the first and last month's rent plus a security deposit before giving you the keys to your new place. That totals approximately three months of rental fees you'll need to have available when you sign the lease. If that little fact suddenly puts the apartment of your dreams out of your range, remember that rental prices can vary greatly within a community. Sometimes a single block divides exorbitant from economical. If the price is right, go ahead and take a look at an apartment in a neighborhood or on a street you're unfamiliar with. The area and property may very well suit your standards. Also keep in mind that prices fluctuate along with the economy. You can sometimes successfully ask for a reduction of the advertised rent during a local recession.

If you still can't afford what you find—or you're willing to sacrifice privacy for savings—get a roommate. A place that's big enough for two will be more expensive overall (unless one of you agrees to sleep in the bathtub), but sharing it with a financially responsible roommate can reduce housing expenses for each of you by a third or more. (If the two of you get along, all the better. For tips on what to look for in a roommate, see page 58.)

UTILITIES

If you've become accustomed to light, heat, running water, and other such creature comforts, then you need to budget for these costs, too. Utilities, which include electricity, telephone service, natural gas or oil, water, and sewer service, typically aren't included in an apartment's rent. In addition to monthly bills, there's a charge for turning on utilities, and deposits are required for new accounts. Some companies will waive your deposit if a customer in good standing (a friend who already has an account, for example) agrees to co-sign on your account. Just be aware that, under this arrangement, any late payments on your bill and the subsequent fees are charged to your friend's account.

Heating and cooling costs are the most expensive utility bills most renters pay, so ask about the space's energy sources, and find out how well insulated the space is. Well-maintained gas furnaces and whole-house air conditioning systems are generally more efficient than electric baseboard for heat or box fans for cooling. High-quality insulation in walls, floors, and ceilings combined with air-tight, insulating-glass windows and solid exterior doors that close snugly translate into energy and money saved. If you can't hold out for the ideal heating and cooling situation, weigh the pros and cons of each residence you look at.

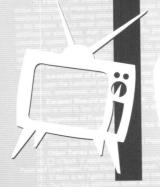

EXTRAS

Can't exist without cable television? Want multiple telephone lines to separate work and personal calls or to accommodate multiple roommates? How about a fiber optic Internet connection or a cable Internet service? These are extras that are rarely included in rental fees. Assess their value to you and your lifestyle, and allocate money for them as you would any other housing cost. Be sure to also include the cost of buying and maintaining necessary equipment and/or making monthly payments for services.

FURNISHINGS

Don't omit the cost of basic furnishings—plus a bit of decorating—from your budget calculations. This isn't just shelter, it's your living space, your very own part of the world. Your days will begin and end here, and so will your moods.

You don't have to furnish and accessorize everything at once. Start small. Make a list of what you have. Make a list of what you need and want. Then start by lining up the essentials—a bed, a chair, a surface for eating. To figure out what your priorities are next, ask yourself some questions. You'll walk your floors each day. Can you live with them the way they are for now, or are you dying to curl your toes in a fluffy rug? You'll see the same windows every day, too. Are the basic white blinds they sport now okay, or are gauzy curtains going to be your first decorating purchase? Give some thought, too, to inexpensive changes you can make to your new living space itself within the terms of your lease. It's amazing how much just a paint job or some new lighting fixtures can perk it up.

Once you have enough basic furnishings to make your home functional, you can add the rest—plants, coffee table, bookshelves, throw pillows—gradually. Budget a small amount to spend monthly, or tackle one room at a time.

the layout

Imagine your first few moments as a new apartment dweller—turning your very own key in your very own lock, and entering an empty expanse that's all yours. Then it hits you. A completely bare room can be a tad intimidating—especially with four or five friends standing beside you, each one holding something heavy and asking where you want it.

Time to impart a logical but often overlooked moving-in tip: sliding tiny pieces of cutout furniture around a drawing of your apartment's layout is so much more fun than dragging bookcases and futon frames from one spot to another, hoping that eventually the scrambled puzzle of furniture and cardboard boxes will work itself out. As compulsive as it sounds, plotting what goes where on a piece of paper before you start unloading the rented truck is actually the easy way out. Here's how.

make a floor plan

Grab a tape measure and measure the perimeters of the rooms you want to make plans for. (Your landlord may even let you into your apartment-to-be briefly before you take over the lease, just to record the measurements.) Then, use a pencil and a ruler to transfer a scaled-down version of each room to a sheet of graph paper—that's the paper with little squares on it that you can buy anyplace that sells office supplies. The squares on graph paper are typically $1/4$ inch (6mm), so the easiest way to create a scaled-down floor plan is to let each $1/4$-inch line on the paper represent one linear foot (30.5cm) of actual wall space in the apartment. Once you've got the walls marked, draw in scaled versions of windows, doors, and any other elements you'll have to work around, such as a fireplace, if you're lucky, or radiators, and label them.

create furniture cutouts

On another piece of graph paper, use the same scale—$1/4$ inch equals 1 foot (6mm equals 30.5cm)—to make tiny versions of all the furniture pieces you plan to move into your rooms. Cut them out, use markers to give them some color, so they'll stand out against the white floor plans, and label each piece.

start moving

Now, in the comfort of a friend's kitchen, your favorite coffee shop, or any other spot with a flat surface, you can experiment with all kinds of furniture configurations without ever putting on a pair of work gloves or remembering to lift with your legs, not your back.

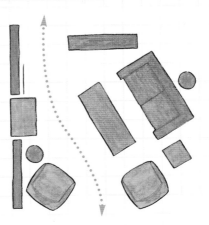

FOLLOWING ARE A FEW POINTERS.

Figure out the focal point for each room—the place around which you want to orient everything else. Most rooms have a logical one: a huge window with a great view, the blank wall where you plan to hang the canvases a friend painted for you or against which you're going to situate the television and VCR.

Play around with your big pieces of furniture first: the couch, the desk, the bed. You'll have fewer places where they'll fit, so it's best to settle them first. Also, their location will typically tell you where other items—the coffee table, the nightstand, etc.—need to go.

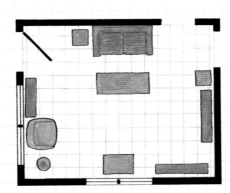

Don't hug the wall. For some reason, lots of first-time furniture arrangers have the idea that shoving most of their furniture up against the walls, so they have maximum floor space, is good. But actually, it often makes your furniture pieces around the rim of the room look isolated and that open floor space in the center seem a little strange. We're not saying sound systems and floor-to-ceiling bookshelves should float in the middle of the room, but some items, such as armchairs and end tables, often look better with a bit of space around them and maybe a floor lamp or plant stand behind them.

Once you've moved a few furniture pieces out into the room, start playing with different angles. Not everything must be parallel or perpendicular to a wall. Experiment with diagonals and with circular and triangular groupings that'll make interaction more comfortable when you have others over.

In the midst of all this experimenting, don't lose sight of the fact that function is at least as important as form. If the arrangement looks great but makes it impossible to see the television from the couch, what's the point? You are going to be living in this space, after all. Think about what kinds of things you'll be doing in each room, then make sure your furniture configuration supports them.

One of the most common activities you and others will carry out in your apartment is walking from one spot to another. Give some thought to what those standard walking routes will be—stove to table, chair to door—and make sure your furniture plan doesn't put a huge piece in the middle of a popular path. Keep those pathways wide enough, too; 2½ feet (76.2 cm) is about the minimum comfortable width.

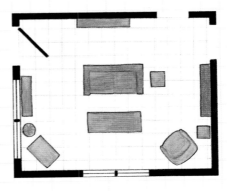

This is also a good time to think about arranging your furniture so it not only makes the most of the features that caused you to fall in love with your apartment, but helps disguise its less-lovable quirks.

IT'S TINY. *Small is beautiful* becomes the buoying mantra of many first-apartment dwellers. If you're making the most of a one-room place or a studio apartment, you've got two workable options. One is to keep the furniture arrangement as open and spacious as possible—the eating and cooking area blending seamlessly with the sitting and sleeping areas. The other is to visually section off one area from another, using furniture such as bookcases, filing cabinets, or even long, narrow tables and couches as dividers. If your landlord will let you mount items on the walls, you can also gain space by trading in freestanding pieces. Sell the bookcase, for example, and buy brackets and shelves instead.

IT'S DARK. If the apartment doesn't get good light, position lamps in the darkest corners. If you've got a choice, go with lamps that have minimal, translucent shades rather than heavy, dark ones. You can also hang mirrors strategically, so they reflect light into darker areas.

IT'S BORING. Maybe the best way to describe your apartment is "boxy": four walls with identical dimensions, and a floor and ceiling to match. Rather than play into the cube-like environment, break it up by setting your furniture off center and at angles, using rugs to split the floor into more interesting sections, and covering one wall completely with a tapestry or hanging mural.

IT'S DESIGNED FOR SHORT PEOPLE. If, even though you'd never make a basketball team, your ceilings feel as if they're caving in on you, arrange some of your lamps so they tilt upward, casting as much light on the ceiling as possible, and draw sightlines downward with interesting rugs, floor cushions, potted plants, and other low-to-the-ground pieces.

sprucing up

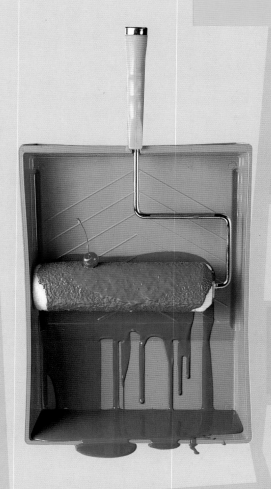

Because you're only temporarily renting someone else's property when you lease an apartment, you have two things to consider when it comes to transforming it into the home of your dreams.

One is how much you're willing to invest in fixing up something you're eventually going to leave behind. You won't benefit long-term from devoting all kinds of time and resources to an elaborate faux-finish paint job on every wall. Then again, if a sunnier color in the kitchen is going to lift your spirits for the next 365 days or so, it's worth repainting it. There are also plenty of simple sprucing-up jobs you can do—then undo and take with you when you go, such as changing the handles on the bathroom cabinets to ones that aren't quite so 1970s, or adding interesting finials (those stoppers on the ends) to the personality-deprived curtain rods in the bedroom.

The other consideration is how much your landlord will allow you to do. Every situation is different. Some landlords have a strict policy against allowing tenants to paint or wallpaper. Others, especially if their rental property is an older building or converted house, are much more lenient. Some have a group of colors for all the apartments in a building, and they'll allow you to repaint if you use a color in that mix. Others are so thrilled that you want to add value to the apartment by giving a few of the rooms fresh coats of paint or wallpaper borders that they'll buy the supplies if you do the work.

Once you know how much you're willing and able to take on, here are the do-it-yourself basics you need to know.

painting walls

One of the easiest and least expensive ways to brighten a dingy room or give a dull one character (not to mention your personal stamp) is to splash a fresh paint color on the walls.

PAINT

You've got two general types of paint to choose from: oil-based (alkyd) and water-based (latex). In most cases, latex is the way to go. Though alkyd paints may be slightly more damage resistant, latex paints today are plenty durable. They're also nontoxic, quick-drying, and they clean up with soap and water as opposed to mineral spirits. The only time you might want to use alkyd paints instead is if you plan to also coat doors, window trim, or other accent spots that'll need a hard finish.

When you buy your paint, the salesperson will ask you what sort of gloss you want. The level of gloss affects the shine and brightness of your walls.

FLAT PAINTS, the most common kind for walls and ceilings, are easy on the eye, reflect little light, reduce glare, and help hide small imperfections.

EGGSHELL, LO-LUSTRE, and **SATIN PAINTS** are good for heavy-use areas that will be subjected to frequent washings—maybe walls around the kitchen counter and stove. They have a slight sheen and hold up a bit better than flat paints.

SEMIGLOSS PAINTS have a slightly greater sheen and can handle a bit more wear and tear than satin paints.

GLOSS and **HIGH-GLOSS PAINTS**, also called enamels, dry to an extremely shiny finish, making them better for woodwork and furniture than entire walls. An enamel surface can withstand heavy use and scrubbing, but it will also reflect any surface imperfection.

ESTIMATING QUANTITY

To figure out how much paint you need, measure the perimeter of your room. Multiply the result by the ceiling height to get the total square feet or meters you need to cover with paint. Don't worry about deducting the space taken up by windows and doors unless they add up to more than 100 square feet (9 square m), which is unlikely in an apartment. Divide your total square feet or meters into the number of square feet or meters your paint can promises to cover. Round up to the nearest whole number to determine how many cans you need.

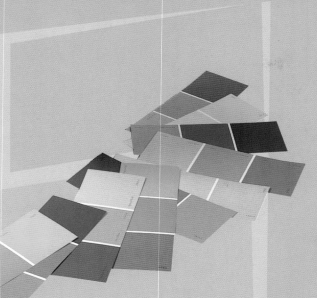

CHOOSING COLORS

First, head to the paint store toting along whatever you want your paint to match or contrast with—a color you clipped from a magazine, a cushion from your couch, one of your electric-green martini glasses. Pick out a bunch of strips of sample colors, and take everything back home. Tack the samples in place on the wall, and pay attention to how they look at different times of day and under different lighting conditions. Start narrowing your choices until you eventually pick the one you'd most like to see in large quantities 24 hours a day. If you simply can't decide—or you're super compulsive—you can always choose two or three paint colors, buy the smallest amount available of each, and apply the paints to scraps of wood. Live with your larger color samples for a day or two before deciding which one you'll use to cover the whole room, remembering that the larger the final painted area, the stronger the color will seem. For a few more tips on choosing colors, see Color Your World, page 108.

MATERIALS & TOOLS

BRUSHES. Nylon or polyester brushes are best for latex paints. Use a natural-bristle brush with alkyd paints. Whichever bristle type you pick, you want brushes with contoured tops that form an oval or a rounded edge. They're best for cutting a fine line along trim and at corners where walls and ceilings meet.

DROP CLOTHS. Disposable plastic drop cloths protect flooring and furniture from paint splatters.

PAINT ROLLERS. Choose a roller with a heavy wire frame and a sturdy, threaded handle that extends (making it possible to easily reach the high spots). The painting surface of the roller is also called a sleeve or cover. It slides on and off the roller cage so you can clean and store it. The length of the nap on sleeves or covers varies; the more irregular your wall surface, the longer nap you'll need.

PRIMER. This specially formulated paint adheres well to bare surfaces and provides an inexpensive base for your more expensive topcoat to stick to.

ROLLER PAN. You need a shallow metal pan with a ramp. You'll run your roller up and down the ramp to evenly distribute the paint on the sleeve.

TRIM GUARD. Also called an edger, this handy hand-held tool lets you shield adjacent surfaces such as window glass or carpeting from the fresh paint you're applying to a wall. It's not essential, but it's a nice-to-have extra.

GENERAL TECHNIQUES

PREP YOUR WALLS. You can paint right over just about any surface, just quickly sponge off any dirt, dust, or mildew first, and let it dry. Also, remove the covers on electrical receptacles, light switches, heating grates, or plate covers from your walls, so you won't splatter them or coat their edges. Cover electrical outlets with masking tape.

PRIME. Apply a coat of primer with a roller or brush. Choose the type that's right for your job; latex primers are for bare wood, others are designed for sheetrock or plaster. Make sure your primer coat is completely dry before you move on.

PAINT. Two simple guidelines will make your paint job a success (and the process more fun): work from top to bottom; and outline first, then fill in second. If you're painting the room's ceiling in addition to the walls, start there. Move on to the walls, and end with door and window trim, doors, and finally baseboards. Use a brush first to outline all the areas a roller can't reach, such as corners, places where the wall meets trim, etc. When you're ready to roll, precondition your roller sleeve by rinsing it with water and spinning it until it's dry. (You don't need to precondition a lamb's-wool sleeve.) Fill one third of your paint tray with paint, load the roller in the deep end of the tray, and smooth it on the sloping end to evenly distribute the paint. Start at the top third of your walls, and work your way down, applying equal pressure and spreading the paint evenly. It's helpful to lay the paint on in the shape of an M or W, then fill in the blank spaces, working from the unpainted areas into the wet paint.

painting floors

If your new place features a wooden floor that's seen better days—or that the previous tenant painted magenta to match her beaded curtains—and your landlord is agreeable, you have the perfect canvas for applying your own color and design.

PAINT

The folks at your local paint store should be able to help you choose the paint best suited for the type and condition of your wood floor. For high-traffic, heavy-use floors, oil-based enamels offer the best durability. You can also find oil-based paint formulated especially for floors and porches, though it's available in only a limited range of colors.

MATERIALS & TOOLS

BRUSHES & ROLLER. The same painting tools you use on walls will work on floors.

FLOOR POLISHER. Tool-rental outlets and even the floor-care centers of many grocery stores rent polishers you can use to roughen up the surface of your floor.

VACUUM CLEANER. You need one to do what it does best: remove dirt and dust, plus sanding residue. A tack rag (basically sticky cheesecloth designed to pick up dust) is a more labor-intensive substitute.

GENERAL TECHNQUES

PREP YOUR FLOOR. Your floor must be free of any gloss or sheen before you apply the paint. Use the floor polisher to buff away the top surface and remove any dirt or grit in the process. When you're finished, use the vacuum to clean up your mess, focusing special attention on cracks and crevices between floorboards.

MARK YOUR PATTERN (optional). If you're painting a design, map it out on graph paper first. Then, use measuring tools and a pencil to transfer the pattern to your floor. If your design features straight lines (a checkerboard pattern, for example), you can use a chalk line to snap the lines according to evenly spaced marks on the edges of the floor.

PAINT. Start by using a brush to outline the perimeter of the floor and to fill in any wide spaces or cracks between floorboards. Once you've got the edges painted, use the roller to fill in the rest of the floor. Working on an area that's about 24 inches (61 cm) wide at a time, paint the entire length of your floorboards, from one wall to the other, then move over to the next strip. Using the edge of a board as your stopping and starting point keeps your wet edge of paint on an even plane rather than in the middle of a board, where lap marks would be visible. Let your floor dry completely between coats if you're adding more than one. For added durability, finish with a couple of coats of matte-finish, non-yellowing polyurethane.

wallpapering

When you want to establish a definite look—art deco, Asian tea room, 1960s retro—wallpaper, with its wealth of patterns and styles, is much more effective than paint. It's also better at hiding flaws in imperfect walls. The downside is that hanging it is a bit more challenging than rolling on paint, but there's nothing so tricky you can't master it.

WALLPAPER TYPES

Save grass cloth, delicate handmade papers, and wall coverings made from pure silk for the home you buy after your trust fund comes through. For now, vinyl wall coverings are more affordable and durable.

PAPER-BACKED VINYL is not only washable and sturdy, it also typically comes in an easy-to-apply prepasted form. Best of all, paper-backed vinyl is available in tons of patterns and in textures ranging from leatherlike to embossed.

FABRIC-BACKED VINYL is a bit more durable than paper-backed vinyl, but it's typically not prepasted.

VINYL-COATED PAPER is the least expensive option, but it's also the least durable. Grease splatters, beverage spills, and the like will leave permanent marks.

MATERIALS & TOOLS

BUCKET & SPONGE. You'll use these as you hang your paper to remove any wallpaper paste oozing from the edges of your newly applied paper.

LADDER. An obvious necessity if you're papering from ceiling to floor.

LEVEL. Anytime you need to determine a straight vertical or horizontal line on your walls, you'll need a level.

PAINT ROLLER OR PASTE BRUSH. If you're not working with prepasted wallpaper, you'll need one of these tools to apply adhesive to the back of your paper.

PLUMB LINE. Simply a weight attached to the end of a string, this tool helps you establish a straight, vertical layout line. Tie the string to a nail near the top of the wall so the weight is just above the floor. When the line stops swinging, align a ruler with the string to mark your layout line.

UTILITY KNIFE. Use a knife with breakaway blades to trim off excess paper at ceiling and floor molding, light fixtures, etc.

SCISSORS. You'll use them to cut your wallpaper strips to size.

SEAM ROLLER. A seam roller is indispensable when it comes to pressing down the seams where two pieces of wallpaper meet.

SMOOTHING BRUSH. The flexible bristles on this brush help you smooth your hung paper so it's free of bubbles and wrinkles.

TAPE MEASURE. When you're measuring and cutting your paper, you've got to have one.

TRIM GUIDE. A painting edger or a broad knife can serve as a trim guide. You'll use it to press your wet wallpaper into a ceiling or wall joint before you trim it.

WATER TRAY. If you're using prepasted wallpaper, you'll need to soak it before hanging it.

ESTIMATING QUANTITY

Using the same system described for estimating the quantity of paint (page 23), figure the total square feet or meters of your room's wall space. Divide your total by the square feet or meters a roll of the wallpaper you've chosen promises to cover. You probably won't come out with an even number; round up to determine how many rolls you should buy.

Go figure: Nobody knows why, but although wallpaper is *priced* by the single roll, it's *sold* only in packages of double rolls—a good thing to know when you're estimating how much you need to buy.

BORDERS

Not ready to tackle an entire wall? Hanging a border is an excellent (and easy) way to test your interest in wallpapering—and it may add all the decorative accent you need. Borders come in all kinds of patterns and various widths for hanging around windows, doors, mirrors, and the tops of walls.

GENERAL TECHNIQUES

PREP YOUR WALLS. Give your walls a good washing down and dry them well, patch any holes or cracks with wall compound, and, after the compound is dry, sand the patched areas until they're smooth. Also, remove the covers on electrical receptacles and light switches, cover electrical outlets with masking tape, and remove any heating grates or plate covers from your walls. If you like to follow all the rules, apply a coat of primer to your walls. Primer is only a must if you're papering over new drywall, but it'll promote adhesion on any type of wall. Finally, apply a coat of wallpaper sizing, a treatment that makes your walls tacky so the wallpaper paste or adhesive has some- thing to bond with.

HANG THE PAPER. Use a level or plumb line to lay out a straight, vertical starting point on your wall. Cut your first strip of wallpaper from the roll. You want your strip a little longer than your wall is tall; you'll trim it later. Soak your strip in water, following your paper manufacturer's instructions, or apply wallpaper paste to the strip. Position the strip at the ceiling joint of the wall, leaving a few extra inches at the top, and carefully align one side with your starting line. Use your hands and the smoothing brush to smooth the strip in place, starting at the top and working down. Once the strip is straight, continue brushing to remove any wrinkles or bubbles. Hang subsequent strips the same way, carefully aligning the seams and using the seam roller to press them in place. As you go, use a wet sponge to wipe up any paste that oozes out of the seams.

TRIM. Where your wallpaper strips meet the ceiling, floor, or any trim, hold the trim guide in the joint, and use the razor knife to cut away the excess paper.

hanging curtains & blinds

Whether your motivation is privacy, decoration, or blocking the sun that streams into your bedroom far too early on Saturday morning, hanging some sort of covering over your windows will likely be one of your first sprucing-up activities.

curtains

MEASURING FOR CURTAINS

Two basic measurements will tell you what size curtains you need.

■ The length of your curtain rod tells you how wide your curtains should be.

■ The length from the mounted rod to the windowsill (for sill-length curtains) or the floor (for floor-length curtains) tells you how long. For this second measurement, measure from the rod itself for curtains with a casing that will be threaded onto the rod; measure from the base of a curtain ring, if you're using rings. For sill-length curtains, deduct $\frac{3}{8}$ inch (9.5mm) from the measurement, so the curtains will clear the sill comfortably, or add 2 to 4 inches (5.1 to 10.2cm), so they'll hang just below the sill. For floor-length curtains, again, deduct $\frac{3}{8}$ inch (9.5mm) from the length for clearance, or add 2 to 8 inches (5.1 to 20.3cm), and let your curtains puddle on the floor.

HANGING THE ROD

The windows in your apartment will probably already be outfitted with rods for hanging curtains. If not—or if you want to replace an existing rod with one you like better—simply center the rod over the window. Place it about 4 inches (10.2cm) above the top of the window, and make sure it extends an equal amount on either side of the window. Rods typically come packaged with the hardware and easy instructions you need to attach them to the wall.

blinds

MEASURING FOR BLINDS

You can mount most blinds on the window trim, on the wall outside the window frame, or inside of the window's recess, which needs to be at least $1\frac{1}{4}$ inch (3.2cm) deep. Decide which option you want, then measure your window. Measure the width at the top, middle, and bottom of the window (warped wood around the windows can affect the width); if the dimensions differ, use the smallest one. Also, measure the length of the window, so you choose a blind with the correct extension amount.

HANGING BLINDS

Blinds come with mounting brackets, most of which have predrilled holes on both ends and on the back. You'll use only one set of holes, depending on which of the three places you're mounting them.

■ Position the brackets where you want them, and lightly mark where you'll screw through the appropriate predrilled holes.

■ Drill pilot holes where you made the marks.

■ Use a screwdriver to install the brackets with screws (typically packaged with the brackets).

■ Push the blind's header bar into the brackets.

■ If necessary, snip the blind cords so your blinds are the proper length; directions for doing so are usually included with the blinds.

 Make sure your landlord approves any drilling in the walls necessary to mount window treatments in your apartment.

fixing up furniture

Unlike walls and floors, tables, chairs, and their counterparts are pieces you will take with you when your lease is up and you move on (assuming you're not renting a furnished apartment). That makes them an especially good focus for your fixing-up time and resources.

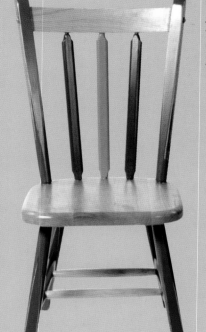

painting furniture

Brushing on fresh paint is the easiest way to give a piece of furniture a new look. You can start with already-painted furniture or with new pieces of unfinished furniture. Flea markets, yard sales, and relatives' attics are great sources for the former. Stores that specialize in unpainted furniture offer a wide selection of the latter, though they're often much pricier than used pieces.

If you're investing in unfinished furniture you plan to have around for awhile, solid-wood pieces are the best choice. While you can find unfinished furniture made of particle board, plywood, and veneers, solid-wood construction is stronger and longer lasting. Depending on where you purchase your unfinished furniture, it can come either assembled or unassembled. If it's unassembled, it should be accompanied by illustrated instructions and all the hardware you need to easily put your piece together.

PAINT

Just as when you're painting walls, you've got a choice between oil-based (alkyd) and water-based (latex) paints and flat, semigloss, and gloss sheens. Again, the advantage of latex paints is that they're nearly odorless, they clean up with soap and water, and they dry quickly. Alkyd paints, on the other hand, are more resistant to wear and tear. For added color options, you may also want to experiment with artist's acrylics, sold in tubes or jars. They're great for painting small areas, detailing a motif, outlining, and highlighting. Artist's acrylics are more concentrated than household paint, so you may want to thin them with water before using them.

FURNITURE-PAINTING MATERIALS & TOOLS

BRUSHES. You probably don't need to invest in specialized decorative painting brushes. A 2-inch (5.1 cm) or 3-inch (7.6 cm) flat paintbrush used for household painting is versatile enough to handle most jobs. A straight-edge brush works well on flat surfaces; an angled brush will be handier when you want to paint clean, straight lines and nice sharp corners. For detail work such as outlining, highlighting, or blending, you'll want a selection of small artist's brushes.

CARBON or **GRAPHITE TRANSFER PAPER.** You'll need this if you're transferring a design to the surface of your furniture.

GLAZE MEDIUM. Formulated to dry more slowly than paint, glaze medium gives you a longer working time for techniques that call for manipulation of the top coat of paint, such as rag rolling or stippling. It comes in either water- or oil-based formulas and dries clear.

DROP CLOTHS. They provide a protective layer between your painting project and your floor. Use an old sheet, purchase an inexpensive plastic cloth, or spread out old newspapers.

RAGS. Lint-free rags are indispensable when it comes to wiping up drips and spills and for cleaning your brushes.

SANDPAPER. Sandpaper is categorized by its grade (coarse, medium, fine, and extra fine) or by a number that indicates the amount of grit used per square inch on the sanding surface (#150 to #200 are considered medium grade, for example).

PRIMERS. If you're working on unfinished furniture, you need a primer to fill and seal the bare wood so the surface will better accept your paint. Choose a good all-purpose primer-sealer formulated for use with water- or oil-based paints.

TACK CLOTH. You'll use this sticky cloth to clean your wood's surface, removing debris and sanding residue before you paint.

VARNISHES & PROTECTIVE COATS. If you want to give your painted surface extra protection, add sheen, or tone down a too-shiny surface, you can apply a few top coats of clear varnish or polyurethane. Varnishes come in water- and oil-based formulas and in sheens ranging from matte to high-gloss.

WOOD FILLER. If your piece features small dents or nicks, natural flaws, or nail or staple holes, use wood filler to even the surface before applying your primer or first coat of paint.

GENERAL TECHNIQUES

Whether you're painting unfinished or already-painted furniture, try to work in a space that's free of drafts and airborne dirt, so specks of dust and lint will be less likely to land on your just-painted surfaces.

PAINTING UNFINISHED FURNITURE

1. Fill any holes or indentations with wood filler, following the manufacturer's instructions for application and drying time.

2. Once the filler is dry, use a fine-grit sandpaper to remove any excess filler and to buff your entire piece.

3. Use the tack cloth to remove any sanding debris.

4. Seal the wood with a coat of primer. Once it's dry, sand again, and again use the tack cloth to remove any debris.

5. Apply your first coat of paint, let it dry, sand your piece again, and wipe it clean.

6. Add your top coat, let it dry, then finish with several coats of varnish if you like.

PAINTING ALREADY-PAINTED FURNITURE

If the existing paint on your piece of furniture is in good condition, just sand the piece thoroughly with medium-grade sandpaper, and apply your new paint. If it features a few chips and cracks, sand the damaged areas smooth before painting. For pieces with more damaged existing paint, use wood filler to even out the nicks and gaps, let it dry, sand it smooth, then apply a coat of primer before adding your paint. It's a good idea, in this case, to apply two coats of your finish paint, sanding between the first and second coat.

SPECIAL FINISHES & DECORATIVE TECHNIQUES

Here are some easy options for adding texture, pattern, and splashes of colorful design to your painted furniture.

WEATHERING

It doesn't have to make sense—some of us simply want our brand-new pieces to look old. Using two paint colors, first paint on a base coat of your lighter color, and let it dry completely. Then use one of the following approaches to "age" your piece.

■ Mix the darker shade of paint with water, and stir well. You'll need to experiment with the ratio of water to paint. For a very thin color wash, use more water. Paint a wash of the darker color over the entire surface of the wood. Allow the paint to sit for a few minutes, then wipe some of the paint away with a clean rag to give it an uneven or weathered appearance. For more color, give the piece a second wash.

■ Apply the darker paint to a paintbrush. Offload the brush onto a rag until it's almost dry. Paint the piece with the almost-dry brush, dragging the tip of the brush in long strokes until the piece is entirely covered. Apply several almost-dry coats in this fashion, building up the layers of top color.

■ Paint the entire piece with the darker paint. Allow the paint to dry thoroughly. Use fine-grit sandpaper to lightly sand away some of the darker color to reveal the lighter shade underneath. Sand very lightly to prevent exposing the raw wood.

STENCILING

Stenciling is simply painting through a hole (or pattern of holes) cut in a piece of stencil material that you've taped against your surface. All you need is a stencil (the pattern of cutout holes), paint (acrylic is most common; specialty stencil paints, paint sticks, and crayons are also available), and a tool for applying the color (artist's brushes, stencil brushes, and sponges are all options). Precut stencils in every design motif imaginable are available at craft stores. You can also design your own stencils and cut them out of a water-resistant material, such as acetate.

1. Use painter's tape or spray adhesive to fix your stencils in place.

2. Dab on paint to fill the stencil's cutout area. Different brushing techniques produce different effects.

DRY-BRUSH application, which involves blotting your brush on a paper towel before applying the paint, creates a soft, muted result.

STIPPLING, or applying the paint in a quick up-and-down motion, creates a fine, textural effect.

SWIRLING, a method of applying a small amount of paint in a downward, twisting motion, creates a smooth finish with dark and light gradations.

Don't ever drag your brush over the stencil; you risk driving paint under the stencil and outside the design's border.

3. Gently remove the stencils, being careful not to smudge the painted design as you do.

SPONGING

Sponging is one of the simplest ways to texturize a surface with paint—a little dipping, a little patting, and you've got interesting patches of color that can serve as your final finish or as a background for additional treatments. Sponging is also a versatile technique. Use a soft touch, and the look is luminous. Apply more pressure and contact to intensify the color in specific areas, and you can create different shades of color. Or, blend several colors into each other, and you end up with a graduated effect. You can use sponges to produce uniform design elements, too; cut dots, diamonds, or any other basic shape from sponges, then use them to stamp your surface.

Kitchen sponges, cosmetic sponges, sea sponges, and sponge mitts all create interesting finishes. You can also "sponge" on paint with everything from crumpled newspaper to nubby fabric—all with their own imaginative effects.

STAMPING

A close cousin of sponging, stamping is another nearly effortless way to add painted accents to any surface. Rubber stamps come in an array of sizes and in designs ranging from spirals and stars to all the letters of the alphabet. Simply dip your stamp in acrylic paint, and press it against the surface you want to decorate.

PICKLING

Pickle a piece when you want it to display a satisfyingly sun-bleached look atop visible wood grain.

1. Using steel wool or a wire brush, open up the grain of the wood by brushing firmly in the direction of the grain. Wipe away all dust and residue with a clean rag.

2. Use an old paintbrush to work the latex paint deep into the grain of the wood. Wipe away the excess paint with a clean rag, leaving the paint in the grain and crevices of the wood. Work small areas at a time; the paint dries quickly. Once you've worked the entire surface, allow the paint to dry thoroughly.

3. Lightly sand the entire surface. Remove all residue with a tack or lint-free cloth.

4. For a more natural look, rub furniture wax onto the surface, then buff the piece. For a more durable finish, apply several coats of varnish, lightly sanding in between coats.

refurbishing wood

Lots of times, varnished wooden pieces you pick up at flea markets or tag sales look as if they need a complete overhaul when they'll actually spring back to life with nothing more than a good, old-fashioned cleaning. To make the process sound like more of a job when you're describing it to others, refer to it by its official name: refurbishing.

1. Applying mineral spirits (paint thinner you can buy at any paint or hardware store) is the best way to remove wax, grease, and grime from old wood. Use a clean cotton rag, and if you're working indoors, make sure you've got the windows open to air out the fumes. Also, because the fume buildup can be flammable, it's a good idea to turn off the pilot light of your stove while you're working.

2. Clean small areas at a time, wiping away any residue with a clean, dry cloth as you go.

3. If your piece is really filthy, you may have to give it a second or even third dose of mineral spirits.

4. Once your piece is clean, you can assess it. You may simply see a few spots where its finish has worn off. If so, slip on some rubber gloves, and use a clean sponge or cloth to dab on some matching stain. Once it's dry, give the wood a top coat of clear, wipe-on finish. If, on the other hand, your assessment tells you your piece still looks pretty shabby, read on.

refinishing or stripping wood

Cleaning off a piece of furniture's dirt and dull top layer of finish may not solve other problems, including extensive cracking or peeling of its remaining finish or stains and water damage. You've got two other more work-intensive choices if your piece needs more help: refinishing, which means removing the surface finish and replacing it with another; or full-blown stripping, taking all the finish out until your piece is stripped down to its bare wood, then restaining or painting and finishing.

While neither option is overwhelmingly complicated—and there are now nontoxic, environmentally friendly products on the market, which make the processes and cleanup more pleasant—each does require specific steps and special tools and materials. Buying a simple guide that focuses on refinishing and stripping techniques will be well worth the small expense. It'll walk you through everything from how to choose the right product for the job to tricks for stripping hard-to-clean crevices.

staining stripped or unfinished wood

In addition to the hundreds of paint-chip samples they stock, paint stores also typically have samples of stains, which come in every wood tone imaginable, plus lots of pastels. You want natural wood colors if your goal is to show off the grain of the wood. Pastels are better at masking imperfections.

1. If your furniture is made of pine or another softwood, apply a coat of wood conditioner before you start. Softwoods have uneven grains that make for uneven stain absorption. The conditioner will help even out the stain penetration.

2. Wearing rubber gloves, pour a small amount of stain into an open pan or paint tray.

3. Dip in a clean sponge, cloth, or paintbrush, squeeze out the excess, and apply the stain to a small area in long, continuous strokes, following the grain pattern of the wood.

4. Wipe the wet stain with a clean, dry cloth to even it out.

5. Apply as many coats as you need, depending on how dark you want your stain. When you're finished, apply a top coat of sealer, varnish, shellac, or polyurethane, depending on the look you want.

If you're staining a piece with doors or drawers, coat all the surfaces, including the insides of the doors or drawers, to keep the wood from warping.

cleaning furniture hardware

Often, the hinges, handles, knobs, and pulls attached to handed-down or salvaged pieces of wood furniture could use some fixing up, too. Use ordinary metal cleaners to clean plated steel pieces. (You can tell they're steel by holding a magnet near one of the pieces; steel attracts magnets.) Clean solid brass, copper, or bronze pieces with brass refurbisher.

1. Apply a thick coat of the refurbisher with a bristle brush.

2. Let it work for about 10 minutes.

3. Wipe off the refurbisher with a clean cloth, apply another coat, if necessary, then buff the cleaned hardware.

removing rust

Wrought-iron outdoor furniture pieces can be transformed into funky indoor accents by cleaning them up and brushing on a coat of paint. If you have a set that's rusting, use a wire brush to remove the loose rust, then lightly sand it or rub it with some fine steel wool dipped in kerosene. Once the kerosene is dry, it's ready to paint.

perking up wicker

Hose off old wicker that looks dusty and tired—a car wash is a good place to do this if you don't have a yard. If your wicker piece needs some extra attention, brush it with a small brush and some dishwashing liquid, then rinse it thoroughly again, and let it dry in the sun. For added life, give your wicker chair or table a thin coat of paint or varnish.

sewing primer

So you didn't win the home economics award in high school. With a simple sewing kit and a few basic techniques, you can reattach buttons and stitch beaded fringe on curtains with the best of them.

the kit

All you really need is an assortment of colored threads, needles of different sizes, and a pair of small, sharp, good quality scissors. In a jam, you'll be glad to find your kit also stocked with a few safety pins, a selection of fasteners such as snaps and hooks and eyes, and buttons in various sizes and colors, particularly white and black. You could also include a thimble (worn on the middle finger to help push needles through thick fabrics), a needle threader, and, if you find yourself cutting lots of lengths of heavy fabric, a large pair of scissors. A tape measure makes measuring soft or curved pieces a cinch. Even if you never pick up a needle, you'll find it useful to have around.

basic stitches

The simplest stitch, a **RUNNING STITCH**, covers lots of ground quickly. Thread a needle and make a knot on one end of the thread. Insert the needle several times through the fabric at evenly spaced intervals, then pull the needle and thread through. Repeat.

A **BACKSTITCH** has more strength than a running stitch. Bring the needle through both layers of fabric you're sewing together, push it back down about 1/8 inch (3mm) in the direction you started from, and pull the thread through completely. Stitch forward the same distance as the first stitch, then backwards 1/8 inch (3mm). Repeat.

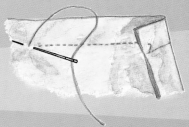

Use a **SLIP STITCH** for hems. Make a small fold that just encases the raw edge of the fabric; press it. Make another fold the size you want the hem to be; press again. Put the needle inside the fold, push it through to the front, and pick up just a thread or two when sending the needle back through to the fold. Don't pull the thread too taut, or the fabric will appear puckered. Repeat.

no-sew alternatives

Let's face it, there are going to be times—perhaps all the time—when you're just too busy to hand-stitch a hem on a piece of fabric to create a tablecloth or to whip up homemade curtains. Here are some easy-way-out alternatives.

■ To avoid hemming altogether, use pinking shears. They cut fabric in such a way that it won't fray, and add a decorative edge at the same time. You can also avoid hemming by choosing the right fabric. Some, such as felt, vinyl, ultrasuede, or fleece, won't fray no matter how you cut them.

■ To join two pieces of cloth that won't need frequent washings, try fabric glue. Its downside is that it can make some fabrics a little stiff.

■ For a more permanent and washable solution, use fusible web. When placed between two pieces of fabric and ironed, this white, mesh-like material melts and bonds to the pieces. Just be careful not to touch it directly with the iron, or it will attach itself to your appliance. Fusible web comes in rolls ½ inch (1.3 cm) wide, or on bolts in wider widths.

■ Snaps offer an interesting alternative for holding fabrics together, and even for hemming. It takes a little planning and care to line the halves up correctly, but you'll need only a hammer to set the snaps. Just follow the directions on their packaging.

sewing on a button

Putting on a button is a snap, and good sewing practice for beginners. After threading the needle, make a knot with both ends of the thread, so you'll speed up the process by sewing with both strands at once. Hold the button in place, and drive the needle from under the fabric, up through one of the holes, and back down through the opposite hole. Repeat four or five times (more if your fabric is heavy). For added strength, poke the needle back up through the fabric, but not through the button, and wrap around the threads twice. Bring the needle back under the fabric and tie off, cutting off the excess thread.

When sewing, use thicker thread and larger needles for heavy fabrics. Likewise, fine needles and thread work better on lightweight fabrics.

APARTMENT DWELLER'S TOOLBOX

The baker's-dozen basics you'll need for simple repairs and decorating.

1 **WORK GLOVES**
They'll prevent calluses and scrapes, and remove the excuse that you can't fix it now because you'll get dirty. Leather and synthetic gloves keep your hands warmer and drier than cotton or canvas.

2 A 16-ounce (448 g) **CLAW HAMMER**
This is a basic carpenter's tool designed for all-around use. It has a flat side for driving nails and a "claw" on the peen side for removing them. Also, buy a supply of various sizes of nails and tacks.

3 **PLIERS**
There's a variety of styles and sizes; you'll need two kinds. Long, straight-nosed pliers with side cutters are great for holding on in tight spaces and for snipping wire. Groove-joint pliers, when opened to their maximum of 2 inches (5.1 cm) wide, resemble the monster in *Alien*. Even cooler, they allow you to grip large nuts and fittings when your hands just won't do.

4 **UTILITY KNIFE**
When scissors won't cut it, a utility knife will, whether you're opening cardboard boxes or trimming wallpaper. Retract the blade when you're not using it.

5 **COMBINATION SCREWDRIVER**
Keep screws of various sizes handy, too, and you'll use this versatile tool often. Its removable heads accommodate several sizes of standard and Phillips-head screws.

6 **PUTTY KNIFE**
Just add elbow grease, and this humble tool removes paint, finish, or glue. A flexible 1½-inch (3.8 cm) blade is good for all-around use.

7 **SOCKET WRENCH SET** with **NUT DRIVER**
A set, with a variety of wrenches and sockets in metric and standard sizes, is most useful. You'll tighten or loosen nuts and bolts on appliances (and vehicles) and be able to reach tight spaces with ease using the ratchet handles and extension shafts.

8 A retractable 25-foot (7.6 m) **METAL TAPE MEASURE**
Precise measurements are key, whether you're designing your apartment's floor plan or installing shelves.

9 A 12-inch (30.5 cm) **COMBINATION SQUARE**
It looks like a triangle, measures 45 to 90° angles and short distances, and has a built-in level for keeping things straight. You can use it for everything from hanging pictures to building furniture.

10 **POWER DRILL** and assorted **DRILL BIT SET**
You'll make up reasons to bore holes or drive screws in wood, metal, and plastic with this tool. A cordless, variable-speed drill with a ⅜-inch (9.5mm) chuck opening is your best bet. (Remember to recharge it after using it.) A more powerful drill will get the job done more quickly and with greater precision. Drills can also convert to sanders and polishers with the proper attachments.

11 **TOOLBOX SAW**
You can use a small, easy-to-handle handsaw for cutting everything from shelving to plywood.

12 **GLUE**
Sometimes a drop of the sticky stuff is all you need. White all-purpose glue bonds wood, paper, and cloth, and cleans up with soap and water. Synthetic resin adhesives, also known as epoxies, provide waterproof fastening. Read labels to determine which types you need for different sticking situations.

13 A can of lightweight **HOUSEHOLD OIL**
A drop of this stops hinges from squeaking, and that makes it worth its weight in gold.

Buy the best quality tools you can afford. Store them together in a toolbox or sturdy basket, always in the same convenient place, so they're both out of the way and accessible.

settling in

No doubt about it, setting up house from scratch can seem overwhelming. You'll brave bewildering expeditions to discount and home accessory stores, spend a lot of money, carry home a lot of heavy bags, then realize you still don't have what you need to open a bottle of wine or dry your hands on something other than a bath towel. The process of settling in becomes much more manageable when you understand that your new home needs a relatively small but essential number of fundamental items to function smoothly. Focus on them first, then add flourishes and embellishments later— or put the extras on your housewarming-party wish list; see page 103.

kitchen

Unless you plan to live entirely on takeout, here are the basics to consider for your kitchen. We'll leave the prioritizing of the extras—from salad spinners and potato mashers to woks and muffin pans—to you.

cookware

12-INCH (30.5 CM) SKILLET. A teflon-coated aluminum skillet, which is affordable, lighter than cast iron, and easy to clean, is a good, all-purpose choice.

STOCKPOT WITH LID. Get one with at least a 6-quart (5.7 L) capacity.

SAUCE PAN WITH LID. One with a 3 to 4-quart (2.9 to 3.8 L) capacity should do.

LARGE COLANDER. Stainless steel has that nice professional-kitchen look, but heavy-duty plastic willl work just fine.

BAKING PAN. A 9 x 12-inch (22.9 x 30.5 cm) rectangle will work for cornbread, brownies, and birthday cakes for friends.

COOKIE SHEET. Round or rectangular; you decide. Either will accommodate nachos, potato skins, and, of course, cookies.

SET OF NESTED BOWLS. Tempered-glass bowls can serve as mixing bowls, refrigerator storage bowls, and serving bowls, plus they're tough enough for a microwave or freezer.

CUTTING BOARD. Plastic is cheaper than wood and (when cleaned) doesn't harbor bacteria. Scrub the board after every use with hot, soapy water. Rinse it with one tablespoon of bleach in a gallon of water.

MEASURING CUPS AND SPOONS. Again, stainless-steel varieties have more flair—especially if they're hanging out on display—but plastic will get the job done.

appliances

BLENDER OR FOOD PROCESSOR. A food processor is more versatile—it purees, grinds, slices, dices, and grates. But a basic blender with only high and low settings will do for most tasks, from mixing smoothies to making pesto.

ELECTRIC MIXER. Freestanding retro-style mixers look funkier, but they also cost a lot more. An inexpensive, hand-held type is plenty sufficient. If you don't plan to bake at all, scratch even the simpler style off your list.

TOASTER OVEN. These convenient multitaskers can toast your bread, bagels, or English muffins, reheat your leftovers, and even bake small items. They heat up faster than conventional ovens and use less energy.

COFFEE MAKER. If you're a coffee drinker and you don't want to live on instant grounds stirred into boiling water, you need some way to brew yourself a cup or two in the morning. Whether you need a bells-and-whistles appliance that also shoots out cappuccino and espresso is up to you.

MICROWAVE. We'll admit the controversy right up front. Some people call them miracle machines and can't live without them. Others find them completely unnecessary. If you demand easy, fast ways to thaw frozen leftovers, reheat your coffee, pop popcorn, melt butter, and cook veggies while leaving most of their nutrients intact, you'll likely get your money's worth out of a small microwave.

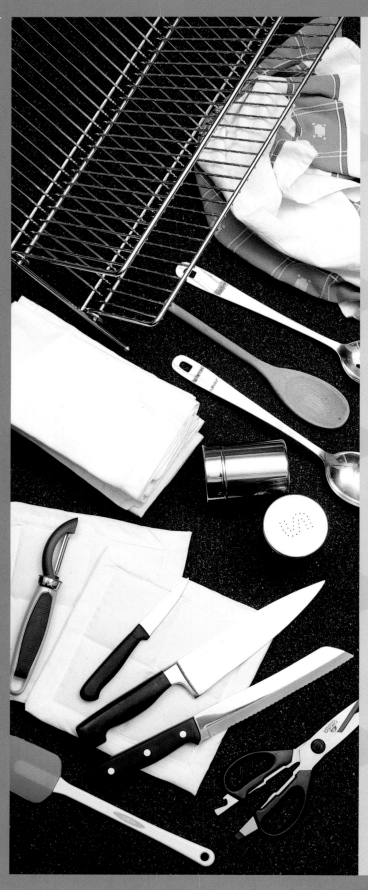

utensils, etc.

KNIVES. Do not make do with the el cheapo knives hanging next to the rubber spatulas in the supermarket; they'll be dull in no time, making all your cutting and chopping a dreaded chore. Save up and invest in a good chopping knife, paring knife, and serrated knife at a department store. Treat them with care, and they'll last you a long time.

SPOONS. A slotted spoon, a ladle, and a large wooden spoon will cover all your basic mixing and scooping needs.

SPATULA. You can choose from either plastic or metal. If you have a teflon skillet, go with plastic. Metal will scrape off the coating, creating tiny flecks of teflon that will float around in your food.

GOOD-QUALITY CAN OPENER. Get one that's equipped with a bottle opener and a corkscrew.

VEGETABLE PEELER. A good one (we recommend a rubber-grip handle) makes it a piece of cake to peel apples for a pie or potatoes for a soup, shave carrot curls into a salad, or carry out other related tasks.

KITCHEN SCISSORS. This inexpensive utensil can make your life so much easier. Without searching for the other scissors you think you left somewhere near last winter's wrapping paper—wherever that is—you can cut open packages of pasta and snip sundried tomatoes into slivers.

DISH DRAINER. Drainers come in all styles, from wooden drying racks to tilted plastic contraptions that guide the drained water right into your sink.

COTTON DISHTOWELS. Buy a stack so you can replace dirty ones frequently. Bonus: dishtowels are a great way to play up (or provide) an accent color in your kitchen.

POT HOLDERS. Don't ruin your dishtowels by using them instead. Go ahead and spring for some flat holders, oven mitts, or both.

CLEANING TOOLS. You'll need a scouring pad and sponge near the sink, and perhaps a rag underneath it for mopping up spills.

SALT AND PEPPER SHAKERS. If it's an extra-long way from stove to table, buy one inexpensive plastic set with handles to use for cooking and another set to keep on the table.

dishes

True, dishes come in all sorts of appealing styles, from fine china to rustic stoneware. But if you've got a finite amount of space in your kitchen and limits to your tableware budget, your best bet is to put together a basic, neutral collection that'll look presentable all by itself and also provide a good backdrop for livelier accent pieces when you add them later.

Piece together a set of basic white or off-white dinner plates, smaller plates that can serve salad or dessert, and soup bowls. Eight of each piece should be plenty to start with, unless you're prone to huge dinner parties or absolutely never do dishes. Not all the pieces have to be the same style; just match the shades of white as closely as possible. You can find plain white dinnerware at kitchen-supply stores, department stores, discount retailers, even thrift stores. It often ranks among the least expensive. Search for simple, classic designs; avoid unusual or trendy looks. You're after a versatile set that will last.

Once you have a white foundation, you can begin to play with color and pattern. Sprinkle in a few pieces of your grandmother's pink Depression glass for a Valentine's dinner, or go ahead and splurge on those small black sushi plates you've been eyeing. Without owning a complete set of anything else, you'll still be able to easily change the mood and style of your table settings.

flatware

It was those pesky Victorians, the same people who gave us frilly trim on houses and books of manners, who came up with the concept of using a different utensil for every single eating activity (think aspic knives, pickle forks, and individual asparagus tongs). Fortunately, the rules have relaxed since the early 1900s. Today, you can get by just fine with nothing more than forks, knives, and spoons—eight of each. If you're feeling expansive, buy smaller salad forks and dessert spoons, too.

You want an all-purpose set of flatware that will go with anything, so stay away from colored handles, gold plating, and unusual designs for your basic pieces. Simple, silver-colored utensils are the most versatile. To get that silver color, you've got several choices: sterling silver, silver-plated flatware, and stainless steel. The first two are more expensive and require polishing (just how you want to spend a free Saturday, right?). Stainless is the way to go. It's affordable, nearly effortless to care for, and comes in styles ranging from sleek and modern to whimsical.

Avoid cheap flatware with thin handles. The poor-quality stuff has little chance of surviving that inevitable encounter with the garbage disposal—not to mention the other pressures of everyday life. Department stores and kitchenware stores typically carry several lines of good-quality flatware.

glassware

As with standard white dishes, plain clear glasses are best if you want a versatile collection of basics. Go ahead and part with the jumbo-sized plastic logo cups you collected over several spring break trips, and buy yourself a set of eight straight-sided tumblers instead. While you're at it, pick up eight short juice glasses, which can double as European-style wine glasses until you're able to invest in stemware.

The same department stores and kitchen stores that sell dishes and flatware carry affordable sets of glasses by the box. With your foundation in place, it's easy to mix in a variety of mismatched pieces, including glasses of different heights, colors, and styles, from antique cut glass to bright painted goblets.

bed

If you're like most people, you spend at least one-third of your life snoozing away in bed. In addition to something comfortable to sleep upon, you need a few other essential items to ensure that the time is well spent.

MATTRESS PAD. Fitted at its corners with elastic, this foundation piece provides a layer between the bottom sheet and the actual mattress. When your bed needs freshening, it's easy to whip off and toss in the wash. Buy one sized to fit your mattress.

SHEETS. Who knows why some people have entire linen closets full of sheets. If you've got two sets, you're covered—one set on the bed, one either camped in your laundry basket or clean and ready to offer to an out-of-town friend who's claimed your couch. Sheets typically come in sets: one fitted sheet, which snugs right over the mattress pad, and one flat sheet, to go on top of it. Cotton-blend sheets are the most affordable and easiest to care for (out of the wash and onto the bed). You might also consider a set of flannel sheets for winter if you live in a chilly

climate. And unless you're absolutely sure you're going to like orange and blue polka dots as much a year from now as you do today, buy sheets in solid, neutral colors or with subtle, classic patterns.

PILLOWS. The range of pillow sizes includes everything from "boudoir" to "king." Though covering your bed with piles of different pillows is an easy way to give it some style, all you really need are a couple of standard-size pillows to prop you up while you read or cushion your head as you sleep.

PILLOW COVERS. Zippered pillow protectors serve the same purpose as a mattress pad—you can remove them and wash them regularly. On top of the protectors, you'll want pillowcases, which typically come in packages of two. Be sure to buy cases that are the same size as your pillows.

BLANKETS AND THE REST. Depending on the weather where you live (and sleep), you'll want either a cotton blanket, a wool blanket, or one of each, so you can switch with the seasons. What you add to the bed beyond that—bed skirt, pillow shams, bedspread, quilt, comforter, or throw—is primarily decor. In other words, if you have to, you can put those purchases off awhile.

bath

Each year, people spend an astounding amount of money on bath paraphernalia, from exotic salts, beads, oils, and soaps to imported sponges and scrubbers. The truth, of course, is that you can get squeaky clean with only a few affordable essential tools.

BATH TOWELS. In 1900, an American towel company invented a thick, pile fabric with loops on both sides. They called it terry cloth, and people around the world have been using the absorbent material to dry their bathed bodies since. Choose your terry-cloth towels in a size that suits your body (you can even find them in extra long, if that's what you need). Solid colors are best for mixing and matching with the other elements of your bathroom, with neutrals, once again, being the most versatile. (Buy purple towels decorated with pink fish, and you have to find a shower curtain and bath mat that don't clash—plus, you're definitely stuck with a theme.) If you hang your towel up to dry right after you use it, then reuse it for a week or so, two to four towels is plenty to have on hand. If you wad it up into a wet pile on the floor after each use, shame on you; you'll need to buy a dozen.

HAND TOWELS. Buy a color and style that match or complement your bath towels. Assuming you wash your hands before wiping them, two to four hand towels is all you need.

WASHCLOTHS. Same story as hand towels. Buy them to match or complement (or buy your towels and washcloths as a set); two to four is plenty.

SHOWER CURTAIN. Unless your bathroom has a shower stall with a door or a tub only, you can't live without a shower curtain. A plain liner-type curtain is all you really have to have to keep water from spraying the room. Add the decorative outer curtain if you want one later.

BATH MAT. Who wants to step out of the shower or tub on a winter morning (or anytime) and feel a cold, slippery floor beneath their feet? Make your bathroom cozy and keep the floor dry with a small mat.

keeping clean

Not long after you take up residence in your apartment, you'll start to notice that you now not only have your very own place, but also your very own dust bunnies, toothpaste splatters, and intermittent colonies of mildew and mold. This is not because you're doing something wrong. Your living spaces have always collected debris. If you're lucky, you've simply had someone else keeping it under control for you until now.

Let go of the fact that you never imagined yourself boning up on grease removal and toilet cleaners. These basic tips and easy tricks for keeping your apartment livable and presentable aren't meant to take over your life, merely to help you make sure a relatively clear path runs through it.

THE NITTY-GRITTY ON DIRT

Every surface collects dust and other deposits, from pet hair and food residue to grit from the outside world. We typically lump it all into the general category of dirt. Places where you regularly put your hands are especially susceptible. Look around the room right now, and you can probably spot signs of use on doors, door frames, light switches, and handles. Other places are less prone to hand smudges but perfect targets for dusty buildup: furniture surfaces, baseboards, the tops of door frames and windows.

SURFACE DIRT that's left alone long enough congeals into nasty grime. (Who likes to be ignored?) Giving all your surfaces a clean wipe regularly, before they have a chance to reach the grimy stage, is one of the most efficient uses of your limited housecleaning time. A good old-fashioned dust rag will do in lots of cases. To remove stickier stuff, maybe on countertops or the refrigerator door, use a squirt of one of the all-purpose cleaning solutions listed on page 51.

FLOORS also provide dust and dirt with one big, convenient surface on which to collect, making regular vacuuming or sweeping and mopping another efficient way to head off major buildup. When you're really going all out, move the furniture and hit those hidden spots that are likely harboring a few crumbs and cobwebs of their own. Take area rugs outside and give them a good shake.

KITCHENS benefit from a little additional scrubbing. Not only does the stove top need to be cleaned (much easier, by the way, if you wipe it down each time you use it rather than every six months), but you'll also want to clean up splattered grease and food off the walls around the stove. If your stove top doesn't have a hood or vent, you should probably run a damp cloth over whatever's directly above the stove, too. The kitchen sink, home on any given day to vegetable peels, food-caked plates, and used coffee filters, will be a much happier place to look at if it's the recipient of a thorough scrubbing every so often. And while you're at it, give the cabinet doors and the surfaces of all your appliances a swipe with a detergent-soaked cloth or sponge. The inside of the refrigerator is a whole other story. Read on.

BATHROOMS are a lot like kitchens. They get super-frequent use, so they need slightly more concentrated cleaning. Bathtubs host soap scum (and mildew, if you wait long enough between cleanings). Sinks can become caked with toothpaste spittle and congested with hair in no time. Toilets—well, we all know what goes in there. Put on some rubber gloves, prepare the cleaning solutions on page 51, grab a sponge and a toilet brush, and have at it every week or so.

cleaning the fridge

If you've recently noticed an odor that surfaces every time you open your refrigerator door—one that's the opposite of appetizing—or if you've become aware of bergs in your freezer that could scuttle the Titanic, it's time to tend to the appliance you depend on to keep your food cool and fresh.

BASIC CLEANING

Unplug the refrigerator and remove everything in it. Pull out the removable parts (shelves and such), and wash them with a mild detergent in warm water. Rinse and dry them. Wash the interior walls and door with 1 to 2 tablespoons (7 to 14 g) of baking soda mixed into one quart (.95 L) warm water. Wipe the surfaces dry and leave the door open to air out the inside. Don't use commercial cleansers, chlorine bleach, or cleaning waxes on refrigerators; they can damage or corrode the plastics.

Maybe you're performing these activities not as a part of basic (that is, regular) cleaning, but as an intervention measure. In that case, the situation might call for a few more steps. If you've removed the months-old carry-out containers and washed the inside of the refrigerator and it still stinks, spread baking soda in shallow dishes and put them on the shelves. Leave the refrigerator open and unplugged for a few hours, and the baking soda should absorb any residual odors. If it doesn't, replace it with kitty litter, imitation vanilla extract, or fresh ground coffee, close the door, and run the refrigerator empty for several days.

DEFROSTING

If you don't have the self-defrosting type, you should defrost the freezer about once a year, unless frost builds up to more than 1/2 inch (1.3 cm) thick before then. Unplug the refrigerator, put on kitchen gloves to protect your hands from freezer burn, and scrape the frost out of the freezer, using a wooden or plastic scraper. Collect the ice chunks in a plastic bowl, tossing them in the sink when the bowl is full. Never use a sharp instrument to scrape with—the freezer coils are easy to damage, and so's your flesh. After you've cleared out all the frost, clean the freezer using the same system described for the inside of the refrigerator.

caring for carpets

If your apartment has wall-to-wall carpeting, you're going to need a vacuum cleaner. Only a few sections of the plush stuff? Then some serious sweeping might suffice. Regardless of the amount of carpet you're dealing with, use the following tips to keep it in shape.

■ To prevent excessive wear, note your frequent routes. Buy cheap, sturdy rugs to place over the carpet in high-traffic areas.

■ If you spill something, deal with it then. Carpets are usually treated with stain-resistant chemicals, so if you act quickly, you should be able to keep it from staining. First, blot the area until it's completely dry with a clean, dry cloth or a paper towel; scrubbing will only spread the stain. As you blot, work from the edge of the spill inward, again, to prevent spreading. If your spill is semi-solid, scrape it gently with a metal spoon after you blot it. Vacuum the area after you scrape as much of the spill off as you can. Next, clean the area with the detergent solution on page 51, or see the tips to the right on removing specific stains. If you decide to use a chemical spot remover, test it on a hidden area beforehand to make sure it won't damage the carpet.

■ Unless you signed a contract requiring you to steam-clean or provide other special cleaning of your carpeting before moving out, don't bother. Consumer studies show that results vary widely, and the service is costly.

REMOVING COMMON STAINS FROM CARPET AND FABRIC

You can either make your apartment off limits to everyone else in the world, then stand completely still in the center of a room while you're there alone, or you can go ahead and live life and use these remedies to deal with any fallout.

WINE OR GRAPE JUICE

Blot up as much of the spill as possible, then neutralize the area with a white vinegar solution: ⅓ cup (90 mL) of white vinegar mixed with ⅔ cup (160 mL) of water. Use the detergent solution on page 51 to remove the stain.

BLOOD

Everything you use on a blood stain must be cool. Heat will set the stain and make it permanent. Blot up as much of the blood as possible, then neutralize it by saturating the spot with an ammonia solution (see page 51). Continue to blot the stain. If this doesn't remove all the blood, try using the detergent solution on page 51—but remember to make it with cold water.

OIL

Oil and water don't mix—that's why it's so hard to clean oil out of anything. Your best bet is to apply isopropyl rubbing alcohol to a clean cloth, paper towel, or cotton ball, and dab the oil spot until it disappears. If this doesn't work, use a detergent solution (see page 51).

RUST

Rust can often form where the metal legs of a piece of furniture rub against the carpet. To remove the rust stains, spray lemon juice on the spot. Saturate it completely, and wait five minutes. Then blot up as much of the lemon juice as possible with a paper towel. Clean the lemon juice out of the carpet using the detergent solution on page 51.

BUBBLE GUM

Rub an ice cube over the gum to freeze it, then shatter the gum and vacuum it up.

WAX

Spread a brown paper bag over the hardened wax, and iron the bag with a warm iron. The paper will absorb the wax.

LAST-DITCH STAIN REMOVAL

If none of these solutions remove the stain, try moistening the area with three-percent hydrogen peroxide. Let it sit for an hour, then blot the stain. Repeat until the stain is gone. You won't need to rinse this solution—sunlight turns hydrogen peroxide into water.

a sensitive subject: you and your toilet

Commode. John. Porcelain God. As with many objects that are important but intimate, we use nicknames for the appliance that services us behind closed doors. But regardless of what you call it, if you don't provide your toilet with a regular dose of basic maintenance, it's not going to keep it a secret (toilets, don't forget, are frequently used by guests). Also, toilets use more water than any other appliance—up to 40 percent of your apartment's total water consumption. If your toilet isn't working properly, you could be flushing a lot of money away.

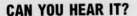

CAN YOU HEAR IT?

Most of the time, fixing a running toilet or one that doesn't flush properly is pretty simple. The first step is to take the cover off of the tank. At the bottom of the tank (all the water in there is clean!) there's a rubber flapper with a chain attached to it. If this chain is too loose, the rubber flapper could get caught between the flange and the gasket, meaning it won't seal the drain and the toilet will "run" or drain constantly. To fix this, shorten the chain by removing a few links with needle-nose pliers. Likewise, if the chain is twisted or kinked up, making it too short and tight, it'll hold up the gasket and let water seep through. Just untangle it.

If the chain isn't the problem, your toilet could be malfunctioning because the water level in the tank is too high or too low. To the right of the handle (again, on the inside of the tank) is an open tube called the overflow pipe. The water level should be ½ inch (1.3 cm) below this opening. If it isn't, you'll need to adjust the floatball (the thing that looks like a rubber balloon). To raise the water level, bend the arm that is attached to the float ball up. To lower the water level, bend the float arm down.

If neither of these things works, make sure there is no buildup on the rubber stopper or the seat that it fits on. Gently scour both the rim of the stopper and the seat so that the stopper will fit snugly. If that doesn't fix your toilet problems, call your landlord.

IT WON'T FLUSH, OR WORSE

If your toilet clogs, get a toilet plunger and put some petroleum jelly on the rim of the cup. Place the plunger over the hole at the bottom of the toilet bowl at an angle. (This will keep air from getting trapped under the cup.) There should be enough water in the bowl to cover the plunger cup. Hold the plunger upright, and push it up and down several times. This should "burp" the clog through and fix your problem. When you finish, rinse your used plunger in a mixture of one part bleach to 10 parts water.

LEAKS, PUDDLES, AND THE LIKE

If the toilet is leaking water onto the floor, it has probably shifted on its base. When a toilet shifts, the wax seal that keeps the water in breaks. To fix this, simply sit on the toilet and twist it back into its proper place. If this doesn't stop the leak, call your landlord.

In the case of absolute toilet chaos, turn off the water supply to the toilet. The shut-off valve is on a silver pipe that goes into the tank (usually on the left). Turn the handle clockwise to turn the water off, then get help from your landlord.

elementary drain theory

The drain is where the water goes after it flows out of the faucet and takes a spin around the sink or tub. That's the idea, anyway. But if food, hair, and other objects have also been filling the drain over time, it will reach a point where it no longer does what its name suggests.

PREVENTIVE MEASURES ARE THE BEST WAY TO AVOID CLOGGED DRAINS.

■ If you don't have a garbage disposal, don't pretend you do. Scrape all food scraps into the trash or compost bin before rinsing dishes. Piling food-laden plates in the sink is only inviting trouble.

■ Don't trim your bangs or shave over the bathroom sink, then rinse all the clippings down. Clean them out with a damp paper towel, and toss them in the trash.

■ Once a month, pour a few gallons of boiling water down each of your drains. The boiling water will dissolve buildup in the pipes.

Once a clog has formed, the best way to unclog it is mechanically (i.e., with elbow grease) rather than chemically. Most chemical treatments can handle minor clogs, but are not very effective otherwise. The more caustic chemicals are also hazardous to use and can even damage the pipes. Instead, try the drain cleaner solution on page 51 first. If the baking soda doesn't clear out the clog, get your plunger and some gloves. Stick the plunger cup to the area over the drain, and fill the sink with enough water to cover the cup. If you have a double sink or an overflow opening, block the second opening with a wet rag. Plunge up and down until the clog comes loose, then discard the debris. Pour boiling water down the drain to flush out any remaining debris.

If the clog in your drain persists despite your efforts, call your landlord. Some of the plumbing may have to be taken apart to find and fix the problem.

bugging out

The best way to keep unwanted guests away, you may have already discovered, is to refrain from supplying them with free meals. In the case of bugs, always store your food (especially sugar and flour) in airtight containers. Clean your counters, tables, and stove top immediately after cooking and eating. If you're going to leave the dishes until the next morning, at least scrape and rinse them.

If you end up hosting insect pests anyway, here are some deterrents, followed by a few "Fatal Final Measures"—for bugs who can't take a hint.

ANTS. Follow the trail and block their entrance with a dab of caulk. If you don't have any handy, squeeze lemon juice into the crack, then cut up the lemon and put it around the entrance. Wash surface areas with equal parts vinegar and water. **FATAL FINAL MEASURE:** *Mix 1 cup (140g) of flour with 2 cups (280g) of borax (which you can typically find at hardware stores or sometimes with laundry soap in the grocery store), and sprinkle the mixture around the foundation of your building (if you're on the ground floor) or around the ants' entrance. (Borax is highly toxic; make sure no child or pet eats it.)*

FLIES. Cover your garbage tightly. When you take out the trash, wash the garbage can thoroughly with soap and water. After it dries, sprinkle dry soap or borax into the can. **FATAL FINAL MEASURE:** *Make your own fly paper. Bring equal parts of sugar, corn syrup, and water to a boil, then spread the mixture onto brown paper, and hang it near problem areas. Avoid walking into it, and change it frequently.*

ROACHES. Never leave food out—not even pet food! Since roaches don't have many friends, all the suggestions we have are **FATAL FINAL MEASURES:** ❶ *If you don't have to worry about children or pets eating toxic substances, mix 2 tablespoons (14g) of flour with 4 tablespoons (28g) of borax and 1 tablespoon (7g) of cocoa. Put the mixture into shallow dishes, and leave it out for a roach's* **Last Supper.** *If you think this would be a terrible abuse of chocolate, mix ½ cup (98g) of borax with ¼ cup (35g) of flour, and sprinkle the powder along baseboards and door sills.* ❷ *If you need a child- or pet-safe solution, mix equal parts of baking soda and powdered sugar. Spread the mixture around the infested area. It will kill the roaches, but only taste terrible to other creatures.*

the only five cleaning products you'll ever need

Perusing aisles and aisles of cleaning products can leave you in a fresh-scented daze. Take heart—there are only five things you'll need to clean anything in your apartment, and you can buy all of them in one quick visit to a grocery store.

1 White distilled vinegar is used in many common cleaning solutions.

2 Dish soap or detergent is another common cleaning substance. Brands that are dye- and fragrance-free and don't contain lanolin or bleach are best for mixing with other products to create other cleaning solutions (read on).

3 Ammonia is also commonly used in cleaning solutions.

4 Baking soda neutralizes acidic odors and is slightly abrasive.

5 Washing soda is stronger than baking soda. You'll find it in the store's laundry section. Always wear gloves when using washing soda.

basic cleaning solutions using your five products

DETERGENT SOLUTION (ALL-PURPOSE)
Mix ¼ teaspoon (1.25 mL) of liquid dishwashing detergent with 1 cup (240 mL) of lukewarm water.

**AMMONIA SOLUTION
(ALL-PURPOSE; ESPECIALLY GOOD FOR KITCHENS AND BATHS)**
Mix 2 tablespoons (15 mL) of household ammonia per cup (240 mL) of water.

**WASHING SODA SOLUTION
(ALL-PURPOSE; GREAT FOR SERIOUS GRIME AND MILDEW)**
Mix ½ teaspoon (2.5 mL) of washing soda with 2 cups (480 mL) of hot water in a spray bottle.

WINDOW CLEANER
Pour ¼ cup (60 mL) of white vinegar, 2 cups (480 mL) of water and ½ teaspoon (2.5 mL) of liquid detergent into a spray bottle.

FURNITURE CLEANER
Combine ¼ cup (60 mL) of white vinegar in a bowl with a few drops of vegetable oil.

SCOURING POWDER
You can use straight baking soda for this.

SOFT SCRUBBER
Mix ¼ cup (35 g) of baking soda with enough liquid detergent to create a frosting-like consistency.

DRAIN CLEANER
Pour 1 cup (140 g) of baking soda down the drain, followed by 3 cups (720 mL) of boiling water.

OVEN CLEANER
Sprinkle ¼ inch (6 mm) of baking soda over the bottom of the oven. Keep the baking soda moist by periodically spraying water on it. Let it sit for six hours or overnight, then scoop the baking soda out and rinse the oven well.

Always rinse all these solutions thoroughly. Any residue will attract dirt quickly.

PROJECTS & IDEAS

We start with your apartment's surface elements: walls, floors, and windows. If you're the only first-apartment dweller in the whole world who's entirely satisfied with these features just the way they are, skip ahead. If not, sift through our plans for doctoring, decorating, and, when necessary, disguising them. After that, we move on to ways you can use lighting, furniture, accessories, and storage tactics to turn your apartment's bare rooms into a home that's undeniably your own.

walls

You can't miss them, so it's best if you enjoy looking at them. We give you ways to both play up your walls and to cover them over, depending on what you have to work with.

paint just one

Dark to airy, or sterile to cozy. The section on wall-painting basics, page 22, tells you how to successfully coat the walls of your apartment with fresh paint. Here are some of the reasons (besides the fact that it's faster and easier) that you might want to stop at one.

DEFINITION. If a room is especially boxy, meaning it's in danger of looking boring, painting one wall a color that's different from the rest is a good way to give it some dimension. It's also an easy way to accent the interesting lines of a room that's anything but boxy, such as the bedroom of the converted attic apartment shown here.

DRAMA. Paint all four walls citron green or the deep red of your velvet love seat, and chances are it'll be too much. But cover just one wall in a brave new color, and you have a definite statement.

SEPARATION. Maybe one section of your small space serves as your home office. Or, perhaps your sleeping and living areas must coexist within the same four walls. Painting one of those walls a different color can help visually separate one area from another.

COHERENCE. At the same time wall colors can help separate the contents of a room, they can also tie them together. Say the only link among your otherwise motley collection of furniture and accessories is the saffron stripe on the sofa that matches the lamp shade on the other side of the room. Splash that same saffron on the wall between the two, and you have instant unity.

clip cord

You have neither the time nor the energy to purchase and mount one of those boring cork-and-wood bulletin boards so you can pin up all your postcards, concert tickets, and bills. Nevertheless, the wall in front of your work space is the perfect holding place for odds and ends like these. Here's the simple—dare we say idiot-proof?—and elegant way out. Tack up one or more clip cords as you need them.

WHAT YOU NEED

Push pins, decorative tacks, screw eyes, screw hooks, or nails

A not-too-stretchy cord: cotton string, nylon cord, picture wire, plastic coated electrical or cable wire are all options

Colored paper clips, bulldog clips, clothespins, decorative bobby pins, etc.

WHAT YOU DO

1 Cut a length of your cord. Three or four feet (90 to 120 cm) will suffice. Too long a cord will droop.

2 Based on your wall (and the terms of your lease), determine what type of anchors you'll use to hang your cord. A temporary, movable, and low-impact choice would be pushpins or tacks. More permanent anchors—nails and screw eyes—will leave larger holes to fill if you move them or leave the apartment.

3 Hang your light bill and the postcards from Cancun from the cord with simple clips. Use only one type of clip on the cord to unify the display; mix clips if you want it more vibrant. Change the display frequently. If you don't pay the light bill on time, display the cut-off notice as a piece of whimsy.

plotting where pictures go

Even though picture-hanging nails are tiny and leave only pin-prick size holes, pounding a bunch of them into a wall, hanging up every framed item you own, *then* standing back to take a look is not exactly the best way to figure out what you want where. Try this instead.

PICTURE THIS

You don't have to own paintings or photographs to cover your walls with interesting colors, lines, and shapes. Wall art comes in all kinds of forms. Try framing and hanging:

Postcards

Maps

Fabric remnants

Vintage game boards

Typed poems

Old letters

Pressed flowers and leaves

Playing cards

Steamed-off labels from bottles of wine or imported olive oil

Blueprints

Old album covers

Pages from a 1950s cookbook, etiquette book, or cocktail-making guide

In case you somehow missed this little gem of information back when you were living in a college dorm, here's one of life's timeless tips: to fill nail holes in a wall, use plain white toothpaste. It won't sink into the holes the way spackling compound often does.

WHAT YOU DO

1 Trace all your pictures onto pieces of paper (paper bags work well), and cut out the shapes.

2 If the backs of the framed pictures are equipped with hanging wire, pull the wire taut on each, and measure from the top of the wire's arc to the top of the frame. On the matching paper template, measure down from the top edge the distance of your measurement, and mark where the picture-hanging nail or hook will meet the wire. If the backs of your pictures feature saw-toothed hangers rather than wire, measure how far down they are from the top edge on each picture, and transfer those marks to the corresponding templates.

3 Use a low-tack tape (both drafting tape and painter's tape work well) to hang the templates on the wall (marked sides facing out), then reconfigure them as much as you like, until you're happy with where each is hanging.

4 Hammer your nails (and picture hooks, if you're using them) through the marks on the templates and right into the wall, then rip the paper off and hang your pictures.

CONFIGURATIONS

STAIR STEPPING. Align the center points of your pictures diagonally.

TOPS OR BOTTOMS IN ALIGNMENT. Draw together a group of various-sized pictures by aligning all their tops or all their bottoms along an imaginary horizontal line.

COMBINATION ALIGNMENT. Divide a larger group of various-sized pictures into two or more rows, and align the tops of the top-row pictures and the bottoms of the bottom-row pictures on imaginary horizontal lines, then line up the sides as well. The grouping on the preceding page is an example of combination alignment.

GALLERY STYLE. Hang identical-sized pictures in a long, neat row, either horizontal or vertical.

MOSAIC. Anything goes, with a bit of method to the madness. Give your mosaic display some balance by aligning the bottoms of some frames with the tops of others and/or by centering some pictures over others. You can also soften a rigid-looking arrangement by adding in a few rounded or octagonal frames.

57

WALLS

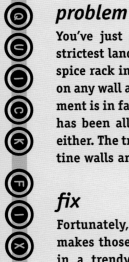

problem

You've just signed a lease with the world's strictest landlord. No painting, no mounting a spice rack in the kitchen, no hanging pictures on any wall anywhere. The upside is, the apartment is in fabulous shape—no previous tenant has been allowed to alter any of its surfaces either. The trouble, of course, is that those pristine walls are awfully bare.

fix

Fortunately, there's a simple solution that makes those bare walls look as if they belong in a trendy gallery: artfully prop pictures, paintings, mirrors, and other framed pieces right up against them. Rest large pieces like this full-length mirror on the floor. Ledges, molding strips, mantles, and the tops of free-standing shelf units, benches, and tables all work well as bases for smaller ones.

five-step plan for finding the right roommate

**So, your budget dictates the need for a roommate.
Thrilled? Terrified? Relax and follow these five steps.**

1. Clarify for Yourself What You Expect

A roommate is a person who shares expenses and space; a roommate is not a guaranteed best friend. However, a roommate must be someone you can trust to respect you, your privacy, and your belongings. Articulate what that means for you. Would you rather your new roommate not have lots of out-of-town visitors who stay with you? Do you expect that you and your roommate will have separate phone lines? What amount of noise is acceptable? At what hour should acceptable noise end so that either roommate can enjoy the silence and work, study, or sleep? Are smoking and drinking acceptable? When and where?

2. Meet the Would-Be Roommates

Depending on your community and situation, you may run an ad, post a flyer, or use word-of-mouth to come up with a pool of potential roommates. Meet with each, ideally in a public place. Share the list of expectations you came up with in step 1. Let her or him know the facts of your lifestyle and the living situation you want, then move on to the discussion items in step 3. If you're interviewing several people, make notes so you remember who said what. If you sense that someone would be a good roommate, collect contact information for references.

3. Five Topics You Must Discuss

These issues come up constantly, regardless of the age or lifestyle of roommates. Talk about them now.

BILL PAYING

You want all bills divided equally and paid on time. Discuss who will make payments and in whose name the lease and utilities will be. (It's best to list all roommates.) Agree that nonessential services (cable television, cable modem, magazine subscriptions) must be negotiated beforehand or will be paid for by the roommate who orders them.

GUESTS

Guests can feel like invaders if you haven't adopted rules to govern their behavior. Agree on the answers to the questions of who, what, when, where, how long, and overnight or not. Also, "house rules" about pets, smoking or drinking, borrowing, and privacy should apply to guests as well.

CLEANLINESS

What's "clean enough"? Who will clean what, and how often? You want chores shared, guaranteeing clean shared rooms (bathroom, kitchen, living room).

PERSONAL POSSESSIONS

If you want to avoid hassles about who ate the last piece of cake and used up the shampoo, agree from the start not to share anything but toilet paper.

SAFETY

Should doors and windows be locked when you're home, when you're sleeping, and/or when no one is home? Where will an extra key be kept? Who else gets a key?

4. Check References

Talk to former roommates, landlords, and the current employer of your would-be roommates. Ask about their bill-paying history. Verify a steady income. Check out any concerns you have.

5. Make the Decision

You've spoken with many interesting people you might never have otherwise met. You've been charmed and repelled. You've checked out their stories. You should be as ready as you'll ever be now to decide whose personality and lifestyle is most compatible with yours.

cover-up message center

If you've got an ugly or even just a blank wall you'd rather not have staring you in the face, here's a useful way to cover a huge portion of it. Frame up a panel of white board next to a panel of steel (you can buy these as big as you like), and you've got one spot for jotting erasable notes and another for sticking lists, both conveniently located right next to each other. Bonus: it's a cinch to make your message center completely your own with a set of personalized magnets.

WHAT YOU NEED

Piece of ½-inch (1.3cm) plywood for the base (This one measures 28 x 34 inches [71.1 x 86.4cm].)

Panel of 26-gauge steel and one of white tile board (These pieces need to cover the unframed portion of your plywood base, with the tile board overlapping the steel by about ½ inch [1.3cm]. The steel here measures 16 x 26 inches [40.6 x 66 cm], and the tile board measures 15 x 24 inches [38.1 x 61 cm].)

2¼-inch (5.7cm) primed molding (You need two pieces to frame the long sides of your message center and two pieces to frame the short sides.)

Liquid nails (the kind in a tube)

Black spray paint

Acrylic paints

Finishing nails

Wood filler

Picture-hanging kit (screw eyelets, wire, etc.)

Handsaw

Miter box (This inexpensive contraption serves as a guide for your saw when you make angled cuts.)

Small artist's brushes

Hammer

WHAT YOU DO

1 The home improvement store where you buy your supplies should be able to cut almost everything to size for you. All you'll have to do is make the 45° diagonal cuts where the molding fits together—known as miter cuts. The miter box will guide your saw so you can cut the ends of your molding pieces (see figure 1).

2 Place the tile board and steel on top of the plywood base. Put the tile board on the left and the steel on the right, with the tile board overlapping the steel by ½ inch (1.3cm). Place the molding around the edges, making sure everything fits before you glue it all together.

3 Remove the molding, and trace the outside edges of the tile board and steel, so you have a guide for putting them back in place.

4 Remove the tile board and steel, coat the back of each panel with liquid nails, and set them back in place. Liquid nails work best if you run a bead of the adhesive about ½ inch (1.3cm) in from the edge of each panel, then drizzle it all over the center. Clean up any misplaced adhesive with hot soapy water right away.

5 Place books or other heavy objects on the corners of the glued panels and down the center where they overlap, and let them dry.

6 Spray the molding black and let it dry. If you like, add detail lines or dots around the molding in other paint colors. The bottom end of an artist's brush is perfect for dabbing on paint dots.

7 Glue the molding around the edges of the message center with liquid nails; it'll overlap both the tile board and the steel slightly.

8 Once the adhesive on the molding is dry, use finishing nails around the edges to further secure it to the plywood.

9 If necessary, use wood filler to spackle any variations in the molding where you pounded the nails or around the corners, then touch up the areas with paint.

10 Install screw eyelets on the back, following the directions on the picture-hanging kit.

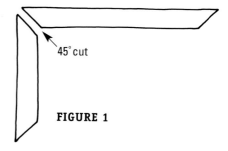

45° cut

FIGURE 1

making magnets

Home improvement stores sell small sets of magnets (rounds, squares, rectangles, etc.), as well as magnetic paper with an adhesive front. To turn these raw materials into one-of-a-kind magnets for the steel side of your message center, either hot glue trinkets (shellacked and painted dog bones, for example) to the magnets, or attach photos to the adhesive side of the magnetic paper, and cut them out.

spiffing up by season

Flip to the opening calendar spread of a certain home decorating magazine (we're not naming names), and, depending on the time of year, you'll be told that October 6 is the day for piling red apples in a wooden bowl or that, come the first Saturday in April, you'd better be coloring eggs. We're guessing that you may not be quite so exacting about plotting what you'll do when. Still, it's nice to do something to celebrate the natural wonder of moving from one season to another.

SPRING

Fasten a row of hand-made straw whisk brooms to your wall. (Great substitute for actual spring cleaning!)

Hand-stitch sheer pockets onto a light-weight curtain, and put pressed flowers (or four-leaf clovers if you can find them) inside.

Put window boxes on your windowsills, and fill them with potted pansies.

Force some bulbs, maybe paper whites or amaryllis.

Weave greenery or budding branches around a light fixture.

Remove the labels from metal cans, paint the cans with a creamy color, and use them as vases for the season's first flowers.

Find an umbrella printed with a motif you like (rubber ducks, multiple Mona Lisa faces, etc.), and place it, opened, in a corner. Skip this one if you're superstitious, of course.

SUMMER

Turn a light cotton tapestry into a no-sew slipcover. Just throw it over a couch or chair, and tuck it in around the edges.

Put driftwood, water-smoothed rocks, and clear bottles filled with sand on display. If you like, drop decorative slips of paper in the bottles, telling where the sand came from or naming the friends or family you were with when you collected it.

Fill a clear pitcher with whole lemons.

String paper lanterns around a room.

Make a bouquet out of nothing but fresh herbs.

Burn candles inside glass lanterns or hurricanes.

Stick pictures from your favorite childhood summer vacations around the edges of a mirror—or upright in a bowl of beach sand.

Pile produce from a local outdoor market in a big bowl for an instant summery centerpiece.

Stack all your favorite summer reads beside a table lamp, then top off the stack with a seashell or two.

FALL

Switch some of your lightbulbs to rose or gold.

String colorful leaves into garlands to hang over doors or windows.

Fill a few interesting jars with nuts still in their shells, and stack them in a clever way on your coffee table.

Add a layer of uncooked wild rice or unpopped popcorn to the bottom of a tray, and nestle votive candles in it.

Use a shallow, open basket as a container for odd-shaped squashes and gourds (you can buy these by the sack at supermarkets).

Laminate some of the prettiest leaves outside your door (a print shop can do this), cut them out, and use them as coasters.

Arrange barley, wheat, or other dried grasses in tin flower buckets (craft stores sell them), or tie them up with raffia and hang them upside down from doorknobs or hooks in the wall.

WINTER

Drape a cozy blanket or shawl over the back of the couch.

Cut out paper snowflakes, and dangle them at different heights by clear thread in your windows.

Dust pinecones, seed pods, and pomegranates lightly with glitter, and show them off in bowls or baskets.

Run a row of poinsettias along a hallway, windowsill, or wall.

Fill a colored-glass cup with a collection of thermometers (even better if some are from an antique shop).

Make a bouquet out of bare, twisted branches.

Create a bowl of good cheer by filling it with tiny, sparkly tree ornaments and a strand of minilights.

Push a bunch of red and white plastic tacks randomly into a wall, and hang candy canes from them.

hanging walls

We all know walls are a good thing to tear down when it comes to divided countries and blocked communication. But in a small, open apartment where you have a lot going on, you may wish you could put a few more up. Floor-to-ceiling sheetrock is probably not an option, but here are two simple fabric partitions that do a fine job of separating one area from another.

hanging walls variation ONE

WHAT YOU NEED

Curtain panels with rod pockets

Wooden dowel (Be sure the diameter fits the rod pocket at the top of the curtain panel. Buy a dowel longer than your curtain panel is wide; you'll cut it to size.)

Wooden lattice strip (Again, buy a strip that's longer than you need so you can cut it to size.)

Wall or ceiling anchors with hooks

Curtain rings with clips

Iron

Measuring tool

Handsaw

WHAT YOU DO

1 Iron your curtain panel.

2 Measure the width of the panel. Add 2 inches (5.1 cm) to the measurement, measure and mark the dowel with this longer measurement, and cut the dowel to size with the handsaw.

3 The lattice strip will weight the bottom of the panel, so it hangs straight and flat. To determine the length you need, slide the strip into the hem casing at the bottom of the panel. Push one end even with the edge of the panel, and mark the opposite end where the other edge of the panel hits. Remove the strip and use the handsaw to cut it just inside the mark.

4 The fabric panels in the apartment shown here hang from an exposed pipe that just happens to span the right portion of the room. If your apartment is missing this handy feature, you can hang your panels from ceiling hooks (the same sort used for hanging plant baskets). Attach the ceiling hooks to the ceiling, spacing them so they'll be a couple of inches (5.1 cm) in from the ends of the dowel rod.

5 Insert the dowel into the rod pocket. Clip each end of the dowel rod with the curtain ring clips, and hang the ring portions from the ceiling hooks.

6 Insert the lattice strip in the bottom hem casing.

Use copper plumbing pipe that's $1/2$ to $3/4$ inch thick (1.3 to 1.9 cm) in place of the wooden dowels and lattice strips, if you want panels with more of an industrial look. You can have your pipe cut at the home improvement store where you purchase it.

If you're on friendly terms with a sewing machine, you can sew your own panels from any fabric you like—or from plain muslin you've dressed up yourself with rubber stamps and fabric ink. Just stitch a simple casing at the top and bottom of the fabric for the dowel and lattice strip.

decorating your first apartment

WHAT YOU DO

1 Measure the height and width of the space where you want your hanging wall. Purchase a pair (or more) of ready-made curtain panels to fit it. Count the number of tabs or ties on each curtain panel; you'll need at least that many pegs. The more pegs you have, the more flexibility you have when you're positioning the panels.

2 Purchase your board and pegs at a home improvement store. Most stores offer free cuts on the lumber you purchase. If you don't want to saw the board to size, have it done at the store.

3 Measure and mark your board at 6-inch (15.2 cm) intervals. Screw the pegs into the board at each mark. To make it easier, make starter holes for the pegs by driving a nail partway into the board at each mark or drilling partway in with a bit about the same size as the screw.

4 Cover your work area, and paint the board and pegs. (Anything goes here: board one color, pegs another; colors that match or contrast with the others in the room; up to you.) Let the paint dry, then recoat everything as needed.

5 Drill a hole at each end of the board with a bit approximately the same size as your drywall screw.

6 Get a friend to help you hold the board in place while you screw it into the wall at each end. Be sure you screw into a stud (a piece of the wooden frame behind the wall) each time. The studs should be right where you need them for a job like this; they're always on either side of windows and doorways.

7 Hang the curtains on the pegs.

hanging walls variation TWO

This variation also makes a good door if you're missing one in a crucial spot (entryway, closet opening, etc.). Or, it can be adapted to work as a window covering.

WHAT YOU NEED

Ready-made tab-top or tie-top curtain panels

Strip of board cut to match the width of the area you want to cover

Wooden pegs with screws

Acrylic or latex paint

Finish nails or drywall screws

Measuring tool

Handsaw (optional)

Drill and drill bits (optional)

Screwdriver

Paintbrush

Hammer

Stepladder or sturdy chair

A friend with nothing to do

home electronics

If recorded music, cable cooking shows, and Internet access seem as necessary to you as indoor plumbing, you're going to have to invest in some gadgetry. What you buy and where you put it will depend on a number of factors: lifestyle, budget, and apartment size—not to mention number of outlets and phone jacks. Here are a few tips for selecting and setting up home electronics.

first things first

Home electronics are generally expensive. Base your buys on what your lifestyle demands and allows. Don't own any compact discs or vinyl albums, and don't expect to anytime soon? Get a clock radio instead of a stereo. If you need to work your way up to a stereo, buy a small boom box that plays cassette tapes and CDs. Are movies at home one of your favorite escapes? Get a television and VCR or DVD player. Let your budget, apartment size, and personal priorities help you decide among a compact unit, an elaborate setup, or something in between. Do you do most of your Internet accessing from home rather than the office, or do you work from home? A hard drive, monitor, and Internet connection via your phone line are basics; a printer, scanner, CD burner, and cable modem are extras to consider, based on your situation.

location, location, location

Don't locate electronic equipment near water sources, such as kitchen faucets, leaky ceilings, or windows that are sometimes open. It's best to set up stereos, televisions, and the like against walls, so you and others will be less likely to bump and damage them. And, here's the big news flash: electronics require electricity. If you don't want cords running across floors or along long stretches of walls, place equipment near outlets. Avoid overloading your wiring, and notify your landlord if you have problems.

special care for specific equipment

STEREO. If you've invested in a full stereo system (receiver, amp, CD player, tape deck, record player, speakers), stack the components, following the manufacturer's recommendations. You may need a multi-outlet extension cord to plug in all the pieces. Place speakers at least 6 feet (1.8m) apart and at the same height, level with where your ears will be when listening. (Most likely, that's seated in a chair or couch 6 feet [1.8m] from and centered between the speakers.) Run speaker wires along wall bases or under rugs.

HOME ENTERTAINMENT CENTER. Store the elements of a home entertainment center (large television, VCR or DVD player, speakers, gaming equipment), in a prefabricated unit, on appropriate shelving, or on sturdy end tables. Again, you may need a multi-outlet extension cord to plug in all the pieces. Position at least some of the room's seating, centered on the television screen, 6 feet (1.8m) away. Lamplight causes less interference with television screens than overhead lighting.

COMPUTER. Treat yourself to some in-home ergonomics, including a desk that doesn't hold your computer so high you have to look up at it and a comfortable chair. Position your setup so your screen isn't hit with direct light from a window. Keep accessories (CD burner, scanner, printer, etc.) off the floor, preferably in a cart. One more time, you'll likely need that multi-outlet extension cord to connect all your pieces to your power source.

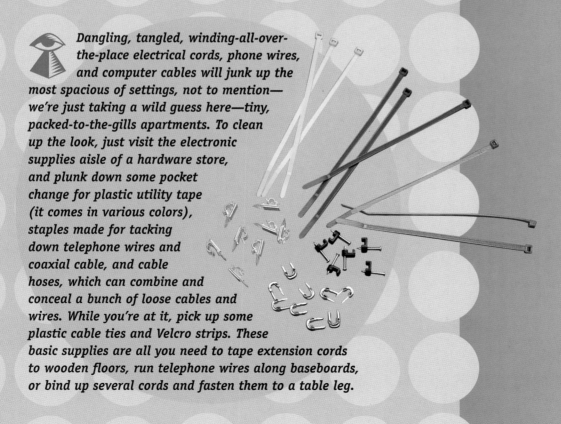

Dangling, tangled, winding-all-over-the-place electrical cords, phone wires, and computer cables will junk up the most spacious of settings, not to mention— we're just taking a wild guess here—tiny, packed-to-the-gills apartments. To clean up the look, just visit the electronic supplies aisle of a hardware store, and plunk down some pocket change for plastic utility tape (it comes in various colors), staples made for tacking down telephone wires and coaxial cable, and cable hoses, which can combine and conceal a bunch of loose cables and wires. While you're at it, pick up some plastic cable ties and Velcro strips. These basic supplies are all you need to tape extension cords to wooden floors, run telephone wires along baseboards, or bind up several cords and fasten them to a table leg.

wall cover two ways

In addition to glaring white, apartment walls can come in the following styles: cracked, scuffed, gouged, peeling, and an ugly color you're not allowed to paint over. Here are two different fabric-based coverups that help disguise a wall that needs it. Depending on the state of your walls, you may want to whip up extra-large versions of both.

wall cover ONE

WHAT YOU NEED

8 metal washers, about 2½ inches (6.4 cm) in diameter

16 metal shower curtain clips

⅝-inch (1.6 cm) inexpensive metal curtain rod

Hammered-metal finish spray paint

1 yard (.9m) of material

½ yard (.45m) of trim material

No-sew hem tape

Iron and ironing board

Grommet kit with ⅝-inch (1.6 cm) grommets

WHAT YOU DO

1 Spray the washers, shower curtain clips, curtain rod and hardware, and grommets with the hammered-metal paint. Let the pieces dry.

2 Cut your larger piece of fabric to the length and width you want, keeping in mind that the finished piece will be approximately 8 inches (20.3 cm) longer with the trim and hanging hardware.

3 Following the directions on the packaging, use the hem tape to finish off the sides of the large piece.

4 Cut two 8-inch (20.3 cm) strips of the trim fabric, making the strips about 2 inches (5.1 cm) longer than the width of the main fabric panel. Fold over the short ends of both strips, and hem them with the hem tape. Make sure the finished length of the two strips matches exactly the width of the main fabric piece.

5 Fold the trim strips in half lengthwise, and press them. Fold the raw edges into the pressed crease, and press again.

6 Place the main fabric on the ironing board. Fit one trim strip over one end of the main fabric, making sure the ends line up, with no overhang, and that the fabric is straight. Attach the strip with hem tape. Attach the other strip to the other end of the main fabric, following the same process.

7 Use the grommet kit and the instructions that come with it to attach grommets to the top and bottom of the wall hanging. Make sure they're evenly spaced and all the same distance from the edge of the hanging.

8 Attach shower clips through the grommets. Thread the curtain rod through the clips at the top of the hanging. Attach the washers through the clips at the bottom.

9 Hang the piece with the curtain rod hardware.

wall cover TWO

You can, of course, simply hang purchased batik panels or tapestries inside old window frames. But if you want to make your own, scan the Batik Primer box below and follow the steps on page 71.

BATIK PRIMER

Batik is a way to resist-dye fabric, with wax serving as the resist. You pour or brush melted wax onto fabric. When it cools, it hardens in position and repels the dye. If you start with undyed fabric, the fabric's original color becomes part of your design. You can also wax areas that have been dyed already, and overdye them. Let's say you wax a circle on a white panel, then immerse the panel in yellow dye. Remove the wax, and you've now got a yellow panel with a white circle on it. Then, suppose you wax a triangle next to the circle and immerse the panel in blue dye. Remove this wax, and you now have a green panel with a white circle and a yellow triangle.

As you can see, this mixing of colors is the fun part, but it also takes some thinking ahead. Take a look at the color wheel on page 108 to figure out what color you get when you mix any other two together, then plot out your color sequence on a piece of paper before you start.

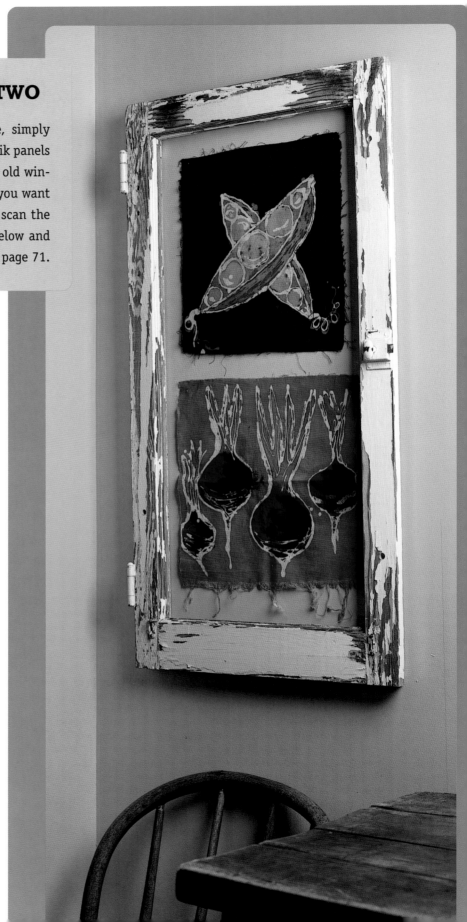

WHAT YOU NEED

Photocopies of images you want to transfer (optional)

Cold-water dyes in as many colors as your design calls for

Panels of 100-percent cotton fabric

Charcoal pen or chalk

Newspaper

Wax (Most craft stores sell batik wax. You need enough to create about 1 cup [240 mL] of melted wax.)

Wax paper

Grocery bags

Mix of half water and half vinegar in a misting bottle (optional)

Salvaged frame (window frame, picture frame, etc.)

Hangers for frame

Pushpins

Wax melter (You need a way to heat the wax slowly without overheating it. An electric skillet or small deep-fat fryer with a thermostatic heat control is ideal, but you'll need to use it for nothing other than wax melting. You can also use a double boiler.)

Several small paintbrushes or a tjanting tool (Tjantings, sold in art stores, have small metal reservoirs that hold the hot wax and heat-proof wooden handles. They create fine, precise lines of wax. They're not expensive, but they're also not essential.)

Iron

Hammer

Drill and drill bits (optional)

 If you use paintbrushes to apply your wax, they won't be usable for other purposes, so just let them cool off in the wax, then heat them up and reuse them for another batik project later.

Some of the wax you apply will crack, creating a spidery or cracked-glass effect where it does. This is part of the charm of batik, not a mistake. In fact, if you really like it, you can encourage cracking by wadding up your waxed fabric before you dye it.

WHAT YOU DO

1 Either sketch out the images you want to transfer to your fabric panels, or cut out the photocopied images you've chosen. Plan the color sequence you want to use when you dye.

2 With charcoal or chalk, transfer the images to the fabric.

3 Mix your dyes according to their package instructions.

4 Cover your work area with newspaper.

5 Melt the wax. It's ready when it flows like water. Test it on a scrap of fabric. If it looks transparent and it saturates the fabric thoroughly, it's ready. If it still looks milky on the fabric, it's not hot enough.

6 Put a piece of wax paper between the newspaper and your fabric, and apply your first layer of wax to certain elements of your design, using a paintbrush or a tjanting. Because wax dries quickly, you need to work quickly. Be sure it saturates the fabric.

7 Saturate the fabric in the first dye, then hang it to dry. Turn the heated wax off while the fabric is drying.

8 When you're ready for the next layer, reheat the wax, paint it over the next elements of your design, saturate the fabric in the second dye, and hang it to dry. Continue this process until you've completed the sequence you mapped out.

9 Once the final dye has dried, put the cloth between two pieces of brown grocery bags (printed side facing away from the wax), set your iron on high, and iron the cloth (with the bags providing protection) until all the wax is soaked up by the bags. If the bags become too saturated as you iron, replace them.

10 Once all the wax is completely removed from the fabric, you can further set your dyes by spritzing the fabric with the water-vinegar mixture and ironing it directly with your iron set on medium high.

11 Hang your frame, using either a hammer and picture-hanging nails or screws and a drill, depending on the size and weight of your frame.

12 Pin the fabric to the wall inside the frame.

floors

You come into immediate, physical contact with your floor every single day. If you hit the jackpot and you're traipsing around on pristine-condition hardwood, skip ahead. If not, here are ways to cover, color, accent, and modernize your area underfoot.

canvas floor cover

Why not pad around on your own little patch of personalized art? This one features a collage of fabric remnants, but you can also paint, sponge, stencil, or stamp on canvas to make lightweight, durable, one-of-a-kind floor covers.

WHAT YOU NEED

Prehemmed canvas (Art and craft stores carry them in a range of sizes.)

Liquid fabric dye in a color of your choice

Fabric remnants cut into rectangles measuring about 4½ x 5 inches (11.4 x 12.7 cm)

Fabric glue

Polyurethane sealer

Iron

Small sponge brush

Small scissors or nail clippers

Large nylon paintbrush

 Use warm soapy water and a sponge to spot clean your floor cover when it needs it.

WHAT YOU DO

1 Dye your canvas in a washing machine, following the directions on the dye packaging. Dry and iron the canvas.

2 Arrange the fabric remnants on the canvas. Eyeballing the arrangement rather than perfectly measuring the placement of each piece gives the floor cover a more casual feel.

3 With the sponge brush, spread an even layer of fabric glue on the back of each remnant, then flip each over and set it back in place on the canvas. Smooth the front sides of the remnants, adding more fabric glue to the tops of the pieces, if necessary.

4 Stand back and take a look. Rearrange any pieces that need it, then let the fabric glue dry.

5 Use the scissors or nail clippers to clip any frayed strings on the remnant edges.

6 Apply a thin coat of polyurethane to the surface of the floor cover with the large nylon paintbrush. Let it dry completely, then add a second coat.

mod floor modules

Seagrass squares come in sewn-together sets you can snip apart or stitch to others to create a floor covering that's the size and shape you need— that much the salespeople at the home decorating stores that carry them can tell you. What they may not know is that the muted, neutral colors those squares come in can be livened up in no time with paint and cardboard stencils.

WHAT YOU NEED

Seagrass squares (They're sold at home-decorating stores and through catalogs, typically in sets of six or so sewn together. Buy as many as you need to create a floor cover that's the size you want.)

Yellow acrylic latex, semigloss (About 1 quart [.95 L] should be enough.)

Red spray paint, semigloss or high gloss, 1 can

Black acrylic paint, 1 tube

2 cardboard squares (One should be the same size as your seagrass squares; the other can be slightly smaller.)

2 guides for drawing circles (glasses, bowls, etc.), one that will make a circle about 1½ inches (3.8 cm) larger in diameter than the other

Drop cloth

Small scissors (optional)

Needle and sturdy upholstery thread (optional)

2 paintbrushes, 1 large and 1 small

Craft knife

WHAT YOU DO

1 If necessary, snip the string holding your seagrass squares together or attach sets of squares to one another, using the needle and upholstery thread, to come up with a floor cover that's the size and shape you want.

2 Dilute the yellow paint, one-to-one, with water.

3 Using the large paintbrush, apply yellow paint to the front, back, and edges of the floor cover. Allow the paint to saturate the fibers, and then dry completely.

4 Use your smaller circle guide to mark a circle in the center of the larger cardboard square. Cut it out with the craft knife. The square with the cutout becomes your template for spraying red dots on each seagrass square.

5 Begin at the center of your floor cover and work outward. Place the cardboard template on a seagrass square, and spray red paint in the cutout circle area. Repeat until you've painted all the squares with red dots. Let the paint dry.

6 Create a second template from the smaller cardboard square. Mark a circle in the center using the larger circle guide, and cut it out.

7 To paint the black rings, go back to the center of your floor cover. Place the smaller cutout circle (from step 4) over the red dot to mask it, and center your new template around it. Press both cardboard pieces firmly in place, and paint the space in between with the black paint, using the small brush. Repeat until you've painted black rings around all the red dots. Let the paint dry.

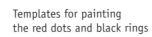

Templates for painting the red dots and black rings

Buy a few extra seagrass squares, and paint place mats or trivets to match your floor cover.

rubber mat kitchen floor

You spent all that time fantasizing about gathering with your friends in your snazzy new kitchen to sip, chat, and whip up fabulously cosmopolitan meals. Now, you're faced with the ugly reality—linoleum in rust or avocado green that looks as if people have been standing on it and throwing together tuna-noodle casseroles for years. Believe it or not, your vision can still be salvaged. Quite easily, as a matter of fact.

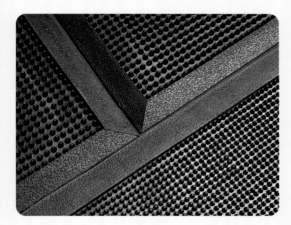

With their utilitarian appeal, rubber floor coverings can instantly modernize the most hopeless of surfaces. You'll find industrial-size rubber mats at restaurant supply outlets; they'll make your floor fit for the best of chefs, should you happen to know some. Or, you can simply use heavy-duty tape, as we did here, to connect the back side of several door mats, creating an urban-look floor cover that fits the size and shape of your space exactly.

first rites

Blessing a new dwelling is an ancient custom practiced the world over. Does it evict the negative energy of previous tenants or portend a comfortable future for you and yours? Maybe. But appropriately christening a new space definitely offers the psychological benefit of a fresh start. Here are some ideas to pick and choose from to create a ceremony that suits you.

CHARMS. Purify your home with natural items. Lay thorny branches near your doorstep, hang a sprig of seaweed in the kitchen, or place lilacs here and there. All are said to dispel evil spirits. A jar of alfalfa in a kitchen cupboard invites prosperous energy to the home. Fresh bamboo is thought to do the same. A sprinkle of sugar or salt (sprinkled, not spilled) is believed to cleanse a room of negative energies.

CLEANING. Unlike an aura, dirt is a residue everyone can see. Clean your new apartment thoroughly. Open all windows and doors, and let in lots of fresh air. Light scented candles and your favorite incense when you're finished, to infuse your new space with the aroma of spices and flowers of your choosing.

CUSTOMS. Many religions have house blessings. Native Americans of the Blackfoot tribe burn sage to purify and cleanse a space. An ancient Hebrew blessing instructs you to bring bread, water, salt, and a candle from your previous living space, make saltwater and sprinkle some on the bread, then light the candle. Improvise a verbal blessing, and take the candle to each window of the apartment. Let the candle shine out each window for a few seconds, then mark the windowsill with the saltwater. Mark all of the doorposts with the saltwater, too. Finally, eat the bread, and return to your old home before moving in.

HERBS. Use the fragrance of herbs to evoke specific moods. Hang a sprig of chamomile (a calming herb) to combat the chaos of unpacking. Let the invigorating scent of cedar bring you strength for all the activity. If you've taken the time to cast out bad spirits, set out eucalyptus oil or leaves to keep them (and, according to folklore, criminals) out. A pinch of thyme eaten before sleep is supposed to bring you good dreams. Why not try it for your first night in your new home?

checkerboard floor

If your landlord says it's okay to splash some paint on your apartment's wood floor (highly possible if it already features a paint job), you've got three choices. You can replicate exactly the bold, graphic pattern shown here. You can scale down this idea and create a painted-in-place checkerboard rug. Or, you can forget this design entirely, and simply use the techniques we describe to paint on a pattern you have in mind—or to roll on a solid color.

WHAT YOU NEED

Wood stripper and/or methylated spirit (optional)

Undercoat or primer

Paint (See page 25 for info on types.)

Roller and brushes

Varnish

Floor polisher (You can rent one at a grocery store. If you're painting only a small area, you can also polish by hand-sanding.)

Pencil

Tape measure and ruler

Chalk line (A handy, inexpensive tool that snaps straight lines. You can get one at a home improvement store. Step 4 tells you how to use it.)

Painter's tape (It's usually blue; you can buy it where you buy your paint.)

A friend who's willing to help (optional)

WHAT YOU DO

1 If the floor has already been painted and you're just painting over it, there's no need to strip the floor. If the floor has simply been varnished or polished, you need to strip the varnish or polish off with wood stripper or by scrubbing it with methylated spirit.

2 Sand the floor lightly just to smooth it; don't try to even out cracks or dents. Vacuum up the residue.

3 Roll on the undercoat, and let it dry.

4 Find the exact center of your floor, so you can mark out your diagonal checkerboard pattern from there. First, measure and lightly mark the center of each wall. Then, connect the marks on opposite walls by snapping a chalk line (see figure 1). To snap the lines, shake the reel, so the chalk inside distributes itself all over the string. Pull out the string and have a friend hold it close to the floor (but not touching) at one mark. (You can also attach the hook at the end of the string around a nail driven at the mark, if you're working alone.) Walk to the opposite mark, unreeling the string as you go. Pull the string taut, lower it to the floor, reach out a couple of feet, and give the string a snap. When it comes down, it'll leave a straight chalk line across the floor

5 From the center point, measure out an equal distance on each of the four lines, and mark those points. If you want to end up with 12-inch (30.5cm) squares, for example, measure out 8½ inches (21.6cm). Use the ruler and a light pencil line to connect the four points (see figure 2).

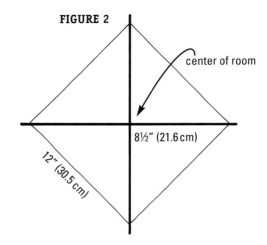

FIGURE 2

center of room

8½" (21.6 cm)

12" (30.5 cm)

6 The square you created in step 5 becomes your center "tile." Extend the lines of this tile out to the walls (again, snapping chalk lines is probably the easiest way), and finish marking off the rest of your squares.

7 Use painter's tape to tape off the inside lines of every other square (all the squares you want white, for example).

8 Paint all the black squares. The painter's tape will serve as an edge guard. Remove the tape, and let the paint dry.

9 Tape off the inside lines of all the black squares you just painted, and paint the white squares. Remove the tape, and let the white paint dry.

10 After the paint is completely dry, varnish the floor, following the varnish manufacturer's directions. You should probably apply several coats, depending on how much wear you expect the floor to take. Again, follow the manufacturer's directions on how long to wait between coats.

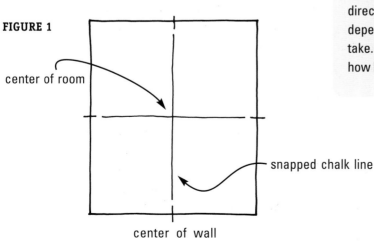

FIGURE 1

center of room

snapped chalk line

center of wall

getting to know your neighbors
(and why)

For people who don't actually live with you, your neighbors have enormous potential to affect whether your daily life is pleasant or not. That's why it's important to get a feel for your neighborhood—before you move in, if possible.

1 IMMEDIATE NEIGHBORS
Try to meet a few of your immediate neighbors (those in your hall and/or those living above or below you) face-to-face by knocking on their doors and introducing yourself. They'll be able to tell you from personal experience about the manager, the landlord, local amenities, other neighbors, and the general living situation in the building.

2 THE BUILDING
Walk around the inside and outside of the building. Is the cleanliness up to your standards? Do residents seem to turn common areas into extensions of their storage spaces (kayaks in the lobby, garbage bags in the hall)? Best to think about whether this bothers you now. Does it seem to be full of activity (maybe lots of small playing children or lots of grown-ups playing musical instruments) or relatively quiet? Consider which atmosphere suits your lifestyle.

3 THE NEIGHBORHOOD
Walk through the neighborhood around the apartment. Junk piles, graffiti, or folks loitering are generally deterrents for a prospective renter. Clean sidewalks, well-tended yards or storefronts, and neighbors conversing with one another suggest a sense of pride and security. If you'll be running or walking for exercise, taking a pet outdoors, or regularly coming home late at night, think about whether you'll feel comfortable carrying out those activities.

WHAT ABOUT YOU?
Evaluate your lifestyle. What kind of neighbor are you? Do you prefer living around families, college students, or young working professionals? Do you like to chat or prefer to mind your own business? If you're a night owl, don't live next door to children who spend the mornings playing outside your window. If you cherish your privacy, don't live in an apartment with a shared bath or shared kitchen privileges.

ONCE YOU'RE IN
As soon as potential neighbors become actual neighbors, it's in your best interest to start acting neighborly. Introduce yourself when you run into other renters at the mailboxes or in the parking lot. Sometimes apartment complexes host social gatherings for residents. Go, and get to know people. If you host your own apartment warming (see page 103), invite your immediate neighbors. These people can become pet sitters and plant waterers when you're away and sources of shared information about building maintenance or safety issues. They'll also likely become everything from business contacts to good friends.

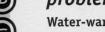

problem

Water-warped wood or linoleum, grimy tile, or—heaven forbid—a carpet-covered bathroom floor.

quick fix

Head to a local garden center, and buy a few of the precast pavers made for laying out a garden path. Bring them back and scatter them strategically so they cover stains, add personality, or provide wet, just-washed feet with a clean place to step. You'll be able to find pavers in squares, circles, hexagons, and other standard shapes, and in a variety of colors and materials, from pressed aggregate (it looks like a bunch of little pebbles all bunched together) to simulated stone. One word of caution: when you place your pavers about, give some thought to whether bare toes might come up against them in the dark of night.

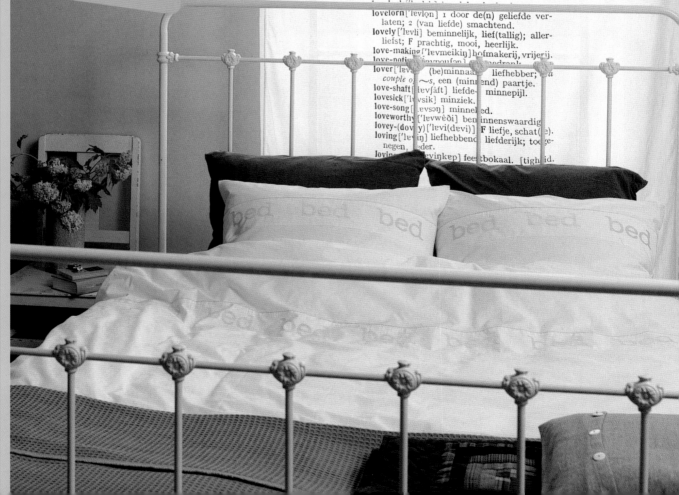

windows

Even if you lucked out and rented a room with an actual view, there are still going to be times you'll want to block it to shade the light or give yourself some privacy. Nice if you can do that in a way that adds to the indoor view, too.

word curtain

Your favorite word spelled out in five languages, the song lyrics that describe how you feel about life these days, or your funniest fortune-cookie predictions—you'll have no trouble finding the raw material for your own version of this printed-word window panel.

WHAT YOU NEED

Curtains
(You can use cotton muslin, if you're up to hemming the ends yourself, or plain, ready-made, rod-pocket curtain panels. Purchase fabric or panels that are somewhat longer and wider than the window you want to cover.)

Pencil and paper

Tacks or pushpins

MATERIALS FOR APPLYING LETTERING; OPTIONS INCLUDE:

Letter stencils, stencil brush, and acrylic paints (Block-letter stencils on manila paper are the easiest to use.)

Rubber stamps and ink pads

Fabric markers

Enlarged photocopies of words and a transfer medium (Check art and craft stores. You can buy bottles of medium that you apply with a brush and blender pens that allow you to transfer a photocopied image by burnishing it.)

WHAT YOU DO

1 On a piece of paper, sketch out the words and layout you have in mind. (Now would also be the time to check your spelling.)

2 Working on a hard, flat surface, lightly pencil guidelines onto the fabric, if you want them. If you'll be printing a poem on the fabric, for example, you might want the lines to be straight. If you're printing single words, on the other hand, maybe you'd rather they be more randomly placed (unless you're using the words *obsessive* or *compulsive*).

3 Print your words onto the fabric, using one of the following techniques.

- Tape letter stencils together to form your words, and stencil them onto the fabric, applying acrylic paint with a stencil brush. In addition to block-letter stencils, you can find letter stencils in cursive and other fancy forms. You can also trace the stencils with fabric markers if you don't want to stencil with a brush and paint.

- Stamp out your words using rubber-stamp alphabets and dye-based or craft inks. Avoid using pigment inks for this project.

- Use permanent fabric markers, and write on the fabric freehand—an especially good idea if you know calligraphy, have a distinctive handwriting style, or have a friend with exceptionally good penmanship who's willing to help. For large-scale, graphic lettering, you can also try writing on blank paper, enlarging the script on a photocopier, and tracing the result.

- Enlarge and make mirror-image copies of a printed page from a dictionary, a book of poetry, or anything else that strikes your fancy. Use a transfer medium to apply the image to the fabric, following the directions on the transfer medium's packaging.

4 Hang your printed panel on a curtain rod (if you used a curtain panel with a rod pocket), or use tacks or pushpins to attach it to the wall above your window.

emergency supply kit

Here are some essential items you might need when your karma runs out (or the power goes off, a snowstorm hits, or you find yourself in some other sort of bind). At the risk of sounding like your father: if you have it, you probably won't need it; if you don't, you'll wish you did. If you like to be super prepared, assemble an emergency kit. Otherwise, at least keep everything well stocked, close at hand, and in a location you can remember.

- Batteries
- Battery-powered clock or watch
- Battery-powered radio
- Candles
- Can opener
- Chocolate (hide it well)
- Duct tape
- Emergency money (for REAL emergencies, not a great poker hand!)
- Escape ladder* (if you live on the ground floor, you can skip this one)
- Extra prescription medication

- Flashlight (one that works)
- Fire extinguisher*
- First aid instruction book
- First aid kit (available premade at your local pharmacy)
- Instant cold pack
- Lighter
- Matches (in a waterproof container)
- Scissors
- Sharp knife
- Smoke detector* (DO NOT ever remove the batteries.)

- In-case-of-emergency phone list: nearest fire department, hospital, landlord, plumber, doctor, power company, phone com-pany, your family's phone number(s), roommate's family's number(s), your phone number and address (in case someone else has to make the call), vet (if your apartment includes residents with fur or feathers), favorite pizza place, your astrologer/psychic consultant

These items should be provided by your landlord.

IF YOU LIVE IN A REGION WHERE THE TEMPERATURE DIPS BELOW FREEZING, BE SURE TO INCLUDE:

- Non-electric heater
- Extra blankets and wool socks
- High-protein emergency food
- Instant hot chocolate
- Snow shovel
- Rock salt or kitty litter (to make icy steps less dangerous)

IF YOU LIVE IN A REGION WHERE THE MERCURY OFTEN AIMS FOR THE TOP OF THE THERMOMETER, BE SURE TO INCLUDE:

- Handheld fan
- Box fan
- Instant lemonade
- Instant cold packs (enough to cover your entire body at once)
- Plane tickets to the frozen wastelands of the north

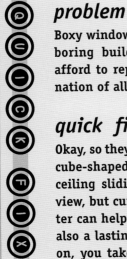

problem

Boxy windows, a boring view of the neighboring building, drab drapes you can't afford to replace, or a devastating combination of all three.

quick fix

Okay, so they're not going to transform your cube-shaped city windows into floor-to-ceiling sliding doors that offer an ocean view, but curtain rods with a bit of character can help perk up your outlook. They're also a lasting investment; when you move on, you take them with you. Home decorating shops and catalogs sell rods made of everything from brushed pewter to antique brass. They also carry finials (those ornamental stoppers on the ends) in all sorts of styles. For a more industrial look, here's an easy do-it-yourself option. Cut copper pipe to size with a hack saw, and hang it from I bolts or coat hooks (top). Or, connect the ends of the pipe to elbow-style plumbing fixtures you can screw into the wall on either side of the window (right and below).

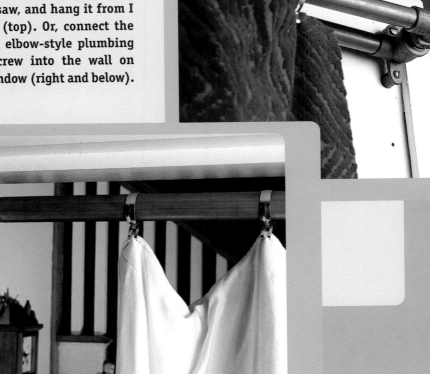

standing sheers

There are lots of reasons—light, drama, distinctive style—that you might want gauzy veils covering your windows rather than big, old, heavy drapes. These fanciful standing panels can move from window to window or room to room, and you can find everything you need to make them at a home improvement store.

WHAT YOU NEED

Sheer panels (Buy them in stores that sell curtains.)

1¼-inch round wooden rods, 2 per panel (This is the most common-size wooden rod sold at home improvement stores. It's possible to find smaller-diameter rods if you want them, but it may take a few phone calls to locate them.)

2½-quart (2.4 L) metal paint pails, 2 per panel

Small bag of quick-setting concrete

Screw eyes, 2 per panel

2-inch (5.1 cm) loose-leaf book rings, 10 per panel

Measuring tape or ruler

Handsaw (optional)

Grommet kit with ½-inch (1.3 cm) grommets

Hammer

Nails

Plastic bucket for mixing concrete

Masking or duct tape

WHAT YOU DO

1 Measure the height and width of the space you want to cover with your panels, jot down the measurements, and take them with you to purchase what you'll need. You may have to buy more than one panel to cover the width of the space. If so, increase the numbers of your other supplies accordingly. Select wooden rods that are equal to or slightly taller than the height of your panels. You may have to cut them to height with a handsaw. Unless you're absolutely sure of your measurements, it's best to cut the rods at home rather than having them cut at the store.

2 Set a grommet in both upper corners of each panel, following the instructions that come with the grommet kit. Then, lay one panel on a flat surface. Mark the positions for four equally spaced grommets down one long side, and set the grommets. Repeat on the other side.

3 Lay a second panel, if you're creating more than one, alongside the first. Mark identical grommet positions down each side of the second panel, and set them as you did on the first panel. Align the panels to be certain that the grommets line up as closely as possible. Continue with as many panels as you have.

4 Use a hammer and nail to punch a small hole in the center of one of the paint pail bottoms. Stand a rod in the pail, and nail it in place. Nail rods in all the other pails, using the same process. Don't worry if the rods wiggle a bit. The nails are simply to help steady them as you pour in the concrete mix.

5 Take the rods and pails outdoors. (Don't attempt to mix concrete on carpet or hardwood floors; you'll regret it.) Follow the manufacturer's instructions for mixing the concrete in the plastic bucket. Pour the mix into each pail almost but not quite up to the rim. If necessary, you can steady the rod with tape to keep it standing straight until the concrete mix sets. Allow the concrete to harden.

6 Place a screw eye at the top of each rod (see the photo below).

7 Open a loose-leaf ring, and thread it through the top grommets of two panels. Bring each end of the ring through the screw eye, and snap them together.

8 Anchor the sides of the panels by connecting the grommet holes with the rings.

9 Connect all your panels, following this same process.

decorating your first apartment

picture
window

Transform the overflow from someone's camera-happy vacation into a window treatment that both flutters and casts color. Look for boxes of transparent slides selling for next to nothing at yard sales, or ask for the contents of the reject bin at your local photo finishing place.

WHAT YOU NEED

Transparent slides

Small S hooks

Decorative curtain rod with ends in a size that fits your window

O rings with clips (Look for them with curtain rods and ends.)

Tape measure

Hack saw (optional; only if you need to cut your curtain rod to size)

Leather punch

Needle-nose pliers

WHAT YOU DO

1 If necessary, cut your curtain rod to fit the width of your window.

2 Measure the window's length, and lay out slides to figure a rough estimate for the number you'll need for each "strand." (Once you make your first strand, you'll know exactly how many slides and S hooks you'll need for each.)

3 Start punching holes in the slides to create as many strands as you need. First, orient each slide image so it's upright, then center the holes in the top and bottom edges of the slide casing. Work gently and slowly as you punch, or you'll split and crack the slide casings.

4 Use the S hooks to connect the slides into vertical strands, squeezing the curved ends of each hook together with the needle-nose pliers. Don't worry about completely closing the hooks, just squeeze them enough that they won't come loose from the slides.

5 Slip the O rings on the curtain rod, and use their clips to hold the top slide in each strand.

 On the top slide in each strand, punch only the bottom hole. On the bottom slide, punch only the top hole.

decorating your first apartment

no-sew exotica curtain

Why in the world would you hang a boring, pre-fab curtain over the focal-point window in your living room (or even over the nearly hidden window in your bathroom), when draping it in silk and beads is such a snap?

WHAT YOU NEED

Piece of fabric to fit your window (See page 28 to measure for curtain size. The key to keeping this easy is to work with the fabric's existing width—typically 45 inches [114.3 cm]—and have it cut about 1½ inches [3.8 cm] longer than you need, so you can hem the ends. If your window is wider than the fabric, use supple fabric that can be bunched together, and make more than one curtain.)

Fusible web

Length of ⅞-inch (2.2 cm) grosgrain ribbon, slightly longer than your curtain is wide

Supply of straight pins

#8 silk beading cord (comes with a wire "needle" attached to it)

1 large bead and 1 seed bead per dangle on the curtain's bottom edge

Tapestry needle

Curtain clips

Curtain rod and hanging hardware

Iron and ironing board

Scissors

Ruler or tape measure

WHAT YOU DO

1 Your piece of fabric will have two finished edges (known as selvege edges in the sewing world) and two unfinished or raw edges. The finished edges are your curtain's sides. The unfinished edges, which you'll hem with fusible web, are the top and bottom. With the fabric right side up, fold either the top or bottom edge over ¾-inch (1.9 cm), so the right sides of fabric are together, and press the fold. Open the fold, and place a strip of fusible web as long as your curtain is wide above the fold line. Fold the fabric back over onto the fusible web, and iron it down, following the fusible web manufacturer's instructions.

2 Cut the grosgrain ribbon in two equal lengths, each a couple of inches (5.1 cm) longer than the width of your curtain.

3 Cut another strip of fusible web as long as your curtain is wide. Line up one edge with the edge of the hem you created in step 1. Place the ribbon over the fusible web, leaving equal amounts of extra ribbon on either side. Iron the ribbon down, following manufacturer's instructions. Flip the fabric over, and use short lengths of fusible web to attach the extra allowance of ribbon onto the back of the curtain.

4 Repeat steps 1 through 3 to hem the other end of the curtain.

5 You'll bead one of the hems to make it the curtain's bottom. Mark 2½-inch (6.4 cm) intervals from one side to the other with pins.

6 Unwind all the silk cord from its spool, and tie a knot in the end that doesn't have the wire attached to it. Using the wire, thread the silk through the tapestry needle. Push the needle through the fabric from the back to the front at one of the pins, about ¼ inch (6 mm) up from the hem edge. Pull all the thread through, and remove the needle. Using the wire, thread a big bead, then a seed bead. Go back up through the bottom of the big bead and pull the thread through, adjusting it so the beads hang ¼ inch (6 mm) below the hem. Thread the silk onto the upholstery needle again, pull the needle and thread through the ribbon hem, from the front to the back, and tie off, being careful not to pull so tightly that the beads no longer dangle below the edge of the hem.

7 Repeat step 6 to attach all your other dangles. Two of them should be on the very edges of the curtain.

8 Attach the curtain clips evenly along the top hem of the curtain, install the rod, and hang it.

problem

You've got a window in dire need of some dressing up, but it's also one of your dark apartment's few sources of natural light, so there's no way you're going to cover it with curtains.

quick fix

Transform your window's panels into faux stained glass. All you need are sheets of colored tissue paper or cellophane, some scissors to cut them to size, and spray adhesive to hold the cut shapes in position on the window's glass. If you've got a multipaned window, fill each section with a different color—maybe alternating mauve and blue, a gradation of green, or a random collage of colors, some layered on top of each other. If your window features one big pane of glass, instead, fill the center with your own design of colored geometric shapes. Nail polish remover will take off any spray adhesive residue left behind when you decide to peel off the colored sheets.

decorative pull

You can live with the simple shades or blinds that were already covering your apartment's windows when you moved in, but your tolerance for minimalism goes only so far. Those plain hanging cords that control them cry out for something more substantial to feel for in the dark (or something more interesting for the cat to bat about while you're at work). Here's an easy reminder that it's the little things that make a home your own.

WHAT YOU NEED

Large, unpainted wooden beads (Look in craft stores.)

Acrylic paints

Acrylic varnish (spray or liquid)

Small brushes

Fine sandpaper

WHAT YOU DO

1 Thin the acrylic paint with water. Apply the thinned paint to the beads with a brush. Let the beads dry.

2 Sand the beads with fine sandpaper, then recoat them with more paint if they look like they need it. Feel free to add dots, swirls, squiggles, or stripes to your beads. Let them dry.

3 Coat the beads with acrylic varnish to protect them from wear.

4 Remove the plastic end from your cord pull by untying the knot that holds it on. Slip the beads onto the cord in its place, and tie off the end of the cord with a simple overhand knot.

If you are, by nature, more of a browser than a crafter, forget the wooden beads and paint. Instead, head straight to a bead store, where you can find pieces made of everything from carved bone to Austrian crystal to thread onto your personal pull.

lighting

Despite the fact that there are expansive stores and hefty catalogs devoted solely to the subject of lighting, it's no more complicated than this: you need it either to see what you're doing or to set a mood. Here are some options for shedding both types of light.

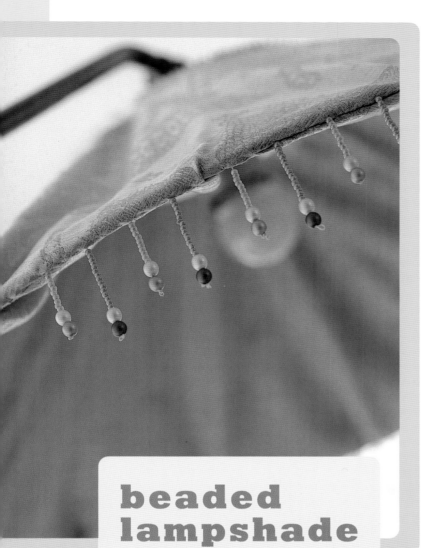

beaded lampshade

Now that most craft and fabric stores sell prebeaded and other types of decorative fringe, you can give any old lamp a touch of flapper-era shimmer, movie-star glamour, or Far Eastern mystery. All you'll need is glue or, if you're really feeling ambitious, a needle and thread and the simplest of sewing skills.

WHAT YOU NEED

Prebeaded fringe

Glue (options include a glue gun or white craft glue) or a needle and thread (Your choice of fastener depends on your shade; see step 2.)

Cloth tape measure or a length of string and a ruler

Scissors

WHAT YOU DO

1 To figure how much fringe to purchase, measure the circumference of the bottom of your shade. Either use a cloth tape measure, or wrap a length of string around the bottom of the shade, mark the string, then measure it with a ruler. The prebeaded fringe comes sewn onto a thin strip of fabric or ribbon. Buy a strip slightly longer than what you need.

2 Decide how you'll attach your fringe. You can glue fringe directly to the inner or outer edge of a paper or plastic shade with white glue or hot glue from a glue gun; hot glue is the easiest method. If you have a cloth-covered shade, you can glue the fringe or, if you're so inclined, stitch it to the shade with needle and thread.

3 Place the shade upside down on a flat work surface. Glue or stitch the fringe in small increments to either the inner or outer bottom edge of the shade. You'll have to hang the beads over the edge of the shade as you work. Keep the bottom edge of the fringe's fabric or ribbon strip parallel to the bottom edge of the shade.

4 Trim the end of the fringe strip so it butts up against the starting point. Turn the shade right side up, and check to make sure your fringe hangs evenly.

wastebasket glow lamps

Sources of direct, utilitarian lighting they're not. But if your goal is to set a mood or soften the harsh reality of unvac-uumed carpet or undusted furniture, these radiating wastebaskets are just the thing.

The "O" decorating the wall just above the glow lamps is an old zinc letter that once helped spell out a company name on a building facade. If your local scrap yard is fresh out of the letters of the alphabet you need, home decorating catalogs now sell them brand new.

WHAT YOU NEED

Clear plastic wastebasket with a frosted finish, 1 per lamp

White craft glue

3 or 4 sheets of colored tissue paper per lamp

Small lamp (You need just the lamp apparatus, no shade. Thrift stores are a good place to find inexpensive lamps.)

Self-piercing plug to fit on the end of an electrical cord

Drill with ⅛-inch (3mm), ⅜-inch (9.5mm), and ¼-inch (6mm) drill bits

Small plastic container with lid

Paintbrush

Heavy-duty scissors

Screwdriver

WHAT YOU DO

1 Drill a hole on one side of the wastebasket, near the bottom; start with a ⅛-inch (3mm) pilot hole, then drill that same hole with a ⅜-inch (9.5mm) bit , and finally drill it with a ¼-inch (6mm) bit.

2 Pour a solution of three parts glue to one part water into the plastic container. Mix it well with the paintbrush.

3 Cut the tissue paper into manageable sections slightly longer than the height of the wastebasket and about 6 inches (15.2cm) wide.

4 Brush glue onto a section of the interior of the waste-basket, and apply a strip of tissue paper. Use the brush to gently flatten the tissue paper and smooth out any air pockets. Keep applying the tissue paper in sections until the entire wastebasket is covered, again using the brush to push overlapping pieces into place. (Don't worry about tears in the paper; subsequent layers will hide them.) Let the glued paper dry overnight.

5 Trim off the top edges of the tissue paper, and use your finger and then glue to smooth any rough areas on the tissue paper. Repeat the process of applying glue and tissue paper, then allow it all to dry again.

6 Apply about three or more layers of tissue to the inside of the wastebasket, then add an extra coating of glue after the final layer of paper. Let everything dry once more.

7 Pierce through the hole in the wastebasket with the screwdriver, working from the outside of the basket in. Using heavy-duty scissors, cut the plug off the lamp cord, thread the cord through the hole, and attach a new plug, following the instructions on the plug's packaging. Place the lamp in the center of the wastebasket, and equip it with a low-wattage bulb.

problem

Stark, overhead ceiling lights that bathe your apartment in an unattractive, interrogation-like glare.

quick fix

Called *uplighters* in interior decorating-ese, freestanding lamps that sit low on the floor and cast light up are one of the quickest ways to give a bland room character. Position them behind plants, under tables or benches that hug a wall, or in corners, and they can create interesting shadows and reflections, light up entire walls to give the illusion of more space, highlight architectural angles or recesses, and even spotlight whatever is hanging above them.

plumbing parts candlesticks

Candlelight is something you're going to want to toss into your lighting mix every now and then, and how you hold the candles in place is a big part of the look you create. These candlesticks made from off-the-shelf plumbing parts will be right at home, whether you live in a converted-factory loft or simply like to pretend you do.

WHAT YOU NEED

2 lead plumbing pipes, ¾ inch (1.9cm) wide
and 5 to 6 inches (12.7 to 15.2cm) long

2 lead flanges

2 large lead couplings

2 lead fittings

WHAT YOU DO

1 Screw one pipe into one flange to create the base of each candlestick.

2 Slide the couplings onto the pipes so they rest on the bases.

3 Screw the fittings to the top of each piece to add definition.

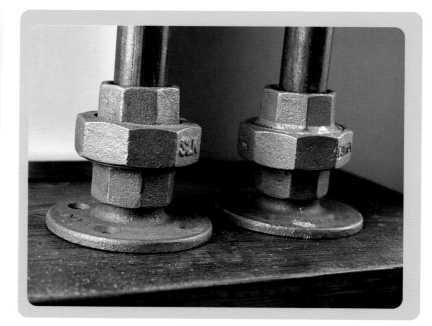

even easier...

We have no idea exactly what these super-cheap parts were manufactured to do, but we think they make terrific candlesticks. (The friendly fellow who helps customers maneuver their way through the plumbing aisle liked the idea, too.) The only assembly required: the addition of a taper candle.

candles by style

TRADITIONAL: Buy a wide wooden baluster at a furniture salvage store (these are the wooden support posts from old handrails). Spray paint it metallic gold or silver. Top it with a thick, chunky square or round candle. If you don't happen to have a baby grand piano, use this as an imposing centerpiece for your table.

ETHNIC: Wrap tall pillar candles halfway up with Oriental rice paper, African mud cloth, or remnant scraps of velvet or raw silk. Tie the wraps with raffia, tassels, or rope, and decorate the ties with beads, coins, or tokens. Roll the wraps down as the candles burn.

ECLECTIC: Group a bunch of mismatched candleholders you picked up in a thrift shop (colored glass, brass, painted wood, etc.), and fill them with candles in different sizes, shapes, and colors.

MINIMALIST: Settle white votive candles into shallow clear bowls filled with pebbles or sand, or use large, flat river rocks as candleholders.

KITSCH: Time to transform your Polynesian-mask cocktail mugs into candleholders, use an old surfboard as an oversized candle platter, or pose Barbie and Skipper so their arms appear to be holding your taper candles upright.

apartment-warming parties

SIX WAYS TO GIVE YOUR NEW HOME THE TOASTY GLOW
GOOD FRIENDS AND THEIR VIBES PROVIDE...

OPEN HOUSE. An especially good plan when you have more friends than chairs. Choose a Saturday or Sunday afternoon, and let guests know they're welcome to come and go anytime within a several-hour window. Set out a simple spread of finger foods and drinks—and make sure you have enough refills on hand to keep the refreshments looking fresh throughout your open-house hours.

POTLUCK. Nothing cozies up a new place like a big, home-cooked meal, especially when everyone who's coming contributes to the cooking. If your new kitchen is not yet overflowing with lots of extra dishes and flatware, make the place settings potluck, too. Invite everyone to bring one, then mix and match all the plates and utensils.

DINNER PARTY. This step up from a potluck is for those landmark times when you have not only a new apartment but also grown-up extras, such as cloth napkins and a set of wine glasses that you're eager to show off. Don't feel you have to go overboard; plan and budget for an appetizer, entree, salad, and a dessert, and you've got a multicourse evening. Though the idea is that you're providing the bulk of the food, it's fine to have guests fill in some gaps (bottle of wine, loaf of bread, etc.). Light some candles, splurge on a bouquet of fresh flowers, turn on some background music, and tell everyone to dress up.

COSTUME OR THEME PARTY. Perfect for establishing your apartment as the party place, one where guests can expect decorations and props, if not games, activities, food, and music to match the mood. If it's a costume party, have plain masks and decorating materials at the door for anyone who arrives in street clothes. Looking for an easy theme? Re-create a kid-style birthday party for a friend who's hitting a 20-something milestone (cupcake decorating contest, musical chairs with gag prizes, hats and horns). Feeling especially ambitious? Send out written theme invitations in advance.

DANCE PARTY. If you don't have lots of furniture to fill your floors, you might as well dance. Base your party on a memorable decade or fad (1950s, disco) or on a celebratory holiday such as Mardi Gras, costumes and all.

FOOD-THEME PARTY. Add focus and embellishment to any potluck or dinner party by setting up a theme buffet. Try make-your-own tacos, and you can also string a piñata, offer Mexican-hat-dance lessons, and have some sombreros handy for your more extroverted guests. Or, put out pita-bread pockets guests can fill with Greek salad as they mingle around in togas.

mini-lights

There are people in the world who believe that little tiny lights should be used only for wrapping around evergreen trees and plastic reindeer—and only once a year. You should feel pity for them. Somehow, they've missed the news that these twinkling, blinking, inexpensive strings can be wound among the leaves of house plants, draped behind sheer curtains, mounded in clear glass containers, and used in countless other ways to provide year-round light and good cheer.

MINI-LIGHTS know exactly how to behave when they're strung among the leaves of something green. Group several small plants in front of an outlet, and use a short string of lights to make them sparkle. Or, turn a tall tree or plant into a living floor lamp. Weave the lights through the leaves and branches, then attach them to an extension cord you can wind around the trunk and off to the outlet.

CREATE a quick table lamp by filling a big glass bowl, platter, pitcher, or urn with a strand of lights and nearly anything else: corks, glass marbles, seedpods, candy with bright-colored cellophane wrappers, or your collection of plastic Barbie doll shoes.

BACK in the aisles you perhaps never visit, home improvement stores sell these minimalist-look steel concrete reinforcement grids. Toss (okay, carefully lift) a couple into your back seat, take them home, and use them as freestanding frames for stringing lights. To make your display even more distinctive, shop thrift stores and antique shops for vintage bulbs like these.

problem

Though you may not have known it had an actual name (it does: task lighting), you do know you need more of it—a directed stream that highlights details when you're reading a book, choosing a CD, or writing in your journal.

quick fix

Clip-on lights will grip the edges of tables and counters, the top of a headboard, the side of a shelf, even the rim of a windowsill. Then, you can swivel them and train them on whatever it is you want to see—or on some decorative item you want to spotlight. Places that sell lighting fixtures carry all sorts of styles, but for good old-fashioned (not to mention inexpensive) metal clip-ons with a no-nonsense industrial edge, you can't beat your local hardware store.

free-form mesh light fixtures

The standard-issue light fixtures in apartments are seldom unbearably bad. They're just boring. Fortunately, most of them can be removed with the simple twist of a few screws. Pack them away carefully, so you can reinstall them when it's time to collect your security deposit and move out. Meantime, here's a two-step plan for putting some pizzazz in their place.

1 Experiment with different bulbs, from round globes to bulbs with frosted and colored finishes. On this bathroom fixture, we replaced the regular bulbs with long, low-watt tubes.

2 Cover the bulbs with contour mesh. This malleable aluminum comes in various colors and finishes. It's sold by the roll at craft stores. Put on a pair of work gloves (the edges can be sharp), and twist, gather, sculpt, and shape it until you've fashioned a shade you like.

COLOR
is one of your most
effective and least expensive
decorating tools. A coat of paint
or a vibrant bouquet of flowers here,
a few colored light bulbs there, and
you can completely change the
feel of a room. Here are the
basics you need to splash
color around with
confidence.

color your world

A SPIN ON THE COLOR WHEEL
...or, what you forgot to remember from art class

PRIMARY COLORS
Red, blue, and yellow; pure colors
that can't be mixed from others.

SECONDARY COLORS
Result of mixing two primary colors;
you get violet, orange, or green.

HARMONIOUS COLORS
Colors adjacent to each other on the color
wheel, such as red, red-orange, and orange.

COMPLEMENTARY COLORS
Colors opposite each other on the color
wheel, such as red and green, orange and
blue, and yellow and violet. When placed
beside each other, they seem to vibrate.
Also known as contrast colors, they are
often used as accents in a color scheme.

COOL COLORS
Those that are more blue than red;
they appear to advance.

NEUTRAL COLORS
Whites, blacks, grays, and browns. They're
considered both "safe" and restful. They can
vary considerably in warmth or coolness. At
their purest, white is cool and black is warm.

WARM COLORS
Those that are more red than blue;
they appear to recede.

COLOR IN THEORY

If you remember mood rings, you know that each color symbolizes something different. (This is not only according to the manufacturers of mood rings. People who actually study such stuff—known as color theorists—say so, too.) Here's a quick breakdown of the effects generally associated with various colors. Toss this info into the mix when you're picking out paints or rugs, but don't worry too much about rules. Better to imagine colors as having personalities, and choose those you connect with.

NEUTRALS

Imply good taste and elegance. Although they might seem understated, don't think of neutrals as bland. White is crisp, refined, clean. Black can represent dignity, serenity, and formality.

REDS

Warm and vibrant, red adds drama and cheer. If you're using lots of it, combine it with accents of white or cream to keep it crisp, or with black for a hint of Asian aesthetic. For an opulent room that's not for the faint-hearted, use only shades of red and deep golds. Mixed as an accent with other colors, red has a playful feel.

PINKS

Fresh and charming. Pastel pinks work well with other soft shades and sometimes feel nostalgic; mix hot pinks with amber, yellow, and coral shades for a taste of the tropics.

ORANGE

Said to stimulate the appetite, orange sometimes gets a bad rap as a faddish color that's hard to combine with others. In the right proportion, however, it can work well with its complements and with neutrals. It's dominant, lively, and fun, especially for bathrooms and work areas.

YELLOW

Bright and cheery, yellow is associated with intellect, power, and creative energy. Lighter, less-radiant shades of yellow are easiest to work with. Most people prefer yellow, like orange, as an accent only.

GREENS

Considered fresh and delicate, greens help reduce nervousness and tension. Dark greens work well in distinguished settings, while soft greens have the most soothing effect. If it were a person, green would be a valued guest at cocktail parties because it mixes so well with others!

BLUES

Evoking images of water, the sky, and nautical themes, blues are used to create harmonious, serene settings. Blues combine well with each other and can soften overly bright rooms. Also, cool blues and white are considered an especially refreshing pair.

VIOLETS

With their strong, majestic tones, violets are powerful accent colors. They also have multiple personalities; the look depends on what you mix them with.

COLOR SCHEMES

● To make a ceiling seem higher, paint your walls in vertical stripes, or, if you have a chair railing, paint the area below it darker than the area above.

● Rooms decorated in dark colors appear smaller than those furnished in light colors.

● To hide architectural flaws, paint a room in a single, distinctive color, which causes the eye to move around the room and not rest on any details.

● If you choose to paint rooms in different colors, use the same color trim to visually connect them all.

● Bear in mind that color is never static. Not only does a color change according to the quality of sunlight bathing it, but it looks different depending on the colors beside it.

decorating your first apartment

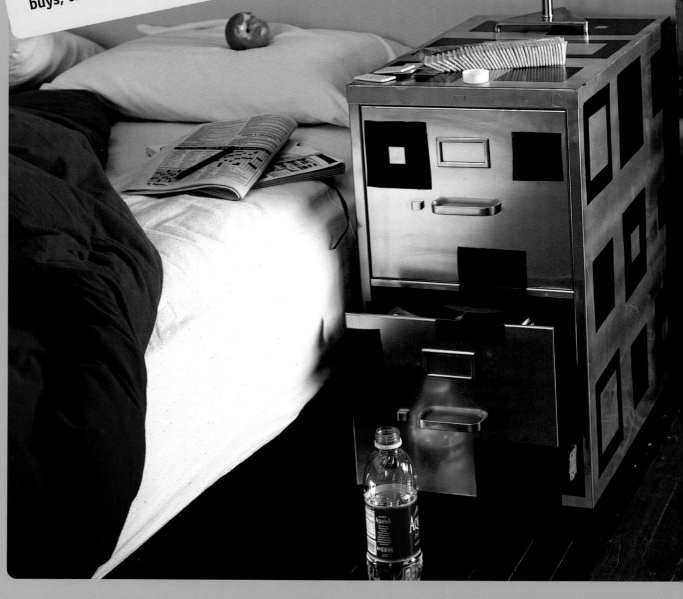

furniture & accessories

You need something to sleep on, something to sit on, some surfaces on which to stack belongings, and a few items to serve as accents. Just because you're meeting all of these needs with a combination of hand-me-down pieces and bargain buys, there's no reason they can't look good.

WHAT YOU NEED

Painted File Cabinet Masking Patterns, page 156

File cabinet

1 can of spray paint (We used chrome on a black file cabinet.)

Acrylic paint that matches the color of your cabinet

Newspaper

Scissors

Masking tape

painted file cabinet

Some people use them to hold actual files (gotta put those college loan records and cat adoption papers somewhere). Others turn them into unconventional dresser drawers (complete with built-in slots for labeling each) or extra kitchen storage containers. But just because file cabinets are so versatile and easy to come by is no reason for yours to look ordinary.

WHAT YOU DO

1 On a photocopier, enlarge the masking patterns to the size you want, and make 12 copies of each. Cut them out with scissors.

2 Attach the patterns in a random fashion to the cabinet, and spread them out evenly, making sure that the same patterns aren't right beside each other. Affix them with masking tape along the edges, making it as straight as possible, but don't worry if it's not perfect. This design is not about precision. Use your fingernail to press down the edges of the masking tape, so the paint won't spray under its edge.

3 Working outside if at all possible, set the cabinet on a protective layer of newspaper, and tape doubled layers of newspaper to all but one side of the filing cabinet.

4 Spray the uncovered side of the cabinet, following the manufacturer' s instructions on the spray can. Let the paint dry completely, then spray a second coat.

5 Once the second coat is dry, cover the painted area with a doubled layer of newspaper, uncover a new side, and repeat step 4. Repeat this process until you've painted all four sides.

6 If necessary, use the acrylic paint to touch up any imperfections.

other ideas to file away

PAINT IT	USE IT FOR
Fire-engine red	CD collection
With over-sized daisies	Towels & toilet paper in the bathroom
Using fern leaves as stencils	Shoes, scarves, umbrellas & hats by the front door
Sheep	Nightstand; store books in the drawers
Random numbers	Phone table

Look Good, Feel Good: FENG SHUI DECORATING

According to the ancient Chinese practice of feng shui, a misplaced bed can make you tired, clutter can cloud your thinking, and a backed-up sink can cause your career to stagnate, just like the water in the basin. On the other hand, if you apply a few basic principles for furniture arranging and decorating, they can help alleviate everything from stress and anger to blocked creativity and blood pressure problems.

The words feng shui, pronouned "feng shwa," "fung shui," or "fung shwa," depending on whether you're Mandarin, Cantonese, or English speaking, mean wind and water. They describe the practice of positioning objects so they take advantage of—and don't block—the chi or energy flowing through the environment. If you've visited a bookstore in the last decade or so, you know that the detailed principles and techniques of feng shui are hardly being hidden away as ancient secrets. Before you buy your own full-blown guide, here's an overview of what it's all about.

BASICS

● Any apartment or house has negative space. You can counteract it by stimulating chi.

● Balancing of the five elements of wood, earth, water, fire, and metal can help bring balance to your living space and your mental and physical life.

● Each element relates to one or more directions in the home (north, south, east, or west). Certain colors, objects, shapes, and ideas exemplify the elements and are used to decorate the corresponding parts of the home. For example, water rules the northern part of the home. Activate that area's chi by using blue tones to decorate. You might also consider furnishing the area with a small table fountain or an aquarium. Detailed feng shui guides will spell all this out for you in charts.

DOS & DON'TS
Do:

● Decorate with art. It can be a potent souce of inspiration and can act as a catalyst for achieving goals.

● Organize and fix up. Physical clutter mirrors chaotic thinking, and lots of unfinished repair work (leaky faucets, wobbly table legs, etc.) can challenge wealth and happiness.

● Tackle work projects in bright, open spaces; they're more energetic.

● Move to more softly lit places when you need to relax or calm down.

● Use bright objects to enhance the energy level in dark corners and nooks.

● Arrange your bedroom symmetrically. Position the bed so it has a clear view of the door but isn't in line with it.

● Consider the energy of shapes. Curves, circles, and ovals are linked with creativity. Squares and rectangles represent organization and rational thinking and stimulate decision making.

● Decorate with tall, upright plants. They have strong, upward energy that counteracts draining energy.

● Place plants next to electrical units to counteract electromagnetic discharges.

● Create a physical barrier between work and home if you work out of your apartment. If you can't shut the work off in a separate room, use a screen or plants to separate it.

Don't:

● Create sharp edges and corners with your furniture placement; they cut off energy. Round out architectural edges with plants or fabrics.

● Place chairs or any seating with their backs to a door.

● Use loud colors or modern prints in the bedroom; they're not restful. You should also avoid lots of vivid color and stimulating decor where you eat, to ease digestion.

● Put up with dead plants or peeling paint near your front door. Keep your entranceway clean and orderly—it's the gateway to your private life. (A Western approach calls for the use of wind chimes near an exterior door, to create positive sounds.)

● Decorate with too much white or black. Use colorful throw rugs, plants, and recent photos to brighten the atmosphere. Avoid blank walls.

● Rely too much on artificial light. Also, consider buying full-spectrum light bulbs; they're the most similar to natural light. They do, however, cost three to five times what a standard bulb does.

nathalie's chair

Nathalie found this chair at a bargain price at a thrift store and had to have it. She fell in love with its excellent bones, but didn't want to live five minutes with its fabric. Though she'd never reupholstered anything before, she figured all she really needed to transform her prize find into the chair of her dreams was some great new fabric and a little common sense. Turned out, she was right. Here's her step-by-step report of how she did it.

WHAT YOU NEED

Chair or other piece of furniture you want to recover (See step 1.)

Upholstery fabric (See step 2.)

Batting (optional) (The piece's existing batting—the stuffing underneath the fabric—may be in good enough shape to reuse; see step 3.)

Straight pins or fabric chalk

Steel upholstery tacks (Reusing the tacks you pulled off the furniture might seem thrifty, but they don't go in straight if they've been bent during the removal process.)

Cardboard or metal tack strips (optional)

Tack puller (This handy gadget easily slips under upholstery tacks, so you can remove them with little effort.)

Lightweight upholstery hammer or regular hammer (Though a standard hammer will work, upholstery hammers have a magnetic tip that holds tacks on the end, so you won't smash your fingers trying to hold them in place while you hit them.)

Scissors

WHAT YOU DO

1 If this is your first upholstering job, too, select simple-lined furniture. This 1950s-era chair has spare but elegant lines that allow the new fabric to take the spotlight. Before buying furniture you plan to reupholster, check to make sure the existing fabric is not sewn on but rather folds into place over the stuffing. Also, make sure the furniture is structurally sound—you don't want to invest all kinds of time in a piece that will quickly fall apart.

2 Choose your fabric carefully. It should be robust enough to withstand daily use, without being so heavy that you can't drape it easily around the furniture's frame. Make sure the fabric is wide enough to fit completely over the elements you're covering. And unless you want to put a lot of effort into matching them, avoid stripes and plaids in fabric patterns. You'll determine exactly how much fabric you need once you've removed the old fabric from the furniture and lined all the pieces in a row (see step 5).

3 Remove your furniture piece's legs, if possible, and begin removing the existing upholstery. The process is much like peeling an onion layer by layer. At each step, carefully examine the furniture to make sure which element is outermost, then remove it. A few suggestions:

■ Keep notes as you go on the order of what you remove; you'll reverse it when you attach your new fabric.

■ As you remove elements, whether legs, fabric, or batting, label them for reference, pinning a piece of paper with the name—*seat* or *front of backrest*, for example—and indicate the front or top of each. In the case of legs, label them and the body of the furniture lightly in pencil where it won't show, so you'll know which slot they screw back into when you're ready to put them back on.

■ Write down measurements related to the placement of decorative elements, such as buttons, so you can put them back where they belong.

■ If there's a particularly tricky way in which something is attached, jot down that information, as well as explanations of where tacks should go. Make marks directly on the frame of the furniture if something has to be attached in a specific spot.

■ If you remove any wooden elements, clean them when they're off the piece, to give them back their luster—and so you won't muck up your spiffy new fabric cleaning them later.

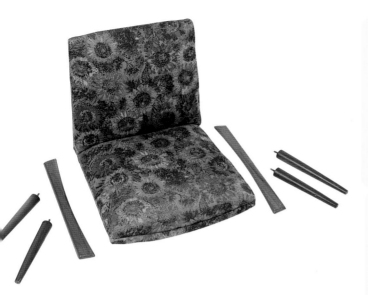

4 Once you've removed all the fabric, assess the condition of the batting. You may have to replace it. If so, use the same quality batting or better. If you're unsure about this, ask for advice at the upholstery section of a fabric store or at an upholstery supply shop.

5 Working in a well-lit area on a smooth, clean surface, lay the fabric pieces you've removed in a row, and press them flat with your fingers. (Don't iron the old fabric; you'll remove folds and creases you might find helpful in determining how to fold your new fabric to shape it correctly around the furniture frame.) Use the pieces as a guide for how much new fabric you need.

6 Lay out your new fabric on the same smooth, clean surface, and use the old fabric pieces as patterns for cutting. You can either pin them to the new fabric or trace them with fabric chalk. As you cut around the patterns, add at least an extra inch (2.5 cm) on each side. You'll find it a lot easier to have too much rather than too little material to grasp when you pull it into place. And you might discover you've made a mistake somewhere that you can fudge if you have a spare inch or two of fabric to play with. You can always cut excess off when you're finished. If your new fabric is ironable, iron your new pieces before moving to the next step.

7 Tack your new fabric in place. Again, a few suggestions:

■ Tack one side of a section in place (the seat, for example), pull the fabric taut, then attach its opposite side.

■ Once you have two opposite sides attached, pull the fabric taut again, tack the center of the third side, and work outward toward the corners, then do the same for the fourth side. After attaching the first piece of fabric, wait 24 hours or so before continuing, to see how the fabric reacts and how your technique holds up.

■ Things get a little tricky if the furniture has an upholstered back. Start by deciding the placement of the top edge. Tack the top two corners down from underneath, then flip the fabric out of the way. With tacks, apply a strip of cardboard across and flush with the back's top edge, to give it a crisp look when you fold the fabric back over it. For the sides, you can use tack strips (strips of cardboard or metal that have tacks already in them, both available at upholstery supply shops). The metal strips will pull the fabric taut more easily, but don't have as smooth a finished appearance. If you don't want to go to the trouble of hidden edges, you can simply cut your fabric with a ½-inch (1.3 cm) seam allowance, iron it under, and use decorative tacks on the outside to affix the material to the back.

■ Ask a friend to help. Though you can do it alone, four hands are more effective than two when it comes to pulling the fabric evenly taut as you attach it. (The fabric will relax a little, so you do need to make sure it's as tight as possible when you tack it in place.)

■ You may have to make notches on the edges of the fabric to ease it around curves or corners smoothly; refer to the original fabric for clues about where this may be necessary.

■ Don't get worked up if you make mistakes: you'll quickly discover that tacked upholstery is very forgiving. Pull up the tacks, perform a dry run of how you think it works, and try again!

8 Reattach your piece's legs if you removed them.

Tie knots at the four corners. You could also use tassels, rope, or hemp to gather the corners.

problem

Take your pick: ugly table (maybe you're the lucky recipient of your parents' plastic patio furniture), boring table (it'd look better beside the bed in a budget motel), table that's the wrong color or style (if only you had decorated everything else in candy-sweet pastel).

quick fix

Buy a floor-length sarong, or pull one out of the closet that you hardly ever wear. These wraparound skirts that come in everything from solid-colored raw silk to bold tropical prints make versatile tie-on table covers.

Make tight rolls on two sides, and roll the ends into rosettes.

Billow two sides, and tie a knot in the center of each.

composition in canvas

On the off chance you're not yet in a position to invest in expensive abstract art, here's a pretty darn impressive alternative. The work involved is fittingly minimal; you're simply painting prestretched canvases. The artistic part is choosing your shapes, sizes, colors, and hanging configuration. Toss around terms such as "nonrepresentational" and "reductionist style" as you go, and you'll have no trouble at all.

WHAT YOU NEED

Primed, prestretched canvases (Both art and craft stores sell these in a variety of shapes and sizes. When in doubt, buy the sizes that are on sale.)

Liquid acrylic craft paint in a variety of colors

Paintbrush

Picture-hanging hardware

Hammer

WHAT YOU DO

1 Apply the paint to the canvases, running all your brush strokes in the same direction and applying the paint evenly. Paint the edges as well as the fronts. Don't use too much paint for your first coat. Let the canvases dry overnight.

2 Apply a second coat of paint to all the canvases, again running your brush strokes in the same direction you did for the first coat.

3 Play with layout patterns on the floor (or use the Plotting Where Your Pictures Go technique, page 55). Experiment with large and small gaps between the canvases, cube-style arrangements, long linear configurations, etc.

4 Once you decide how you want your canvases grouped, use the picture-hanging hardware to hang them.

botanicals under glass

Yellowing documents, mass-produced watercolors of sunsets, needlepoints of kittens in baskets—framed versions of all kinds of bad art are going cheap somewhere at a yard sale or secondhand store near you. Forget what's inside; you're after the inexpensive frames. Here's how to use them to create a classy set of pressed ferns floating between panels of glass.

WHAT YOU NEED

Picture frames with glass

1 fern leaf or other flattish plant leaf per frame

Small bottle of black craft paint

Glass cleaner

Sheets of green vellum paper, 8½ x 11 inches (21.6 x 27.9 cm), 1 per frame

Sheets of heavy white paper, 8½ x 5½ inches (21.6 x 14 cm), 1 per frame

Glue stick

Field guide to wild plant identification

Fine-point pen

Glazier clips, 8 per frame (You can buy these little metal fasteners where glass is sold.)

Chrome ball chain, approximately 4 feet (1.2 m) per frame

Pliers

Small paintbrush

Screwdriver with flat blade

Staple gun

WHAT YOU DO

1 Use the pliers to remove the glass and backing from the frames. Take the frames to a glass shop, and order an additional piece of glass cut to fit each.

2 Press your ferns or other leaves between the pages of a phone book weighted down with other heavy books. They should be pressed and dried in about five to seven days.

3 Clean the frames, and paint them all black.

4 Clean all your glass.

5 Position each fern or other leaf on a sheet of white paper, and secure it with a bit of glue. Print the Latin name of the fern or leaf across the bottom of the white paper (this is where the field guide comes in handy).

6 Center each white sheet of paper on a sheet of green velum, and secure it with a dot of glue.

7 Center each leaf-and-paper grouping on a pane of glass. Place another piece of glass on top of each, then place each "sandwich" in a frame.

8 Use two glazier's points per corner (one on each side) to secure the glass in the frames. The points push in easily with the flat blade of a screwdriver.

9 Attach the ends of 4 feet (1.2 m) of ball chain to the back of each frame with a staple gun.

pillow talk

Scatter them on the floor around a low table; you have dinner seating. Toss a couple of red ones onto your couch; instant seasonal decorating. From dainty throw-pillow size to full-blown floor cushions, pillows are one of the easiest ways to cozy up a room, reinforce a color scheme, carry out a theme, or make a place look lived in. The plain-Jane, discount-store variety of pillow is also the perfect canvas for adding some personal panache.

buying tips

The way a pillow is constructed will dictate which techniques you can easily use to embellish it. If its cover is removable—look for buttons, a zipper, ties, or an overlapped opening on the back—anything is possible (and simpler), from stamping to beading. If the cover is sewn closed, you can still add all kinds of surface decoration. Or, if you're determined and even mildly sewing savvy, you can carefully rip out the stitching on one side of the pillow, remove the cover, decorate it, then stitch it back in place.

simple pillow transformations

WHAT YOU CAN USE

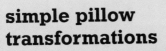

Premade tassels
Buttons
Upholstery trim
Ribbons, rope, twine, etc.
Embroidered or sequined appliqués
Beads
Vintage handkerchiefs
Silk flowers
Fabric paints
Rubber stamps and fabric ink

WHAT YOU CAN DO

Sew one (or more) matching or contrasting tassels to each corner. Or, stitch a passel of tiny tassels all over the pillow.

Stitch big, bold buttons around the front edges of a pillow, or remove and replace your pillow's existing, boring buttons.

Make a bold move, and neatly stitch a length of bright ball fringe or rickrack around the edges of your pillow.

Center an embroidered appliqué or a colorful handkerchief on the pillow, pin it on, and stitch it.

Cut out simple geometric felt shapes if you can't find them precut. Pin them randomly onto the front of the pillow. Use a blanket or running stitch to attach them to the pillow. Contrasting thread is a nice touch.

Stitch on straight lengths of ribbon, yarn, rope, or twine. Tie bows, and stitch their knots in place to secure them.

Sew tiny, glimmering seed beads all over the pillow. This option is primarily recommended for those with plenty of perseverance and time on their hands (or a good long movie ready to pop into the VCR). Still, if it's the glittery look you're after, this is it.

Sew on bunches or rows of silk flowers—they lend themselves to looks ranging from cute to campy.

Remove the pillow cover, slip a folded newspaper inside it to protect the back side, and paint designs on the front with fabric paint. If your cover isn't removable, go ahead and dab designs on it anyway.

Use fabric inks or dye-based inks and rubber stamps to stamp on a design. Alas, this last is recommended only for removable pillow covers, since you need a flat, sturdy surface to effectively stamp on.

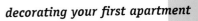

Q
U
I
C
K
F
I
X

problem

In your mind's eye, your apartment features just a few bold, dramatic decorative flourishes. Unfortunately, the sports trophies and tiny keepsakes you have to work with in real life aren't making the statement you want.

quick fix

Here's an inexpensive and accessible way to create a contemporary, graphic display. Gather a dozen or more simple black-and-white images from any low-cost source—clip them from fashion magazine ads, illustrated calendars, or used books. Trim them all so they measure 8 x 10 inches (20.3 x 25.4 cm), and stick them in matching, unadorned frames. (Watch discount stores for sales, and you'll be able to buy a bunch cheap. You want black-rimmed frames or all-clear frames that close with metal clips.) Fill most of a wall with three or more evenly spaced rows of your framed pictures.

furniture on the move

Equip a piece of furniture with wheels, and it not only takes on an air of industrial chic, but it also becomes a more versatile, flexible unit that's happy to change location to meet your changing needs. Baskets and bins that have been outfitted with casters allow you to wheel a supply of books or magazines right up next to your chair and then out of the way when you're finished. Small tables and benches on wheels make it possible to roll televisions and sound systems from spot to spot—or completely out of sight. And low platforms like this one (consider old doors or legless tabletops) can serve as everything from coffee tables to under-bed storage pallets.

adding casters

To make your furniture go places, simply attach small wheels on swivels that support moveable weight. Casters are categorized according to how heavy a load they can handle (100-pound [45 kg] load-bearing casters, for example). They also come in two primary styles: one with fixture plates that you screw in place and the other with stems you insert in drilled holes. Screw-in-place casters work best on pieces that feature a flat base area, such as a platform or a wastebasket. If you're adding casters to individual furniture legs, stem-type casters provide sturdier support.

reincarnated table

Using little more than sandpaper and fresh paint, we brought this weather-beaten hand-me-down back to life as a sleek worktable. You can use the same resurrection technique on chairs, benches, stools, shelves, you name it.

WHAT YOU NEED

Small table

Wood filler (if necessary)

Primer (Use gesso as your primer; you can find it at art and craft stores. That way, if the paint already on the table is oil paint, you won't have to remove it first.)

Acrylic paint

Water-based polyurethane

Plastic scraper

Sandpaper (fine and medium grit)

Tack cloth

Paintbrush and/or sponge brush (Brushes that are about 1 to 2 inches [2.5 to 5.1 cm] wide work well on smaller furniture pieces.)

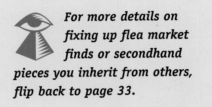

For more details on fixing up flea market finds or secondhand pieces you inherit from others, flip back to page 33.

WHAT YOU DO

1 Don't worry if the table has paint on it from its previous life; there's no need to strip it down to bare wood. Just scrape off any cracked or chipped paint, and fill in any cracks, dents, or holes with wood filler.

2 Sand the table with medium-grit sandpaper first, then use a fine-grit sandpaper to smooth the surface.

3 Wipe down the table with the tack cloth to remove all the sanding dust.

4 Coat the table with primer. Once it's dry, you may need to lightly sand the primer layer with fine-grit sandpaper, so it's smooth. Again, remove all the sanding dust with the tack cloth.

5 Paint the table with the acrylic paint.

6 Let the table dry for at least 24 hours, then coat it with polyurethane. You can apply a second and even third coat of polyurethane if you want the table to be super wear resistant. Wait 24 hours between each coat.

decorating your first apartment

artificial turf trays

If you don't want your guests to take you too seriously, serve them their fruit-punch cocktails atop an artificial garden, aquarium, or night sky under glass. You can use these kitschy compositions as portable trays. Or, mass a collection of them close together on TV-tray stands, and you've got a coffee table that also serves as a conversation piece.

WHAT YOU NEED

Artificial grass in green, blue, and black (Choose the type with the lowest grass height—which is also, oh happy coincidences, the cheapest.)

Plastic trays with lips

⅛-inch (3mm) glass or plastic, cut to fit your tray (You need one piece per tray. Look for glass suppliers in the phone book; they'll sell you the glass or plastic and cut it to size for a small charge.)

Artificial daisies, sheet of orange craft foam and fish stencils, wiggly eyes, silver star garland and gold confetti stars, or any other flat trinkets that suit your fancy

Craft glue

Needle and black thread

Scissors

Craft knife (optional)

Hot glue gun and glue sticks

WHAT YOU DO

daisies on green

1 Use the scissors to cut the green mat to fit the recess in your tray.

2 Pull the daisy heads off their stems, and pull any green plastic off the bases of the flowers, to make them as flat as possible. Trim any amount of stem remaining on the bases of the flowers to about ⅛ inch (3mm).

3 Place the flowers randomly on the mat. Hot glue them in place, if you like.

4 Lay the glass on top of the flower-studded grass.

fish on blue

1 Use the scissors to cut the blue mat to fit the recess in your tray.

2 Trace several fish shapes and sizes onto the foam, and cut them out with scissors or a craft knife. To give them added dimension, hold the knife at a 45° angle while you cut, with the point aiming toward the inside of the fish shape. Flip the angle-cut fish over before you use them.

3 Hot glue wiggly eyes on some of the fish, if you like.

4 Arrange the fish on the mat, and glue them down with hot glue.

5 Lay the glass on top of the fishy mat.

stars on black

1 Use the scissors to cut the black mat to fit the recess in your tray.

2 Arrange the silver star garland on the mat. Use the needle and thread to tack it down every few inches.

3 With craft glue, glue down the garland's stars. You'll probably have to hold them down or put a light weight on top of them until they adhere to the mat. You might also want to pull off extra stars that make the look too busy.

4 Sprinkle gold stars on top of the display.

5 Lay the glass on top of the starry sky.

problem

Cabinets and drawers in your kitchen and bath that feature the same dull, sea-mist gray veneer as the cabinets and drawers in every other cookie-cutter apartment in the city. Or (you decide which is worse), cabinets and drawers that look as if they were salvaged from the kitchen of the camper your parents bought when you were seven.

quick fix

Replacing the handles and knobs of the doors and drawers you open every day can do wonders to liven them up and make them look like your own. Home improvement stores carry a huge variety of both industrial-look and contemporary styles. At smaller home-decor shops, you can find everything from painted-glass knobs to hammered-metal handles. Best of all, you can remove these custom pieces and take them with you when you move on.

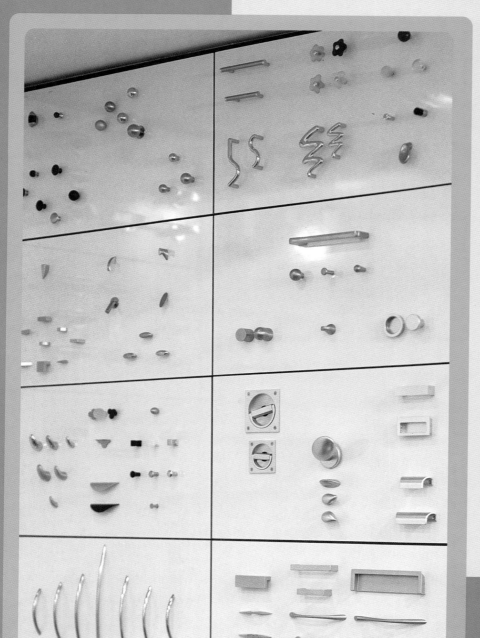

urban jungle

Even if you're cultivating a look that's ultra modern, somewhere amid all the steel pipe, glass block, and shiny metal, you need some living, oxygen-emitting green. Plants are one of the most effective accent pieces you can invest in if you want atmosphere. They can fill bare corners, drape tendrils along bookshelves, climb lattice in windowsills, and cast interesting shadows when lit just right. They look best doing all of this if they're sitting in something other than the plastic containers they're sold in. Here are several suggestions for easy, less-predictable ways to contain plants.

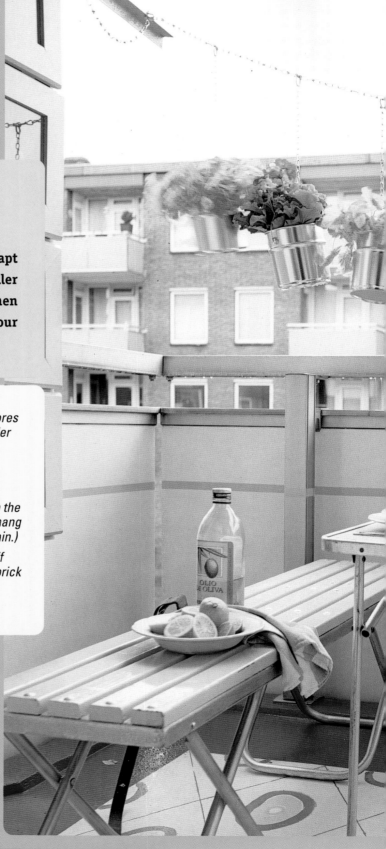

hanging buckets

If you don't have a balcony, adapt this idea—perhaps using smaller buckets—to fit across your kitchen windows or along the wall in your steamy, well-lit bathroom.

WHAT YOU NEED

Galvanized paint pails (Hardware stores are the place for these. For smaller pails, try craft stores.)

S hooks, 2 per pail

2 screw hooks, heavy duty

Length of chain (Buy enough to span the space you want to cover and to hang each bucket from the central chain.)

Drill and drill bits (Use masonry bits if you're hanging your buckets on brick or concrete-block walls.)

Pliers, for tightening S hooks

WHAT YOU DO

1 Before you head out to buy your supplies, measure the width of the space you want to span, and jot down the measurement. Also, decide how many buckets you want to hang in the space and how far you want each to hang from the central chain. When you purchase the chain, the person helping you at the home improvement store will have to cut it from a roll. With your measurements in hand, you can ask the helpful salesperson to make your job easier by cutting one long length for your central chain and multiple short lengths for your hangers.

2 Determine how high you want to mount your long chain. Drill pilot holes in the wall, screw in the screw hooks, and hang the chain from the hooks.

3 Attach a short length of chain to the central chain with an S hook. Hang a bucket on this short length with another S hook. Hang all of your buckets following this same process.

4 If the long chain droops too far, simply adjust the chain at either end until you're satisfied with its amount of sag.

5 You can plant directly into the buckets if you're hanging them outside, just pierce drainage holes in their bases with a hammer and nail first. If you're hanging them inside, put your plants in small plastic containers with drainage holes, then set them down in the buckets.

vintage canisters

Flea markets and yard sales are overflowing with colored-glass containers once used to hold flour and sugar. We turned ours into a windowsill garden that does a spectacular job of catching the afternoon light. Simply wash the canisters well in hot, soapy water, and fill them with potting soil and plants. To add to the sparkly effect of these, we mixed iridescent glass discs (the kind sold to hold flower stems in place) with the soil.

containers within containers

Put your plant in any old nondescript pot. Put a drip tray underneath it, and set it down inside something—almost anything—else. If they don't have to be in direct contact with dirt, roots, and water, all sorts of unusual objects can become holders for plants.

ANTIQUE BIRD CAGES
   (Leave the door open, and let the plant weave its way out.)

CERAMIC CHIMNEY FLUES
   (Check salvage yards.)

OLD ENAMEL PITCHERS AND WASH BASINS

SHOPPING BAGS LINED WITH BRIGHT TISSUE PAPER
   (Imagine a tree-sized plant popping out the top.)

WOODEN CRATES
   (Try fruit and vegetable stands as sources.)

LARGE OUTDOOR URNS
   (Garden centers sell them. They can fill big, undecorated voids in your apartment with rustic, Tuscan-villa flair.)

A WICKER PICNIC BASKET

AN UPSIDE-DOWN SOMBRERO
   (Think cactus.)

BUBBLEWRAP ENVELOPES
   (Graphic, urban, high tech.)

apartment-friendly plants

Here are five recommendations—all appropriate for beginning indoor gardeners—for the greening of your apartment.

PHILODENDRONS

Among the easiest houseplants to grow, many philodendrons tolerate low light and lots of neglect. Treat yours well, however, and it'll be beautiful for years.

The name philodendron actually refers to a diverse group of plants whose vines feature heart-shaped leaves ranging from 3 inches (7.6cm) to 3 feet (.9m) long. Some types have glossy, solid green leaves, others have velvety leaves with patterns, and still others have deep red leaves and stems. You can limit the size of vining types by keeping their supports small and by training and pruning. The self-heading types eventually can become very large and need ample space. Locate these plants out of heavy traffic paths.

Most philodendrons prefer indirect sunlight and can survive in low light. The common heartleaf philodendron is particularly forgiving of dim environments. Philodendrons like night temperatures of 65 to 70°F (18.3 to 21°C) and day temperatures of 75 to 85°F (23.9 to 29.4°C). Water them frequently enough to keep the soil evenly moist, but not soggy. Never let your plant stand in water. High humidity is ideal for best growth, but philodendrons will put up with the low level of humidity in most homes. Fertilize philodendrons regularly with a dilute water-soluble houseplant fertilizer, following the manufacturer's recommendations, or use a time-release fertilizer.

SPIDER PLANTS

There's one main reason spider plants are one of the most common houseplants: instant gratification. Spider plants grow quickly and easily to 2 to 2½ feet (61 to 76.2cm) wide and 2 to 3 feet (61 to 91.4cm) long when grown in hanging baskets, and they're especially speedy when it comes to forming new plant shoots. Their long, grassy leaves can be green or striped yellow or white. Long wiry stems appear on healthy plants, with many small white flowers and miniature plantlets sprouting off their tips. These new plantlets will root if they touch soil. Detach them to produce new plants, or leave them on to create a very full basket.

Spider plants grow best in bright, indirect light. They can tolerate some direct sunlight, but midday light may scorch their leaves. They prefer temperatures between 65 and 75°F (18.3 and 23.9°C) during the day, and 50 to 55°F (10 to 12.8°C) at night. During the winter, move spider plants a few feet from windows to protect them from drafts. These plants should dry out briefly between watering. During times of active growth, feed them a water-soluble or a time-release houseplant fertilizer, following the label recommendations.

RUBBER PLANTS

Excellent plants for beginners, rubber plants grow well in a variety of conditions. Their glossy, leathery leaves vary in color from dark green to deep maroon, and sometimes have yellow, cream, pink, or white markings. The trees easily reach 6 to 10 feet (1.8 to 3 meters) or more indoors if they have enough space; support them with a stake. You can prune them to reduce their size or to rejuvenate them (which may be necessary in the spring).

Rubber plants prefer bright light, but will adapt to low light. They grow best with the morning light from an east window. Their ideal temperature ranges from 60 to 65°F (15.5 to 18.3°C) at night and 75 to 80°F (23.9 to 26.7°C) during the day. Water rubber plants thoroughly, letting the soil dry somewhat between watering. They prefer humid conditions, but tolerate the dry air common in homes. Wash the leaves with water when they get dusty to keep them looking healthy. Fertilize your rubber plant regularly with a water-soluble houseplant fertilizer during active growth, following the manufacturer's recommendations. Fertilize plants growing in lower light less often.

WHEAT GRASS AND SPROUTS

Growing grassy plants inside in everything from collections of ceramic bowls to long metal troughs is an especially contemporary way to add living green to your indoor environment. It's also a great reminder of one of the benefits of apartment dwelling: no mowing.

Soak wheat berries (you can purchase these at health food stores) overnight at room temperature. The seeds will double in size. Fill the container you want to plant them in with 2 inches (5.1cm) of soil, and water it well. Cover the soil completely with seeds, so you can't see it, then cover the seeds with a light sprinkling of soil. Mist the top layer of soil with a water bottle, and put the container in filtered sunlight (in front of closed blinds, for example). Mist the soil daily, but don't soak it. The seeds should sprout within four days; place them in sunlight and keep misting. They should reach a height of 6 inches (15.2cm) within a week to 10 days. For different plant textures, you can also sprout alfalfa seeds or lentils.

FERNS

Ferns with tough, leathery foliage usually adapt better to typical household conditions than feathery, delicate types. Most ferns prefer moderate, indirect light inside; direct sunlight will damage the foliage. Close to a north-facing window is an ideal spot for a fern. Never put one directly in a south or west-facing window. Because fern fronds are sensitive to rough handling, you should also keep ferns out of high-traffic areas where they might be brushed up against regularly.

The ideal temperature range for most ferns is between 60 and 70°F (15.5 and 21°C) during the day, and about 50 to 60°F (10 to 15.5°C) at night. All ferns love moisture, but the amount they need varies among the many different types. Some like being kept almost wet, while others should dry slightly between waterings. Don't allow any fern to dry out completely, though. Likewise, don't allow water to stand in pots; it can lead to root damage. Also, lightly mist your fern occasionally to replicate its natural environment. Homes usually have too low a humidity for fine, thin-leafed ferns, and in the winter, the humidity level drops even lower—a good time to move your fern to your most humid room: the bathroom. Fertilize most ferns lightly once a month, from April through September only. Apply liquid houseplant fertilizers at about half the recommended rate. Their leaves will scorch if they're fertilized too heavily.

wild side table

When all your carefully selected neutral colors and go-with-any-thing styles start to make you feel you're living in an environment that's a tad too tame, fol-low these four easy steps. They tell you how to turn an ordinary-looking end table or other piece of paintable furniture into something much less civilized.

WHAT YOU NEED

Table

Photo or drawing of animal stripes or spots you want to copy

Pencil

Acrylic primer

Acrylic paints (You need one light color such as white or cream and one dark color such as black or brown. If you're tackling a design with more than two colors—maybe leopard spots—you'll also need some in-between shades such as caramel or dark gold.)

Paintbrushes

Sandpaper

Tack cloth

WHAT YOU DO

1 If your table is made of raw, unpainted wood, you'll want to give it a coat or two of acrylic primer. If it's already been painted or varnished, sand it to give it "tooth" to accept new coats of paint, wipe up the sanding residue with the tack cloth, then add a coat of acrylic primer.

2 Give the table a base coat of your lighter paint, and let it dry. Give the table a second coat of paint. Let the second coat dry as well.

3 Study the design you want to copy. You'll see that it's composed of broad areas of one color and accented with other colors. A zebra design is the simplest in terms of color: you'll use black and white. A tiger or ocelot design may use three or more colors. Lightly sketch the large stripes or spots of your design onto the table. Don't be too precise. Concentrate your design on the top of the table, then extend it to the legs, wrapping the design around each leg.

4 Outline the stripes or spots with a small brush and your darker color of paint, then fill them in. Stand back, squint your eyes, and see if you think you need to add smaller, thinner stripes or spots in places. Just take it gradually; it's easier to add accents than it is to remove them. Let the paint dry. Give the stripes or spots additional coats of paint, if necessary.

flea-market shopping

With their one-of-a-kind finds and bargain prices, flea markets are a great place for taking some decorating risks on fabric, furniture, and accents. Here are tips for making the most of a flea-market trip.

● Dedicated flea market shoppers are up at the crack of dawn. Arrive early so you're there for the best selection.

● Take a list of your needs for each room. Do let the spontaneous spirit of flea-market shopping guide you, but don't stray too far from your list. (A collection of Neil Diamond eight-tracks might make an interesting living room centerpiece, but it doesn't satisfy your need for a coffee table.)

● Take a set of room photos, paint chips, or fabric swatches if you're trying to match colors.

● If you're shopping for furniture, be sure to drive to the flea market in a vehicle equipped to transport your purchases home with you.

● Take cash in small bills. Some sellers can make change or will take checks; others can't or won't.

● Negotiating prices is usually acceptable, so use this as an excuse to sharpen your bargaining skills.

● Sometimes, the only way to know if the pink chenille bedspread or the mirror whose frame could use some polishing is right is to take it home, clean it up, and give it a try. Give yourself a "why not?" budget for seductive finds that you just aren't sure about.

● Beware of furniture made with veneer (a thin layer of wood applied atop the basic structure) or particle board (chips of wood glued together). You generally can't refurbish either.

nesting tables makeover

You've seen them. Every mega-discount store with a furniture aisle sells them—styleless table sets with a shiny finish that look as if they should be displaying business cards and brochures in some office lobby. Upside: they're affordable and handy. Downside: woefully ordinary. Here's a smashing way to overcome that little problem with a bit of paint and decoupage gloss and an extra-large photocopy of a face.

WHAT YOU DO

1 Create two large copies of your photo. Enlarge the photo first on a standard photocopy machine, then make two larger copies of the enlarged image on a poster-size copy machine (you can find them at commercial copy shops).

2 Sand your tables thoroughly, to cut through whatever finish is already on the wood (it'll keep your paint from adhering well). Use the tack cloth to wipe the sanding dust off the tables.

3 Apply primer/sealer to all parts of the tables with the paintbrush. Let it dry. If much of the table is showing through, apply a second coat to the table you'll be painting white. Clean the paintbrush.

4 Paint your tables: one white, one black, and one red. Start with the tables upside down, and paint the undersides of the tops, the aprons, and the legs. When the tables are dry enough to flip over, do so and paint the tops. You don't need to paint the areas where you'll apply the images. Simply paint a border of approximately ⅛ inch (3 mm) on the top surfaces. Clean your brush between colors and when you finish.

5 Measure the area you want to cover on each tabletop. Using the measurements, mark out the areas you want to cut from the photocopies. You'll cut the eye area from one photocopy, the mouth area from the other photocopy, and the nose area from the first photocopy. (The parts you want to cut of the nose and mouth area will likely overlap; that's why you need the two photocopies.) Cut out the face pieces.

6 Apply the decoupage gloss to the tabletop areas you'll be covering, using the paintbrush and following the instructions on the bottle. Place your images, smooth out any air bubbles, and let everything dry.

7 Brush decoupage gloss over the images and onto the painted border, to seal the edges. Let everything dry.

WHAT YOU NEED

Black-and-white photo of your face or another you won't mind looking at regularly

Set of nesting tables

Water-based primer/sealer

Acrylic latex enamel in gloss white, gloss red, and gloss black

Decoupage gloss medium

Acrylic paint in silver and gold

Clear acrylic enamel spray (glossy)

Sandpaper, fine

Tack cloth

Paintbrush, 1 to 1½ inch (2.5 to 3.8 cm)

Ruler

Craft knife or scissors

Plastic lid or something similar to use as a paint palette

Small, round artist's brush

Rectangular kitchen sponge

8 Pour a bit of gold paint into the plastic lid. Load one end of the rectangular sponge with paint, and sponge it lightly on the aprons of the tables. The right angle on the edge of the rectangle shape should fit the apron perfectly, creating clean sponged edges. Let the paint dry.

9 Decide where you want to add star and dot accents on the decoupaged images. Pour some silver paint in your plastic lid, and paint them on with the small artist's brush. Use the end of the brush dipped in paint to create the dots (moving it straight up and down). You can either paint the stars freehand or cut out a star image and lightly trace it onto the tables first.

10 Spray the tables all over (tops, aprons, and legs) with clear acrylic spray. It'll help with durability and take away the tacky feel of the dried decoupage gloss.

storage

Never mind *how* someone with zero discretionary income can accumulate so much stuff. You can. You likely already have. And without some clever storage solutions, it'll clutter up every spec of your cozy little living space.

shelving five ways

Sure, your apartment may have a lot of what a professional organizer would call "underutilized storage space." Trouble is, it comes in the form of a long, skinny strip of wall above the bedroom door or a narrow nook between the stove and fridge, and you can't find shelves to fit. Good news from the do-it-yourself front: if you can nail four pieces of wood together, you can make your own shelves to fit wherever you want them.

WHAT YOU DO

1 Smooth the edges of the brackets and the front and side edges of the shelf with sandpaper. Leave the back edge of the shelf and the top edges of the shelf back unsanded; they need to be square so they'll fit together accurately. Finish sand both sides of the brackets, the top of the shelf, and the front of the shelf back.

2 Fasten the brackets to the ends of the shelf back by applying a small amount of wood glue first, then using three or four nails on each end. Be sure to align the top and rear edges of each bracket with the top and rear of the shelf back.

3 Fasten the shelf to the back and brackets, again using glue first, then nailing.

If you're a perfectionist, buy or borrow a tool called a nail set, which you can use to drive the nails below the wood's surface. You can then fill the nail holes with wood filler, so all the edges are smooth.

WHAT YOU NEED

2 pieces of wood, one to be the shelf top and one that's a bit shorter in length to be the back (Paint-grade lumber and medium-density fiberboard are both fine choices for shelves you plan to paint or finish in some way. You can either buy your wood cut to size or cut it yourself with a handsaw.)

2 wooden brackets (Home improvement stores sell manufactured wooden brackets in a range of styles.)

Sandpaper

8d finish nails

Wood glue

Hammer

four easy variations on the theme

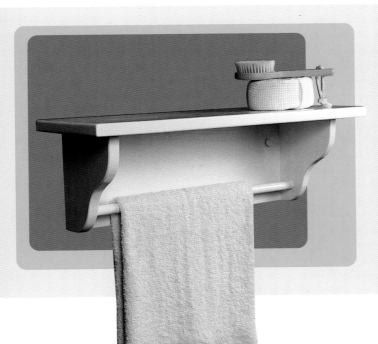

VARIATION 1:
ADDING A TOWEL BAR

Before assembling the shelf, drill two ¾-inch (1.9 cm) holes ⅜ inch (9.5 mm) deep in the two end brackets. Position the holes 2 inches (5.1 cm) from the back edge of the brackets and 1½ inches (3.8 cm) from the bottom, and be sure you drill in opposite sides of each bracket, creating mirror-image pieces. Insert a ¾-inch (1.9 cm) hardwood dowel into the holes, then assemble the shelf.

VARIATION 2:
ADDING A LOWER SHELF

Cut a board to size. Sand the top, the bottom, and the front edge, but leave both ends and the back edges square. Decide where you want it to attach to the brackets. Using a square, lightly draw a line at that point on each bracket, making the line perpendicular to the rear edge of the bracket. You'll use the lines to align the bottom edge of the shelf with the brackets while nailing. Use a couple of nails in each end and across the back to fasten the lower shelf in place.

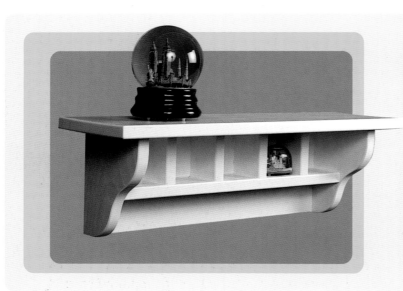

VARIATION 3:
ADDING PIGEONHOLES

Add the lower shelf in Variation 2, then measure the opening between your lower shelf and the top one to determine the height of your pigeonhole dividers. The length of the dividers should match the depth of the lower shelf. Cut the number of dividers you want. Using a square, mark guidelines where each divider will go, making the lines perpendicular to the front edge of the lower shelf. Sand the dividers, position them, then drive a couple of nails through the top and bottom shelves to fasten them in place.

VARIATION 4:
ADDING PEGS

Figure the number of pegs you want, purchase them, then make evenly spaced marks for each on your shelf back, about 1 inch (2.5 cm) up from the bottom edge. Drill holes the size of the ends of your pegs at each mark. Add a small amount of wood glue to the holes, then insert the pegs.

hanging shelves

How you secure a shelf to a wall depends on what type of wall you've got.

● If you're working with a hollow, wood-frame wall, the easiest approach is to drive support screws through the shelf and the plaster or drywall and into a piece of that wooden framing. Make sure that at least half the screw's length extends into the framing piece. If you're mounting your shelf to a hollow part of the wall (where there's no framing member to screw into), you need to first drill holes in the wall and insert anchors (see the next point). They'll help hold your screws or bolts in place.

● If you're working on solid masonry walls, the screws or bolts you use to hang your shelves need to work in conjunction with some sort of anchor that expands and grips inside the wall. Lead anchors and expansion shields are both standard choices. Hardware stores sell them.

A basic home improvement book will provide you with an illustrated chart of wall fasteners and tell you what sort of wall and shelf weight each is best suited for. The folks at your local hardware store can also help guide you toward the right fastener for the job.

energy savers

There are plenty of ways to lower your energy bills without cramping your style. Here are both year-round and seasonal habits you can cash in on.

YEAR-ROUND:

● Turn off all lights, stereos, and other electrical equipment when you're not using them.

● Turn the heat down or the air conditioning up a few degrees while you sleep and before you leave home for the day.

● If you have access to your hot water heater, keep the temperature at 110°F (43°C). You'll still enjoy steamy showers, but you'll have a lower energy bill.

● Install aerators in all your faucets and a low-flow showerhead to reduce the amount of water you use. (These are inexpensive and easy to install. Just be sure to choose a good brand that guarantees decent water pressure. If it doesn't deliver, return it.)

WINTER:

● If you've got a window-unit air conditioner, wrap it in plastic and seal the edges with duct tape. This will keep warm air from leaking out around it.

● Weatherstrip your windows. Weatherstripping is a modern plastic creation available at all hardware stores. It seals the cracks around windows where air can sneak in or out. Make sure the surfaces where you want to apply it are clean and dry and that it's at least 20°F (-7°C) out, then follow the directions on the product's box.

● If your apartment is especially drafty, seal entire windows with clear plastic sold at hardware stores and home centers for this purpose. First, clean and dry the molding around your window. Next, apply a line of double-sided tape along the entire window frame. Press the plastic wrap firmly to the tape, covering the entire window. The plastic will wrinkle; don't worry about it. Finally, use a hair dryer on its highest setting and blow hot air evenly over the entire covering. The hot air will shrink the plastic wrap, sealing your window completely. At the end of the season, remove the plastic and the tape.

the indispensable
(and amazingly easy to build) cube

Build one. Admit how easy it was—and how great it looks. Build a bunch more, and paint them all different colors. Hang your cubes and organize your heart out.

WHAT YOU NEED

2 pieces of ½-inch-thick (1.3cm) wood for the cube's sides

2 pieces of ½-inch-thick (1.3cm) wood for the cube's top and bottom (These pieces need to be 1 inch [2.5cm] longer than the two side pieces.)

1 piece of ¼-inch (6mm) plywood for the back (This piece should be a square, with its sides the same length as your top and bottom pieces.)

Wood glue

Hammer

8d finish nails

⅝-inch (1.6cm) wire nails or brads

Sandpaper

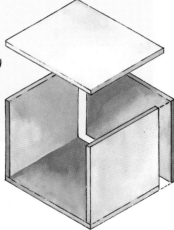

WHAT YOU DO

1 Brush wood glue onto the edges of your pieces, then nail the top and bottom to the sides.

2 Check to make sure your cube is square, then apply a small amount of glue to the edges of the back piece and nail it in place, using ⅝-inch (1.6cm) wire nails or brads.

3 Smooth all the edges of the cube with sandpaper.

problem

You don't consider it a problem, exactly. You like to think of it as being well prepared: a different pair of sunglasses for every mood, bracelets to match any out-
fit, enough beer mugs to host the whole volleyball team. Nevertheless, coming up
with places to put all these reserve supplies is somewhat of a dilemma.

quick fix

Fortunately, one person's storage problem is another's decorating device. If your
items can be loosely grouped into something resembling a collection—hats, scarves,
flower vases, you get the idea—pull them out of your overflowing closet or cabinet, and put them front and center. That can mean everything from hanging them
on hooks you mount in the hallway to lining them up on a sunny windowsill.

making the
one-room efficiency work

"Studio living" seems chic when you read about it in magazine spreads accompanied by glossy photos of airy, high-ceilinged, chrome-and-white interiors. But in real life, the experience can be just plain crowded. Here are some tips and simple decorating tricks for helping a one-room apartment both look and feel more livable.

PAINT. A neutral tone will help your place seem as expansive as possible. Still desperate for color? Paint one wall to contrast with the off-white or cream of the others. Just avoid dark colors; they tend to swallow space.

LAYOUT. Dividing your apartment into sections can create the illusion of a much larger space. Strategic placement of a couch can say: "This is the living area, back there is the bedroom." A standing divider or a few tall plants can screen off where you sleep from where you eat and entertain. The trick is not to go overboard. Too many dividing devices, and you'll feel as if you live in a maze.

ORGANIZATION. Clutter is your enemy. Avoid knickknacks, letting just a few bold pieces of artwork or decoration add flavor, color, and pizzazz instead. Mount shelves on the wall to free floor space. Select kitchen appliances that fit under cabinets, so they're not filling up your small amount of counter space. Invest heavily in hooks, hangers, knobs, and specialty storage pieces designed to keep the tools of daily life in their place and, when possible, out of full view.

STORAGE. Use your interior cabinet space to the max. Hooks or magnetic strips will make it possible for you to hang mugs and utensils inside the doors, freeing shelves for other items. If you don't have lots of cabinet and closet space, minimize your supplies and possessions to what you absolutely need. Put what you have to on "display" (think flea-market dishes, canned and boxed foods with pretty labels, decorative boxes holding winter sweaters, etc.).

FURNITURE. Select furniture that does double duty. Chairs with removable seats can conceal extra sheets and blankets. Stools and ottomans with detachable lids are excellent hiding places for office supplies, books, and odds and ends. A futon that folds up into a couch and down into a bed is a great idea for a small room. Keep a table uncluttered so it can be used as a food preparation area, an ironing board, and a craft area. Cover it with a bright tablecloth that matches your decor.

ILLUSIONS. Create space out of thin air. If your one-room palace didn't come with a closet, several extra-long pegs can double as coat hooks and a closet area. (You can even fit a stack of several skirts or pairs of jeans on top of side-by-side pegs.) Drape a tapestry or pretty piece of fabric to protect your clothes from dust and mimic a closet door. For a room without a view, paint a window on a wall. (You can even adjust the view to suit the season.) Faking a doorway is just as easy. Both options are surprisingly effective at relieving that cramped feeling. They also show what a good—and good-humored—sport you are.

storage in disguise

In the space-deprived reality of first apartments, few storage containers are as handy as those that masquerade—and do double duty—as something else. Create a coffee table out of a wooden trunk, for example, and you've got a flat surface for drinks, candles, or plates of food on top, but also a nice hollow space hidden below for stashing winter blankets, yearbooks, or a few pieces of camping gear. What makes this arrangement so apartment friendly, of course, is that the multitasking trunk does all of this without demanding a single inch more of your precious floor space than most standard coffee tables would.

Here's a starter list of other unconventional storage containers that can successfully pose as everything from coffee tables and nightstands to end tables and bases for televisions and sound-systems:

- Metal file bins
- Lidded wicker baskets
- Wooden wine cases
- Barrels
- Wall-mount kitchen cabinets (unmounted, of course)
- Stacked sets of secondhand suitcases
- Large aluminum tool chests (the kind designed to fit in the back of pickup trucks)
- Displaced wooden drawers fitted into plywood boxes

lattice organizer

Got a tall, skinny stretch of wall or a long, narrow strip that you know would be the perfect place for hanging pots and pans or back scrubbers and towels? This eclectically studded strip of lattice is the way to make use of it. The bare lattice comes ready-made at home improvement stores, and it's easy to saw to size yourself. Then you screw all your showy hangers into it, rather than into the wall. Landlord is happy. You're happy. And everything has a place to hang.

WHAT YOU NEED

Ready-made lattice
(Buy a strip that's close to the size you need; you can trim it when you get it home.)

Pickling stain

Liquid dye in any color you like

Variety of hangers
(Here's your chance to show off a few funky [and pricier] drawer and cabinet pulls or knobs, plus hooks, handles, pulleys, etc. You don't need a whole expensive set of anything, just one of each.)

Handsaw

Paintbrush

Rags

Screwdriver

Drill and small drill bits (optional)

WHAT YOU DO

1 With the handsaw, cut your lattice to fit the nook or cranny in which you want to position it.

2 Paint the front and all the edges of the lattice with the pickling stain. As you work, wipe off excess pickling stain with a rag every three to five minutes. Let the stain dry while you clean your brush.

3 Paint the dye over the pickling stain, wiping it randomly in various places, so more of the white pickling stain shows through here and there. This gives your organizer a washed-out, weathered look. Let the paint dry.

4 Screw your hangers where you want them on the lattice. To make this easier, you can first drill pilot holes one size smaller than the screws you're using.

 Don't screw or drill too closely to the lattice's edges or the wood will split.

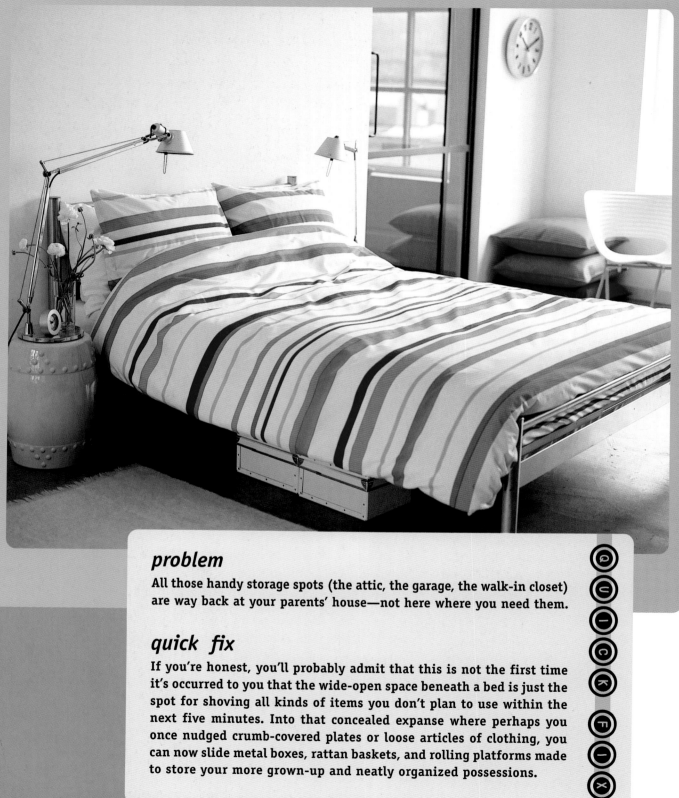

problem

All those handy storage spots (the attic, the garage, the walk-in closet) are way back at your parents' house—not here where you need them.

quick fix

If you're honest, you'll probably admit that this is not the first time it's occurred to you that the wide-open space beneath a bed is just the spot for shoving all kinds of items you don't plan to use within the next five minutes. Into that concealed expanse where perhaps you once nudged crumb-covered plates or loose articles of clothing, you can now slide metal boxes, rattan baskets, and rolling platforms made to store your more grown-up and neatly organized possessions.

QUICK FIX

coffeehouse magazine racks

Whether you keep up with vegetarian cooking, snowboarding, international politics, or the local arts scene, chances are you have at least one or two magazines appearing in your mailbox every month. Then there are the extras you grab at the newsstand, the alternative weekly you pick up for the movie reviews and horoscopes, and the catalogs full of the supplies you need for the cooking, snowboarding, or whatever.

If, like the owners of well-kept coffeehouses, you don't want all this glossy paper and newsprint cluttering your tables, couches, and floor, follow their lead and install a few wall-mount hanging racks. Home improvement stores carry a huge selection of towel racks, in styles ranging from rustic to high tech. Simply use the screws that come with them to attach them to a wall, and you have a place to keep all that must-have reading material for the 23 hours a day you're not curling up with it.

when all else fails, shop

With companies out there devoted solely to creating custom-shaped gizmos for storing everything from spoons to shoes, it's likely that one or two of the items they've come up with are just what you need to put your place in order. You'll find storage solutions for sale in three basic categories.

freestanding storage

The main advantage of freestanding storage is that it's portable and therefore adaptable. Bookcases, carts, metal shelving units, and furniture pieces such as tables equipped with drawers or doors all fall into this category. For even more flexibility, opt for freestanding storage pieces that feature adjustable components (such as shelves you can move to meet your needs) and that are outfitted with wheels, so that rolling the piece here and there (and out of the way) is a no-fuss job.

compartmentalized storage

Many times, simply keeping items separated is the key to storing them neatly and efficiently. A drawer divided into distinct sections of rubber bands, paper clips, thumbtacks, and staples, for example, is easier to navigate than one full of a nondescript mass of home-office supplies. Anything that helps segregate pieces into those helpful, partitioned sections can be thought of as compartmentalized storage, from baskets, jars, and bags to hooks and pegs.

item-specific storage

These storage pieces are specially designed to perform specific functions, such as organize your CD collection, keep all the shampoo and soap in one place in the shower, or store your cooking supplies and gadgetry close at hand but not all over your one tiny patch of counter space. Sometimes, an item-specific storage piece is all you need to quickly solve a straightforward storage problem.

buyer beware

When you're confronted with all the alluring options, from crates, baskets, trunks, and boxes to bags, racks, and bins, it's tempting to load up on snazzy-looking containers that end up creating even more clutter in your small space—without meeting your actual storage needs. The best defense against this is to have a clear idea of those needs before you hit the store aisles or dial up the catalog company. Buy a box for storing sweaters if that's what you need, not the electric-green canister set that you love but you're not sure what to do with. Also, don't waste precious space housing oversized storage containers. Match the size of your container to the thing to be contained.

pattern for

Painted
File Cabinet

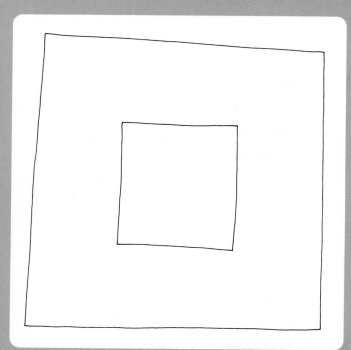

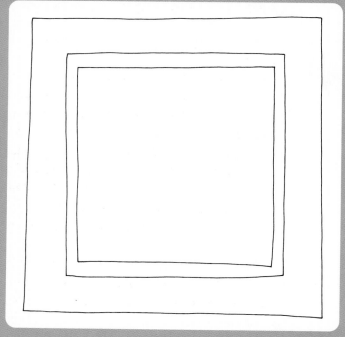

enlarge 200%

acknowledgments

An especially tasteful group of apartment dwellers helped us develop some of our early ideas for this book. Thanks to them all: Cindy Burda, Dietra Garden, Veronika Alice Gunter, Emma Jones, Michelle Keenan, Shelly Mehlen, Charlie Pierce, and Heather Smith.

And while we're at it, extra amounts of very special thanks must be heaped upon Veronika Alice Gunter, research maven, gifted writer, in-house hipster, and, helpfully, a landlord who has rented her share of apartments. She made all the nifty sidebars throughout the book happen.

a note about suppliers

Usually, the supplies you need for making the projects in Lark books can be found at your local craft supply store, discount mart, home improvement center, or retail shop relevant to the topic of the book. Occasionally, however, you may need to buy materials or tools from specialty suppliers. In order to provide you with the most up-to-date information, we have created suppliers listings on our Web site, which we update on a regular basis. Visit us at www.larkbooks.com, click on "Craft Supply Sources," and then click on the relevant topic. You will find numerous companies listed with their web address and/or mailing address and phone number.

contributors

If there's something these amazingly talented people can't whip up with paintbrushes, needles, hammers, glue, and a very strict budget, we'd like to know what it is.

SHEILA ENNIS is a writer and artist living in Boston, Massachusetts. She teaches writing at a local community college and has a small business as a decorative paint finisher. She applies her enthusiasm for crafts to anything that involves paint. Sheila's work appears on page 101.

DIETRA GARDEN lives in Asheville, North Carolina, where she teaches visual arts to elementary-age students. She has worked in the art field as a professional since 1990, teaching in public schools and summer camps, and offering private studio lessons. She also does commissioned work and has recently had her art featured in Art-O-Mat vending machines. Dietra's work appears on pages 59, 70, 73, 74, 90, 135, and 150. She'd like to give special credit and thanks to artist Anna Morgan, who created the batik print in the project on page 70.

DIANA LIGHT lives and works in the beautiful Blue Ridge Mountains of North Carolina. Her home/studio, like her life, is surrounded by glittering glass in hundreds of forms, styles, and types. After earning her B.F.A. in painting and print-making, she extended her expertise to etching and painting fine glass objects. She has contributed to numerous Lark books and is the coauthor of Lark's *The Weekend Crafter: Etching Glass*. Her work appears on pages 122–23, 128, and 140.

SHELLEY LOWELL, of Columbia, Maryland, is an award-winning graphic designer, illustrator, and fine artist. Her paintings and sculpture have been exhibited in museums and galleries in many cities throughout the United States. She has contributed to Lark books ranging from The *Ultimate Clock Book* and *Painting on Glass* to *Creative Candleholders*. Shelley consulted on the projects on pages 78 and 126.

NATHALIE MORNU studied fine craft for five years before pursuing a writing career. The chair on page 113 was her first foray into affixing fabric to furniture. The rest of Nathalie's work appears on pages 92, 98, 110, and 118.

ALLISON SMITH lives in Asheville, North Carolina. Her home-based business specializes in providing deluxe tourist accommodations in remote locations around the world. She is an avid crafter and designer in addition to being a full-time mother. She has created projects for numerous Lark books including *Decorating Baskets*, *Girls' World*, and *Decorating Candles*. Her work appears on pages 68, 117, 120, 131, and 134.

TERRY TAYLOR lives and works in Asheville, North Carolina, as an editor and project coordinator for Lark Books. He is a prolific designer and exhibiting artist, and works in media ranging from metals and jewelry to paper crafts and mosaics. Some of the most recent Lark books to which he has contributed include *Creative Outdoor Lighting*, *Salvage Style*, and *The Book of Wizard Craft*. Terry consulted on the projects on pages 54, 62, 65, 85, 88, 95, 97, 122–23, and 138.

SKIP WADE makes a living making people and places look good. Specializing in fashion and domestics, he works in both still photography and film as a photo stylist, prop master, wardrobe manager, and location scout. He and his partner live in Asheville, North Carolina, where they're continually renovating a 1920's house. He has contributed his talents to several Lark books, including *The New Book of Table Settings*, *Decorating Porches and Decks*, and *Decorating with Mini-Lights*. His own designs appear on pages 82, 87, 94, 100, 106, 107, 124, and 153, and he contributed his styling talents to projects throughout the book.

INDEX

acknowledgments, 157
appliances: electronic, 66-67; kitchen, 39
artwork, displaying, 55-56, 57-58, 147-148

bathroom, necessities, 45
bedroom, necessities, 44, 152
budgeting, 16-17

carpets, cleaning, 48
cleaning: basics, 46-47; products, 51
clogged drains, 50
color, 108-109
contributors, 158-159
cookware, 39
curtains, hanging, 28

darkness, alleviating, 20
dishes, 41

efficiencies. *See* one-room living
electronics. *See* appliances
emergency supply kit, 86
energy, conserving, 145

feng shui, 112
finding an apartment, 11-12
flatware, 42
flea markets, 139
floor lights. *See* projects, uplighters
floor plan, 18-20
furniture: cleaning, 33; placement, 18-20

gardening. *See* projects, plants
glassware, 43

handles, cleaning, 34. *See also* projects

improvements, 24
insects, 50

kitchen, necessities, 39-43
knobs, cleaning, 34. *See also* projects

landlords, 13
leases, 14
lighting, 98-99, 106, 104-105. *See also* projects
low ceilings, tips for, 20

neighbors, 81

one-room living, 20, 148

patterns, 156
parties, 103
plants, apartment friendly, 136-137

projects:
artificial grass, 128-129
artwork, 70, 120

blinds, 28
buckets, 132-133
bulb cover, 107-109
bulletin board, alternative to a, 54

candlesticks, 101-102
canisters, 134
canvas, 73, 118-119
casters, 125
chair, 113-116
cover-ups, 59, 68-71, 117
cubes, storage and display, 146
curtains, 68-71, 84, 85-93, 88-89, 90-91

dividers, 62-65

fabric, 92-93, 113-116, 122-123
file cabinet, 110-112
finials, 87
floors, 72-73, 74, 76-77, 78-81, 82-83
furniture, 126-127, 138-139, 140-141

handles, 130

knobs, 130

lamp, 98-99
lampshade, 97
lattice, 150-151

magazine racks, 153
magnets, 60
message center, 59-61
mini-lights, 104-105

organizer, 150-151

pavers, 82-83
plants, 131-135
picture frames, 120-121
pictures, hanging, 55-56
pillows, 122-123
photographs, 124
pulls, decorative, 95

quick fixes for any room, 57-58, 82-83, 87, 94, 100, 106, 117, 124, 130, 147, 152

rolling furniture, 125
rubber mats, 76-77

screens. *See* dividers
seagrass, 74-75
serving trays, 128-129
shelving, 142-146

slides, 90-9
stained glass, faux, 94

tables, 126-127; 138-139; 140-141
task lighting, 106
temporary walls, 62-67
trunks, 149

uplighters, 100

walls, 53, 54, 55, 56, 59-60, 62-65, 68-69, 70-71
wire mesh, 107-109

techniques:
batik, 70
beading, 95, 97, 122-123

decorative finishes. *See* pickling, sponging, stamping, stenciling, weathering
decoupage, 140-141

painting, 22-25, 29-31
pickling, 33

refinishing wood, 34
refurbishing wood, 33

sewing, alternatives to, 36; basics, 35-36
sponging, 32
staining wood, 34
stamping, 32
stenciling, 32
storage options, 142-146, 149, 152, 154-155

upholstering, 113-116

wallpapering, 26-27
weathering, 31

refrigerators, cleaning, 47
rental costs, 16
renter's insurance, 15
rituals, 77
rods, curtain, 29, 87
roommates, 58
rust removal, 34

seasonal decorating, 61
security deposits, 15
storage options, 142-146, 149, 152, 154-155
studios. *See* one-room living

toilets, cleaning, 49
tools, recommended, 37

utensils, 40
utilities, 13, 16

wicker, cleaning, 35